By

STREAMLINER
New York to Florida

JOSEPH M. WELSH

D1616348

ANDOVER
JUNCTION
PUBLICATIONS
P.O. BOX 1160   ANDOVER, NJ 07821

To the memory of John J. Welsh
a great father, railroader and writer who introduced me to the Champion

ANDOVER JUNCTION PUBLICATIONS
P.O. BOX 1160   ANDOVER. NJ 07821

PUBLISHING DIRECTOR
Joyce C. Mooney

PUBLISHER
Stephen A. Esposito

EDITORIAL & ART DIRECTOR
Mike Schafer

DESIGN & LAYOUT
Rick Johnson

Most illustrations in this book are property of the author.

COVER: The warm, cozy confines of the Florida-bound *Silver Meteor* streaking along Pennsylvania Railroad's electrified New York-Washington main line offer both refuge and transport to travelers seeking relief from frigid northern climes. Tomorrow, lofty palm trees and warm sands rather than swirling snow will surround these travelers as they step off the *Meteor*—or other streamliners of their choice—in the Sunshine State.—MAIN RENDERING AND INSETS BY MITCHELL A. MARKOVITZ.

TITLE PAGE ILLUSTRATION: Florida's breeze-swept palms seduced not only passengers but Budd Company's renowned artist Leslie Ragan, who idealized rail travel in Florida in this idyllic portrait of the northbound *Champion* speeding along the Atlantic Ocean on the Florida East Coast Railway.—FEC, COLLECTION OF WILLIAM F. HOWES JR.

PHOTO ABOVE: During its southbound flight on the Pennsylvania Railroad, the *East Coast Champion* catches the afternoon light as it crosses the Raritan River at New Brunswick, N.J., in May 1963.—VICTOR HAND.

FOREWORD

I rode in many trains between 1940 and the start of Amtrak in 1971. Each had a personality which reflected the individual companies which ran them. The *20th Century Limited* gave me the feeling of the grandest aspects of New York City, Park Avenue elegance and everything done in a first-class and professional manner. Its great rival, PRR's *Broadway Limited*, was a businessman's train which was every bit as good as the *Century*, although until its very last years didn't carry as many passengers. DL&W's *Phoebe Snow* was a pleasant lady who took you on a beautiful daytime journey, while Santa Fe's *Super Chief* was a speedster which raced two-thirds of the way across the continent while providing its guests safe haven from the wild country through which it traveled.

No trains, however, in the opinion of this observer, had more personality than those which ran from New York to Florida. Although there were a number of ways to make this journey, taking the train was the best. For many years in a row, our family escaped winter's stormy blast for several weeks in the Miami Beach and Fort Lauderdale area. Getting there by train was as much an adventure as the vacation itself. In the mind's eye of my remembrance, we left Newark each time in the afternoon and during the worst weather imaginable—rain, snow and cold. As soon as we boarded the train, our vacation began in the new world of Pullman warmth, security and comfort.

I recall a flight through wintertime cold and gathering darkness punctuated by a wonderful evening meal in the dining car. Those of the Atlantic Coast Line had a subtle, yet inviting atmosphere I have not experienced elsewhere. It was a chorus of wonderful cooking aromas including roast stuffed turkey, hot buttered toast and spices unique to the style of cooking which had evolved aboard the cars during the previous 50 years.

Both employees and passengers shared a sense of expectancy because they knew their Florida vacation was imminent. But it was still cold as PRR turned our train over to the RF&P in Washington. The train was on its way to Richmond as we returned to our accommodations, usually a drawing room in a heavyweight car, and found that the porter had transformed the space into a cozy sleeping apartment with crisp fresh linen and warm blankets. After Richmond, when ACL was in charge, sleep came quickly from the steady clickety-clack of the wheels rolling fast over rail joints.

Within a few short hours we awoke in a different world. Our train was speeding south of Jacksonville and heading for our destination. Sometimes the porter opened the top of the vestibule dutch door during station or other stops, and we were greeted by the delicate scent of orange blossoms in a bright setting of clear blue sky, warm sunshine and quiet Florida landscape.

Dinner is served aboard a Seaboard diner in Silver Fleet service circa 1960.

Atlantic Coast Line funneled its (East Coast) trains onto the Florida East Coast; both had beautifully ballasted double-track main line all the way. Seaboard, by contrast, had but a single track which seemed to wander through a wilderness away from the center of things. We traveled Seaboard only a few times, and it was a different operation, marked by streamlined cars and a different—though no less pleasing—dining-car cuisine.

During the 1960's, as passenger trains in the U.S. were fading in popularity, the Florida traffic remained strong, and this observer took serious steps to both investigate and record all that was transpiring. The trains, the cars, their environment and their employees all came under scrutiny just before they vanished. Now Joe Welsh has drawn much similar information together in this wonderful and long overdue book, and I am pleased to provide a small historical preface to it.

Peter Tilp
Short Hills, N.J.
February 1993

CONTENTS

Seaboard Air Line train 7, the Sunland, Coleman, Fla., 1964.—David W. Salter

ACL E3A No. 501.—Mike Schafer

West Coast Champion on ACL near Jacksonville, 1965.—David W. Salter

"Streamlining through Wonderful Florida"

By "Streamliner" Thru Tropical Florida

ACL and SAL postcards circa 1940.—Collection of the author.

Seaboard's Palmland at Miami, 1961.—John Dziobko Jr.

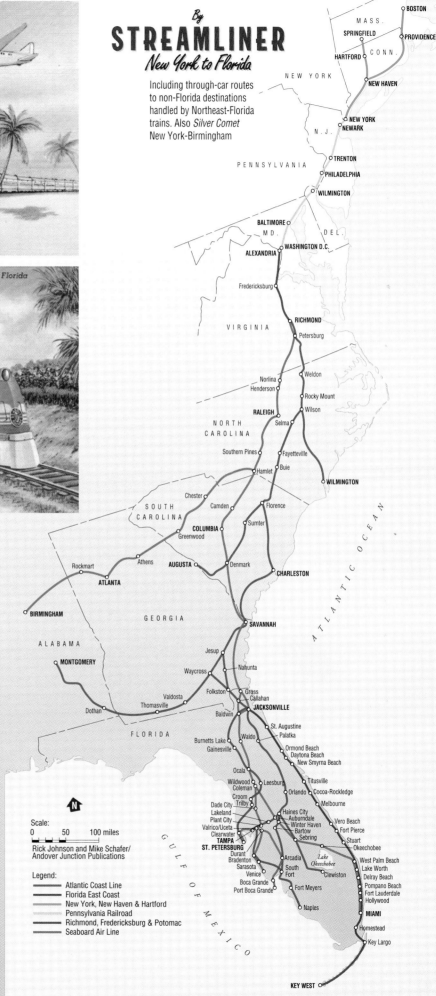

By
STREAMLINER
New York to Florida

Including through-car routes
to non-Florida destinations
handled by Northeast-Florida
trains. Also *Silver Comet*
New York-Birmingham

N

Scale:
0   50   100 miles

Rick Johnson and Mike Schafer/
Andover Junction Publications

Legend:
— Atlantic Coast Line
— Florida East Coast
— New York, New Haven & Hartford
— Pennsylvania Railroad
— Richmond, Fredericksburg & Potomac
— Seaboard Air Line

INTRODUCTION

Thousands lined the tracks all up and down the Pennsylvania Railroad, RF&P and Seaboard for a look at the brand-new *Silver Meteor* in 1939. This is the southbound *Meteor*'s first arrival in Jacksonville on Feb. 3, 1939.—CSX TRANSPORTATION.

*T*hose of us who toiled in the railroad passenger business through the 1960's were, frankly, quite envious of Jim Getty and Ken Howes, our counterparts at the Seaboard Air Line and Atlantic Coast Line, respectively (after the 1967 merger, they both worked together at the newly formed Seaboard Coast Line). Their streamliners linking the Northeast with Florida's resorts and retirement communities were well-patronized year-round while ours rolled much of the time with anemic loadings and mounting deficits.

This had not always been the case, of course. Through much of railroading's "Golden Era," the Florida carriers were plagued with a highly inefficient seasonal traffic pattern which boomed during four balmy months each winter and languished in torrid doldrums the rest of the year. Things began to change in the 1930's when air-conditioning and off-season hotel rates opened Florida to summer vacationers of modest means. Just as Henry M. Flagler had developed rail routes around the turn of the century to bring the nation's affluent to his winter playgrounds along Florida's East Coast, now the state's business and civic leaders were looking to the railroads to bring in the masses.

Enter the Edward G. Budd Manufacturing Company promoting economical, lightweight stainless-steel trains, plus the Seaboard Air Line Railroad struggling to climb out of its Number Two position in the Florida travel market, and in February 1939, the Sunshine State had its first streamliner, SAL's all-coach *Silver Meteor* from New York. Sensing market loss to its arch rival, the conservative Atlantic Coast Line and its partner, the Florida East Coast, introduced later the same year their Budd-built all-coach *Champion*s between the Northeast and Florida and FEC's *Henry M. Flagler* between Jacksonville and Miami. The streamliners were immediate hits with the traveling public and soon prompted a new, year-round demand for additional coach capacity. More equipment was ordered and schedules expanded.

Intense competition between the ACL/FEC and SAL for the exploding Florida market drove the roads to ever-higher levels of service. Taking advantage of its route across the flat Atlantic coastal plain, ACL's Champion McDowell Davis squeezed fractions of degrees (and thereby precious minutes of time) from curves on his road's Richmond-Jacksonville main line in his quest for a 24-hour run between New York and Miami. Aboard its trains, the Coast Line received high marks for its dining-car cuisine and recreation cars. Meanwhile, Seaboard combined modern, innovative equipment and attentive on-board services with aggressive marketing to successfully challenge the larger ACL. Both roads effectively used their passenger services to win favor with freight shippers and on-line communities.

Despite the steady popularity of Florida service and enthusiastic support of ACL and Seaboard managements, storm clouds moved in during the 1960's as strike-bound FEC broke its through runs with the Coast Line, and the flagging interest of the Pennsylvania Railroad—and outright hostility of Penn Central—hampered operations between New York and Washington. Nevertheless, patronage remained remarkably strong. What distinguished the Florida service from the rest of the nation's fast-fading network of long-distance rail passenger operations, however, was not the respective biases of rail managements, but rather the inherent strength of this particular market. Surprisingly, the story of pre-Amtrak rail passenger service between the Northeast and Florida has not been thoroughly documented. Happily, Joe Welsh has now corrected this oversight.

William F. Howes Jr.
Former Director of Passenger Services
Baltimore & Ohio Railroad
Chesapeake & Ohio Railway

GLOSSARY

Buffet-lounge: A lounge area that features a counter for serving refreshments.

Compartment: A compact private room for two occupants, with sofa by day and two foldout beds at night.

Double bedroom: A private room for two occupants, with a chair and sofa or two chairs by day and two fold-out beds at night.

Drawing room: A private room for three occupants, with chairs and sofa by day and three foldout beds at night.

Duplex roomette or duplex single room: Slightly smaller than a roomette, a private room for one person, with a built-in chair that folds down into a bed, covering the toilet. Duplex roomettes are arranged within a car such that alternating rooms are above car-floor level, accessible by a step arrangement.

Master room: A spacious private room sleeping two travelers, with chairs and sofa by day and fold-out beds at night. Master rooms often featured a shower.

Roomette: A private room for one person, with a built-in chair that folds down into a bed, covering the toilet.

Sections/private section: Open facing seating for two by day that is transformed at night into upper and lower wide berths made private by heavy curtains. By design, a private section offered more privacy.

Single bedroom: A spacious private room for a single occupant, with a sofa or chair by day and a foldout bed. Unlike the roomette, the toilet remains accessible when the bed is down.

A WORD FROM THE EDITOR

Throughout the chapters of this book, the reader will find numerous references to a myriad of sleeping-car types. For many passenger-train afficionados who have purchased this book, the term "10-6" (or sometimes "10&6"), for example, is a familiar reference to the famous 10-roomette, 6-double-bedroom sleeper—a car type which after World War II became the standard-bearer sleeping car for railroads everywhere. Even on Amtrak, as the 20th Century wound down, 10-6 sleepers were the norm on single-level overnight trains such as the *Broadway Limited* and *Silver Meteor*.

But, what in the world, many of you may ask as they peer at various consists in this book, is a "5-1-4-4" or a "6-d.br. lounge"? In many cases, space does not permit us to spell out what each is, hence this handy glossary. Also, many of the consists within include city codes which designate a car's operating endpoints. For the most part, we have adopted Amtrak's three-letter city code to indicate various endpoints and at the same time save considerable space.

A final note about that word "consist." In the real world out there, it's usually used as an intransitive verb, and as such, it is pronounced con-SIST; e.g., "The train consists of two locomotives and 12 cars." However, in the small world of the passenger-train/car enthusiast, the word is often freely used as a noun (a use of this word that many dictionaries do not even acknowledge!). In such usage, the pronunciation reverses: CON-sist. ("The train's consist includes two locomotives and 12 cars.") We cringe at how often we hear the former pronunciation applied to the latter usage. Of course, it's a free country, so pronounce it any way you want when silently reading this book. But if we hear otherwise, we may have to ask you to turn in your stepbox.

— Mike Schafer, Editorial & Art Director

Heavyweight sleeping-car types
1-1 lounge obs: 1-drawing-room, 1-single-bedroom buffet-observation
2-1 lounge: 2-compartment, 1-drawing-room buffet-lounge
3-1 lounge: 3-compartment, 1-drawing-room buffet-lounge
3-2 lounge: 3-compartment, 2-drawing-room observation-lounge
5-cmpt. buffet-lounge: 5-compartment buffet-lounge
6-3: 6 compartments, 3 drawing rooms
6-4-4: 6 sections, 4 roomettes, 4 double bedrooms
6-6: 6 sections, 6 double bedrooms
6-cmpt. buffet-lounge: 6-compartment buffet-lounge
6-s.br. cafe-lounge: 6-single-bedroom cafe-lounge
7-2: 7 compartments, 2 drawing rooms
7-cmpt. buffet-lounge: 7-compartment buffet-lounge
8-1-2: 8 sections, 1 drawing room, 2 compartments
8-1-3: 8 sections, 1 drawing room, 3 double bedrooms
8-5: 8 sections, 5 double bedrooms
8-sec. lounge: 8-section buffet-lounge
8-s.br. lounge: 8-single-bedroom lounge
10-1-1: 10 sections, 1 compartment, 1 drawing room
10-1-2: 10 sections, 1 drawing room, 2 compartments
10-2: 10 sections, 2 drawing rooms
10-2-1: 10 section, 2 double bedrooms, 1 compartment
10-4: 10 sections, 4 private sections

10-sec. lounge: 10-section lounge
12-1: 12 sections, 1 drawing room
12-1-4: 12 roomettes, 1 single bedroom, 4 double bedrooms
12-2-3: 12 roomettes, 2 single bedrooms, 3 double bedrooms
13 sec.: 13 section (tourist car)
14 sec.: 14 sections
14 s.br.: 14 single bedrooms

Lightweight sleeping-car types
2-1 lounge-obs: 2-master room, 1-double-bedroom lounge-observation (PRR View series assigned to SCL)
2-2-1 bar-lounge: 2-double-bedroom, 2-compartment bar-lounge
4-1-7-3: 4 sections, 1 compartment, 7 duplex roomettes, 3 double bedrooms (GN cars in Florida assignment)
4-4-2: 4 double bedrooms, 4 compartments, 2 drawing rooms
4-4: 4 compartments, 4 drawing rooms (ACF rebuild)
5-1-3 dome: 5-roomette, 1-single-bedroom, 3-compartment dome (leased from B&O, purchased by SCL)
5-1-4-4: 5 double bedrooms, 1 compartment, 4 roomettes, 4 sections
5-d.br. lounge: 5-double-bedroom lounge
5-d.br. lounge-obs: 5-double-bedroom lounge-observation
6-5-2: 6 roomettes, 5 double bedrooms, 2 compartments
6-d.br. lounge: 6-double-bedroom lounge
7-2: 7 double bedrooms, 2 drawing rooms (ACL rebuild)
10-5: 10 roomettes, 5 double bedrooms (PRR cars in Florida service)
10-6: 10 roomettes, 6 double bedrooms
11 d.br.: 11 double bedrooms
12-4: 12 duplex single rooms, 4 double bedrooms (PRR cars)
12-5: 12 duplex single rooms, 5 double bedrooms (PRR cars)
13 d.br.: 13 double bedrooms (PRR/NYC cars in Florida assignment)
14-2: 14 roomettes, 2 drawing rooms
14-4: 14 roomettes, 4 double bedrooms (NH or SOU cars in Florida assignment)
16-4: 16 duplex single rooms, 4 double bedrooms (ordered by SAL from Pullman-Standard but never built)
16-4: 16 duplex roomettes, 4 double bedrooms (leased from B&O, purchased by SCL; also GN cars in ACL service)
16-4 BRC: Budget Room Coach redesignated from 16-duplex-roomette, 4-double-bedroom sleepers leased from B&O and bought by SCL)
21 BRC: Budget Room Coach redesignated from ACL/RF&P/PRR 21-roomette cars)

CITY CODES
AUG	Augusta, Ga.	PBG	Port Boca Grande, Fla.
BHM	Birmingham, Ala.	RVR	Richmond, Va.
BOS	Boston, Mass.	SPG	Springfield, Mass.
CHI	Chicago, Ill.	SRA	Sarasota, Fla.
FLO	Florence, S.C.	STP	St. Petersburg, Fla.
JAX	Jacksonville, Fla.	TPA	Tampa, Fla.
LAK	Lakeland, Fla.	WAS	Washington, D.C.
NAP	Naples, Fla.	WIL	Wilmington, N.C.
MGY	Montgomery, Ala.	WWD	Wildwood, Fla.
MIA	Miami, Fla.	VEN	Venice, Fla.
NHV	New Haven, Conn.		
NYP	New York City/Pennsylvania Station, N.Y.		

RAILROAD/MANUFACTURER CODES
ACF	American Car & Foundry
ACL	Atlantic Coast Line
B&M	Boston & Maine
B&O	Baltimore & Ohio
Budd	Edward G. Budd Company
C&EI	Chicago & Eastern Illinois
C&O	Chesapeake & Ohio
CofG	Central of Georgia
GN	Great Northern
IC	Illinois Central
L&N	Louisville & Nashville
NC&StL	Nashville, Chattanooga & St. Louis
NYNH&H	New York, New Haven & Hartford Railroad
NYC	New York Central
PC	Penn Central
PRR	Pennsylvania Railroad
P-S	Pullman-Standard
RF&P	Richmond, Fredericksburg & Potomac
SAL	Seaboard Air Line
SCL	Seaboard Coast Line
SOU	Southern
UP	Union Pacific

1 DIAMONDS IN THE ROUGH
Early Trains to a Blossoming Florida

Near Ormond, Fla., on the Florida East Coast, the legendary *Florida Special* is a thing of beauty in this view taken circa 1925. FEC Mountain No. 447 leads a consist which includes a Pullman baggage-club at the head end and at least one vintage transom-windowed sleeper.—DeGoyler Library, Southern Methodist University. RIGHT: The back of this postcard from the Roarin' Twenties is imprinted "Having a wonderful time on this marvelous train with its music, games and lovely hostess."—Author's collection.

IN St. Augustine, the past and present meet as nowhere else in the bounds of our whole country. Where the din of battle between mailed Spanish conquistadors and Huguenot chevaliers resounded, the joyous laughter of daintily-clad women resounds. Somewhat less tropical than farther south, it is a favorite place to tarry going down the coast and returning. Its quaint narrow streets and buildings, the two rivers and harbor waterways, give much to see.

A palace, luxurious and royal in its rich appointments, is the Hotel Ponce de Leon. It is that and more, for it presents appropriate symbolism and decoration completely harmonious to its origin and environs.

Built of native shell rock material and set amid its beautifully laid out semitropical gardens, its architecture and adornment harks back and embodies the history and tradition of its connections with old Spain.

Florida, that seductive land of tropic breezes, palm trees and sunshine, has been one of America's favorite destinations for over a century. Long before the proliferation of interstates and airlines, people were lured to the state, America's Riviera. Most came by train.

If not the first, perhaps the most important person ever to visit Florida was Henry M. Flagler. Partner to John D. Rockefeller in a colossal enterprise known as Standard Oil, Flagler had retired at 60 with an enormous fortune. Like most visitors to Florida, he came for the climate, specifically the warmth which comforted his ailing wife. Unlike any other tourist, Flagler did something singularly amazing: He developed most of the state.

Charmed by the beauty of St. Augustine, then a town of only 2,500, Flagler was dismayed by the lack of suitable hotel accommodations. So he built one.

LEFT: Florida East Coast spared no expense in producing this elegant 12-page brochure in 1911, enticing travelers to the new Florida paradise. Between the booklet's gold-embossed covers were descriptions of the noted hostelries that awaited passengers alighting from Florida East Coast trains. Elaborate duotone artwork on each page included the likes of the Ponce de Leon resort (ABOVE) at St. Augustine, Fla. Views also included the Inner Harbor at Key West and the port of Havana, Cuba. On the inside covers were diagrams of the golf courses at Ormond Beach, Palm Beach, Miami and Nassau on the Bahama Islands. Hotels of the Florida East Coast Hotel Company were located at St. Augustine, Ormond, Palm Beach, Miami, Long Key and Nassau.—VIC RAFANELLI COLLECTION.

THE FOUNDATION FOR ONE PIER REQUIRED A MIXTURE OF SAND, GRAVEL, AND CEMENT EQUAL IN BULK TO THE CARGO OF A FIVE-MASTED SCHOONER

LONG KEY IS LINKED TO GRASSY KEY BY THE MARVELOUS LONG KEY VIADUCT

FLORIDA EAST COAST RY.
KEY WEST
EXTENSION

When FEC's Key West extension opened in 1912, the company released a handsome 38-page booklet detailing the construction and layout of the line. The last two pages (ABOVE) were actually a foldout that included a map of the extension as well as a construction scene of one of the piered segments of the "over-sea railroad" and a view of a train entering Long Key Viaduct.—COLLECTION OF VIC RAFANELLI. RIGHT: Looking more like an Irish poet than the man who helped transform Florida from a malarial swamp into a world-class tourist mecca, Henry M. Flagler surveys the progress of his overseas extension at Knights Key, circa 1908.—COURTESY HENRY M. FLAGLER MUSEUM, PALM BEACH, FLA.

When it was completed in January 1888, at a cost of $1.5 million, the Hotel Ponce de Leon, patterned after a Moorish palace, was one of the most-opulent resorts in the world.

Convincing wealthy northerners to travel to this wonderful establishment required adequate transportation, so in 1885 Flagler did something equally amazing: He purchased a railroad—the narrow-gauge Jacksonville, St. Augustine & Halifax. In 1890 Flagler would bridge the St. Johns River in linking Jacksonville and St. Augustine, convert his railroad to standard gauge and rename it the Florida East Coast Railway. Through-car service from Jersey City began in December 1884 with the extension by ACL of a Jersey-Waycross, Ga., sleeper to serve Jacksonville. In November 1886, a Jersey City-Tampa sleeper was established via ACL.

On Jan. 9, 1888, deluxe through passenger service began between Jersey City and Jacksonville with the inauguration of the *Florida Special* via the Atlantic Coast Line Railroad which operated between Richmond, Va., and Jacksonville. Other partners in the service were the Pennsylvania Railroad, which handled the cars between Jersey City and Washington,

D.C., and the Richmond, Fredericksburg & Potomac between Washington and Richmond.

The *Special* was comprised of six wooden Pullman Palace cars, including a baggage car which housed a dynamo to generate electricity for lighting the train, making for one of the first electrically lighted trains in the country. The train also featured a smoking/library/refreshment car, a dining car and three 10-sec-

ABOVE: Greatest of the "overseas" fleet in the 1920's and 1930's was the *Havana Special*. The train carried sleeping cars from New York and Washington to Key West where passengers transferred to Peninsular & Orient steamships for a sail to exotic Havana. Shown circa 1930, the *Special* is moving over the 2½-mile Long Key Viaduct. Passengers crowd the parlor-observation platform to take in the experience of a morning at sea from the rear of the train.—COURTESY OF THE HENRY M. FLAGLER MUSEUM, PALM BEACH, FLA. FAR LEFT: The train's appointments were highlighted in this now-rare brochure which featured color artwork. NEAR LEFT: This special menu was issued for President Coolidge and his party's rail/steamship trip to Havana for the International Conference of American States.—BOTH BROCHURES, AUTHOR'S COLLECTION.

tion, 2-drawing room sleeping cars. In addition to the novelty of electric lighting, the *Special* was also one of the first vestibuled trains in the country.

Aboard the cars for the 31¼-hour journey were a host of dignitaries including no less a personage than George M. Pullman, whose company had built the train. On the menu were such delicacies as roast antelope, which passengers enjoyed amidst the overstuffed plush and Victorian elegance that typified cars of this vintage. Chandeliers, French glass windows and polished woods such as Spanish mahogany completed the interior amenities. It was the beginning of an era.

There would follow an unparalleled period of growth, both for the railroads and for the state itself. Flagler would bejewel the East Coast of the state with

Text continued on page 14

Predating Jacksonville Union Station, which opened in 1919, was this mission-style Union Depot built in 1904. The colorized postcard view is postmarked, on the back, Nov. 5, 1909, and includes a handwritten message: *"Am this far on my way and am now in this depot."* It was addressed to a Miss Louise Shephard in Petersburg, Va., by a Miss Parham, who we may presume had come down from Virginia and was perhaps changing trains at Jacksonville.—AUTHOR'S COLLECTION.

LEFT: As the end of the 20th Century drew near, trains still called at the modest brick structure serving as Tampa Union Station. The outward appearance of the headhouse changed little from this postcard view dating from the 1920's where a cluster of women await a jitney to whisk them to their final destinations.—AUTHOR'S COLLECTION.

RIGHT: Palm trees line the streetside of the Seaboard Air Line depot at West Palm Beach. The structure's bell tower was its hallmark, showing up in numerous photos taken at the station over the years (see pages 16-18). Stucco Spanish-style depots like this were *de rigeur* at numerous passenger stations on all railroads throughout Florida.—AUTHOR'S COLLECTION.

LEFT: We're at Auburndale, Fla., in 1935, and Seaboard Air Line Mountain No. 224 has a roll on a 12-car *Orange Blossom Special.*—SMITHSONIAN INSTITUTION. BELOW: The back page of Florida East Coast's timetable issued on Jan. 6, 1929, featured a contemporary rival of the *Orange Blossom*, the *Miamian* of Atlantic Coast Line and FEC.—VIC RAFANELLI COLLECTION.

FLORIDA EAST COAST RAILWAY

FLORIDA EAST COAST RAILWAY · FLAGLER SYSTEM

PASSENGER TRAIN SCHEDULES

EFFECTIVE JANUARY 6, 1929
INCLUDING COMPLETE WINTER SERVICE

SUBJECT TO CHANGE WITHOUT NOTICE

WM. P. KENAN, JR.
President

H. N. RODENBAUGH
Vice-President

J. D. RAHNER

THE TRAIN OF TRAINS TO FLORIDA

"Only One Night Out"

9:15am Lv. New York (Penn Sta.)	Ar.	7:20pm
11:13am Lv. North Philadelphia	....Ar.	5:21pm
11:25am Lv. West Philadelphia	....Ar.	5:09pm
1:28pm Lv. Baltimore	............Ar.	3:00pm
2:45pm Lv. Washington	..........Ar.	1:40pm
5:45pm Lv. Richmond	............Ar.	10:40am
5:30am Lv. Savannah	...........Ar.	10:50pm
9:05am Ar. Jacksonville	.........Lv.	7:20pm
9:30am Lv. Jacksonville	.........Lv.	6:45pm
10:25am Ar. St. Augustine	........Lv.	5:50pm
f11:00am Ar. Ormond	.............Lv.	f4:44pm
11:36am Ar. Daytona Beach	......Lv.	4:31pm
12:01pm Ar. New Smyrna	........Lv.	4:05pm
3:00pm Ar. Fort Pierce	..........Lv.	1:15pm
4:30pm Ar. West Palm Beach	.....Lv.	11:45am
6:15pm Ar. Miami	...............Lv.	10:00am

No Extra Fare
But ALL the Luxury of Travel

Finer and faster . . . THE MIAMIAN operates over the only continuous double-track, automatic signal equipped route between New York and the East Coast of Florida.

Superior Pullman equipment . . . club and observation cars between New York and Miami . . . open section, drawing room and compartment sleepers . . . ladies' lounge and shower baths. Excellent dining-car service.

The MIAMIAN

From the Heart of
NEW YORK
Leaves Pennsylvania Station, 7th Avenue and 33rd Street, New York, at 9:15 in the morning.

33 HOURS

To the Heart of
MIAMI
Arrives Florida East Coast Railway Terminal in the center of Miami at 6:15 the next evening.

FLORIDA EAST COAST RAILWAY
FLAGLER SYSTEM
A Modern Transportation System

50 YEARS OF SAFE TRAVEL 1888-1937

YOUR WINTER HOLIDAY BEGINS WHEN YOU BOARD THE TRAIN

The FLORIDA SPECIAL

"Aristocrat of Winter Trains"

PROVIDING A CLEAN COMFORTABLE RIDE ON A DOUBLE TRACK ROCK BALLASTED RAILROAD PROTECTED BY AUTOMATIC SIGNALS AND TRAIN CONTROL

IN THE UNIQUE RECREATION CAR

One of the many reasons why Florida Travelers choose the Florida Special season after season for their trip to and from Florida—Orchestra—Hostess— Dancing—Games

---

For the *Florida Special*'s golden jubilee year, 1937, Atlantic Coast Line issued a gold-and-purple brochure that provided prospective travelers with a history of the train, a description of its appointments, a schedule and an historical overview of Florida. The brochure's centerspread (ABOVE) heralded the *Special*'s most-unique feature, the recreation car, replete with "orchestra, hostess, dancing and games."
—COLLECTION OF THE AUTHOR.

Continued from page 11

a series of world-class hotels while extending his railroad ever southward. On the Gulf Coast, Henry B. Plant, owner of the Southern Express Company, was doing the same. By the late 1800's, Plant had extended his own rail network—the Plant System—through the northern part of Florida. In 1884 he built into Tampa, where in 1891 Plant would open the sumptuous Tampa Bay Hotel, rival to the Ponce de Leon.

By the turn of the century, the newly formed Seaboard Air Line would enter Tampa (through the acquisition of stock in the Florida Central & Peninsular) providing another link between Richmond and Florida. At this time, too, Seaboard's through passenger service to Florida blossomed. In 1903 SAL's first winter-season all-Pullman train, the *Seaboard Florida Limited*, debuted, initiating a rivalry with the *Florida Special* which would later be taken up by the *Orange Blossom Special*.

By 1902, ACL had swallowed up the Plant System and most of Florida's rail system was in place. In 1904, Flagler's Florida East Coast began an incredible journey, a trip which took the railroad to sea. In one of the great engineering feats of its time and an eight-

year project, FEC extended its line to Key West nearly 100 miles at sea in the Gulf of Mexico. The object was to move people and freight southward to Key West where steamships would take over for the journey to Latin America.

Knights Key was reached in 1908. For the winter season of 1908-09, the *Florida Special* was extended south to serve the burgeoning resort community of Palm Beach, with cars for West Palm Beach and Knights Key where passengers bound for the exotic port of Havana transferred to Peninsular & Occidental steamships for a sail over the Spanish main. Along the way to Knights Key, the *Special* made a stop (at 3:20 a.m.) at a little place called Miami, then still in its infancy. The city had been reached by the FEC in 1896. On April 16 of that year, regular passenger service had been established, no doubt to support Flagler's new Royal Palm Hotel then under construction.

FEC inaugurated the completed Key West extension on Jan. 22, 1912. Regular passenger service began the same day. For the next 23 years, until a hurricane severely damaged the line causing the end of rail operations, FEC trains operated over the 128-mile extension, leap-frogging over 37 miles of open ocean on an

island-hopping adventure to "America's Gibraltar."

Greatest of the "overseas" fleet in the 1920's was the *Havana Special*. A descendant of the *New York & West Indian Limited*, inaugurated in 1878, the *Havana Special* was re-equipped and rededicated for the 1926-27 season, carrying new mid-train lounges like the *Camaguey* and the *Cuba*. In addition to a separate men's and ladies' lounge, the cars featured a soda fountain. Also available were a bath and shower as well as valet service and a ladies' maid. Routinely, a pink Atlantic dawn would find the *Special* trundling over the Long Key viaduct en route to Key West, its passengers gathered on the observation platform to take in the spectacle of a morning at sea from the rear of a train.

The quiet splendor of the pre-World War I era was replaced by the Roaring Twenties. Florida continued to grow at an unprecedented pace, becoming the playground for an America obsessed with the quick buck. Jacksonville, always a key transfer point, had become the state's revolving door. As one postcard had it, "More millionaires passed through the terminal than any other in the world."

Passenger traffic increased spectacularly, peaking in the winter season of 1924-25 when three quarters of a million passengers arrived on the cars from as far away as Montana and Quebec. The state was growing at a frantic pace. The passenger and freight crush spurred FEC to double track its main line. As on the Florida East Coast, the Florida land rush triggered a building spurt on the SAL. In 1924 Seaboard affiliate Florida

Western & Northern started construction of a 204-mile line to connect Coleman, Fla., with West Palm Beach. By 1927 the railroad would reach Miami.

It was at this time that Seaboard inaugurated what may well have been the greatest of all the winter-season Pullman heavyweight trains to serve Florida—the *Orange Blossom Special*. Entering service on Nov. 21, 1925, with cars for St. Petersburg and West Palm Beach from New York, the train offered a ladies' lounge, bath and maid service as well as what Seaboard modestly referred to as "unrivaled service." But by the time the *Blossom* arrived, the party was almost over. As quickly as the boom had come, bust followed. Florida's economy sagged, as did its tourism market. Following on the heels of the Florida bust, the nationwide Great Depression took a big bite out of the railroads as well. By 1930 Pullman traffic had been nearly halved. That same year, Seaboard entered receivership.

By the mid 1930's, despite the Depression, Pullman traffic had rebounded sufficiently to enable ACL's *Florida Special* to routinely operate once again in sections, including a record seven in one day on Feb. 29, 1936. The fundamental problem, however, was encouraging the average passenger, impacted by the Depression or smitten with the automobile, to return to the rails in numbers sufficient to make up a frightening shortfall. By mid-Depression, the nation's railroads' passenger earnings had been cut in half. No run-of-the-mill marketing efforts would make up that gap. Necessity had become the mother of invention.

The *Florida Special* circa 1937 at Jacksonville. The high-windowed observation car is probably a New York Central-assigned *Valley*-series 1-drawing-room, 1-bedroom car from the *20th Century Limited* pool. The Latino string band was a fixture in the recreation car, and the observation platform was a favorite posing spot for the FEC photographer. The drumhead *Florida Special* lent a cachet of elegance to an even ordinary occasion.—COURTESY OF THE HENRY M. FLAGLER MUSEUM, PALM BEACH, FLA.

2 METEORIC SUCCESS
Seaboard Air Line: 1939–1945

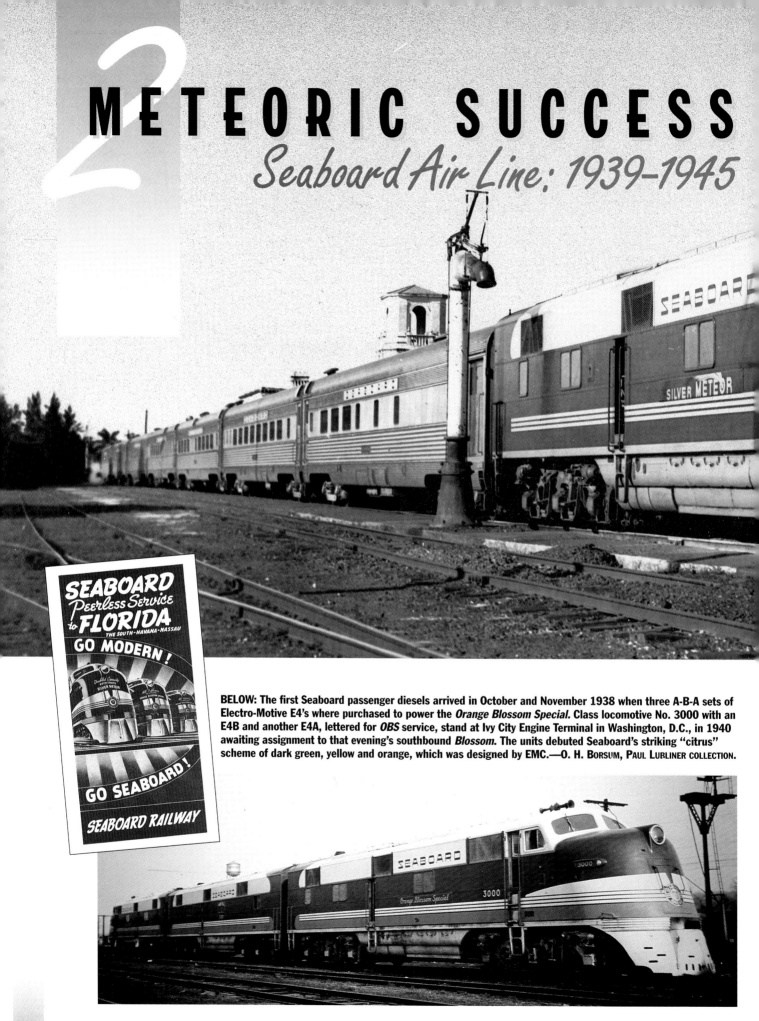

SEABOARD
Peerless Service
to FLORIDA
THE SOUTH—HAVANA—NASSAU
GO MODERN !
GO SEABOARD !
SEABOARD RAILWAY

BELOW: The first Seaboard passenger diesels arrived in October and November 1938 when three A-B-A sets of Electro-Motive E4's where purchased to power the *Orange Blossom Special.* Class locomotive No. 3000 with an E4B and another E4A, lettered for *OBS* service, stand at Ivy City Engine Terminal in Washington, D.C., in 1940 awaiting assignment to that evening's southbound *Blossom.* The units debuted Seaboard's striking "citrus" scheme of dark green, yellow and orange, which was designed by EMC.—O. H. BORSUM, PAUL LUBLINER COLLECTION.

Glistening in the Florida sun, Seaboard's new *Silver Meteor* pauses at West Palm Beach in March 1939. Unit 3006, an Electro-Motive E4, was built expressly for the new all-coach streamliner and carries the *Silver Meteor* name on a letterboard on its flanks.—CAL'S CLASSICS.

At the beginning of March 1938, the *Miami Daily News* kicked off an unusual editorial campaign entitled "Streamliners for Miami." Why would a major metropolitan daily tackle such an obscure subject? After all, newspapers were supposed to editorialize on community issues.

Well, if you lived in Miami, tourism *was* a community issue. One of the principal economic pillars of the city—and indeed the state—tourism had been flagging as a result of the Florida bust of the 1920's and the Depression. The cost of a Florida vacation was out of the reach of the ordinary traveler. It didn't help that Miami was served only by traditional heavyweight trains, while elsewhere across the nation lightweight streamliners flashed to and fro making household names of the cities they served. It was time to get aggressive.

Firmly backed by the business community, the campaign quickly received public support, and the paper sent reporter Warren Smith off to Chicago and Denver for a look at the various lightweight wonders crisscrossing the West and a talk with the folks who ran them. In a series of four "On the Road" articles, the *Daily News* scribe documented the experiences of CB&Q President Ralph Budd, Rock Island's top man, the head of the Denver Chamber of Commerce and actor George Arliss—a neophyte streamliner expert, having just arrived in Chicago on Union Pacific/Chicago & North Western's lightweight *City of Los Angeles*. Not one among them spoke less than euphorically on the issue of streamliners.

Budd detailed the savings afforded by the speed and efficiency of diesel-electric power, Denver businessman Stanley Wallbank dwelt at length on the issue of the Mile High City's newfound status as a "suburb" of Chicago thanks to the faster schedules of the new trains, and Arliss waxed eloquently on the

On what may have been the same day that the *Silver Meteor* photo on the previous pages was recorded, the *Southern States Special* strikes a stately pose at West Palm Beach. SAL Mountain No. 224 gets its tank filled as the engineer oils the spotless 4-8-2. The date is March 1939 and, save for the *Meteor* and the E-units on the *Orange Blossom*, this is state-of-the-art railroading, Seaboard style.—Cal's Classics.

comforts he had encountered on his recent trip.

Clearly, the words which carried the most weight were those of the railroad men. Of these, an interview with Rock Island's J. D. Farrington caught the attention of Seaboard Air Line. Like the Seaboard and many other American railroads, Rock Island was in serious financial trouble as a result of the Depression. Farrington had beseeched the Rock's creditors for enough funds for six streamliners to boost passenger revenues. With grave reservations, the bankers lent the railroad the money. By the end of 1937, a scant three months after delivery, the new *Rocket* trains were turning a substantial net profit.

While delivering positive information like this to the folks back home, Smith was also wielding the pen to refute the claims of the conservative Atlantic Coast Line that lightweight streamliners worked best "out West" where distances between stops were longer. Florida, the railroad said, was virtually commuter territory, a "pickup and distribution" state and no place to use diesel streamliners efficiently. Smith casually rebutted these statements and, using Burlington's *Denver Zephyr* as an example, patiently explained the numerous stops it made—including one not 30 miles out of Chicago. Going one step farther, the reporter showed how the speed and efficiency of diesels helped Rock Island operate its Chicago-Des Moines *Rocket* on a daily roundtrip while a steam-hauled FEC local completed a similar distance run in Florida only one way per day.

In defense of ACL, not all railroads had embraced lightweight streamlining. Part of the reluctance was due to the "experimental" nature of the beast, but by 1938 that tag had worn thin. Even such conservatives as Pennsylvania and New York Central had invested heavily to streamline their flagships. A more-probable cause for ACL's hedging was the obdurate nature of its mechanical department. As late as

1938, four years after the official dawn of the streamlined era at the Chicago Railroad Fair, ACL was busy purchasing a series of heavyweight day coaches.

Not everyone in the South was this resistant to change. If ACL was unwilling to take the plunge on streamlining, underdog Seaboard would. In late 1936 and early 1937, SAL had received its first lightweight cars—six coaches and four combines based on a pioneering lightweight design introduced by the New Haven Railroad and Pullman's Osgood-Bradley plant. The sleek, turtle-roofed cars went into service on SAL's *Orange Blossom Special*.

This was not the first streamlined equipment in the South. In July 1935, the Gulf Mobile & Northern had introduced a non-articulated streamliner, the *Rebel*, built by American Car & Foundry. Operating between Jackson, Tenn., and New Orleans, La., the three-car, silver-and-red "pocket streamliner" proved to be highly economical and very popular.

With lightweight, diesel-hauled trains proving their success nationwide and in the South, and with community leaders pressing for action, SAL considered its situation. In 1934, four years after the road threw itself on the mercy of the courts, the road's net income deficit had been a staggering $8 million. Since that time, the loss had never been under $4 million. Despite these gloomy numbers, passenger revenues *had* been on the increase, but in 1938 they too went on the decline, finishing the year $10^{1}/2$ percent lower than 1937. Something had to be done.

Paradoxically, it was the lack of income which spurred Seaboard to spend more on improvements. In the fall of 1938, SAL acquired nine Electro-Motive E4 diesel passenger units in three A-B-A sets. The justification for the purchase was an expected reduction in operating expenses thanks to the efficiency of diesels. The shortening of schedules made possible by the units' ability to maintain higher sustained speeds with less maintenance also allowed for expansion of service.

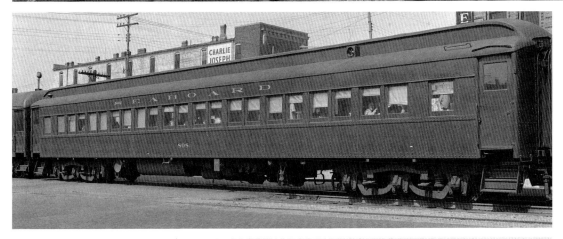

In that year, the *Orange Blossom Special*, the train for which the diesels had been purchased, began handling through cars to Boston, thanks to the faster schedule.

The real problem, however, was how to attract riders back to the rails. In 1929, passenger revenues were $874 million nationally. Just four years later, reflecting the Depression and the inroads of the automobile, that figure had shrunk to $329 million. Seaboard had never ceased trying to fill its trains and worked within its means to air condition its own cars while handling air-conditioned Pullmans over its route. But clearly something more was needed, something dramatic to improve its image and attract more passengers. A

coach streamliner between New York and Miami seemed the answer.

All-coach trains were, on the whole, more profitable than all-Pullman or combined operations due to higher capacity. A wider range of potential travelers could also be targeted with luxurious, affordable accommodations. Too, the luxury-coach concept seemed an excellent way to entice the budget-minded traveler to Florida in the "off" season of summer when hotels went unfilled and the rates were lower. This could be a way to break the annoying cycle common to heavy-in-winter, light-in-summer Florida travel. The imbalance affected everything from the

The fellows in the Chevy —and especially the chap in the rumble seat—are getting a great view of a 4-8-2-powered *Orange Blossom Special* as it cuts a swath across their path. The location is somewhere in Florida, and the date, pegged to the auto license and the lack of diesels on the head end, is probably 1937.—BARRIGER COLLECTION, ST. LOUIS MERCANTILE MUSEUM.

A guide for "southern vacationists" published by Seaboard in the 1930's. —COLLECTION OF WILLIAM F. HOWES JR.

utility of railroad-owned passenger equipment to the staffing and operation of dining service. The Florida roads often found themselves leasing off-line diners and employing dining-car crews from other roads as well each winter.

The natural model for a Florida coach streamliner was Santa Fe's *El Capitan*. The Budd-built, five-car, luxury-coach operation had been in service between Chicago and Los Angeles since February 1938 and was succeeding splendidly. The key to attracting riders had been "luxury"—a word which, until recently, had rarely been used in the same sentence with "coach." From a marketing standpoint, Santa Fe had benefited by paying attention to the unspoken needs of the coach traveler and in turn had discovered a rich source of ridership.

After conducting extensive inquiries of the other roads operating streamliners to confirm its idea, Seaboard petitioned receivers L. R. Powell Jr. and H. W. Anderson, the security holders and the courts for permission to purchase a streamlined coach train. Approval was granted to acquire one "experimental" trainset.

Enter the Budd Company, midwife to a host of railroads who had given birth to the streamlined era. By 1938, the Philadelphia car builder had produced entire lightweight trains for Santa Fe, Reading, Rock Island and Burlington, including the first diesel-powered streamliner in the world—CB&Q's *Pioneer Zephyr*. Along the way it had perfected the use of stainless steel in car-building, developed a standard exterior design for a carbody and become a formidable competitor of Pullman-Standard and ACF.

Budd's hallmark was its shining stainless-steel trains. But the hard-to-work metal was also more expensive than the standard lightweight alloy of the time, Cor-Ten Steel, favored by Pullman-Standard. Budd's engineers argued persuasively that although their train was more expensive to build, it cost a quarter cent less per mile to operate. After a computable number of days, so the explanation went, there was a break-even point, and after that a Budd-built train actually saved money.

Armed with this argument and an impressive record as the premier builder of coach streamliners, Budd captured the SAL contract. (In point of fact, Seaboard had waited for the Pennsylvania Railroad's approval of SAL's new venture before committing to the deal.) With all parties in agreement, SAL finalized its order to Budd on Oct. 12, 1938. As soon as the basic engineering aspects such as car types and improvements to roadbed were covered, the project was turned over to Budd's talented architects Paul Cret and John Harbeson. The team had created such marvels as the *Pioneer Zephyr* (it was Cret who helped design Budd's fluting) and the original Santa Fe *Super Chief* with its exquisite wood-toned interiors and Navajo themes.

Creativity didn't come at the expense of a deadline, however, and the men always worked under the gun. In a letter, John Harbeson explained the process of creating a streamliner:

"We usually had no more than three weeks to do a train. . . In the office we had a 'train crew' made up of my former [architectural] students at the University of Pennsylvania who were willing to work nights and weekends and became proficient in working fast.

"We started with a few geometricals to determine basic shapes and then went immediately to perspectives over which we made tracing-paper studies in pastel to study color. Three weeks was the limit of time we had, not only for the presentation of perspectives, but also the accompanying 'color and material' paste-ups. . . It made a good presentation—went over well.

"We believed in decoration to interest the passenger but also to give the advertising men something to advertise. Thus, for the Santa Fe, we had Southwest Indians, Kachina dolls, etc. . . We made small-scale studies of bar fronts, of glass partitions, etc. Then giving dimensions of space we asked Bourdelle, Harriton etc. to make sketches using their own talent, within the agreed-upon general field of history, locality, etc.

"The 'team,' having gained experience, produced miracles quickly. There were always a number of trials—the better were chosen, the rest dropped."

If there was leeway in the interior design, there was very little in the exterior. By 1938 Budd had returned to the modified Pratt truss sideframe after experimenting unsuccessfully with upright channels for side support on Santa Fe coach 3070. The Pratt truss and a new, heavier centersill design added structural strength at the cost of added weight. SAL's first coaches for the *Meteor* weighed in at nearly 51 tons—almost nine tons heavier than Santa Fe's experimental coach. Having invested heavily in jigs, presses and brakes, Budd was comfortable with a fairly standard car design. Any major changes in the pattern, beyond a point, would be unjustifiably expensive.

The construction process involved shaping thin sheets of 18/8 stainless steel (18 percent chrome and 8 percent nickel) into the various structural components of the cars. The material, first produced in Germany in 1912, had fascinated Edward G. Budd for its properties of light weight, high strength and corrosion resistance. Convinced it was a natural for aircraft and railroad-car construction, Budd challenged Col. E. J. Ragsdale to find a way to successfully fasten the material without inhibiting its strength. The answer was the "shotweld," a precisely controlled "shot" of electricity. The key was the quick timing of the weld. Budd was justifiably proud of this patented technique and used it as an advantage over the competition.

In the capable hands of the folks at Budd's Hunting Park (Philadelphia) plant, the then-nameless

LEFT: Trainside on the *Orange Blossom Special* at West Palm Beach in the late 1930's. Redcaps push baggage carts, porters stand at attention beside rivet-sided heavyweight Pullmans and passengers take in the balmy breezes of Florida on the grounds of Seaboard's Spanish-style stucco depot. Note the minstrel strolling the platform with a guitar. It was all part of the service.—Barriger Collection, St. Louis Mercantile Museum.

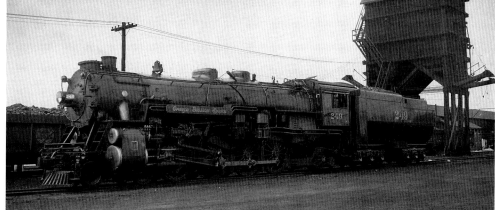

RIGHT: Seaboard's 200-class Mountains typically provided the power for the *Orange Blossom Special* in the 1930's prior to the arrival of diesels. Name boards identifying the *Blossom* were common on the Mountain-class engines as well as on light Pacifics which handled the West Coast section between Wildwood and St. Pete. —California State Railroad Museum, Gerald M. Best.

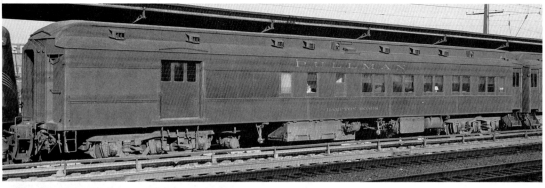

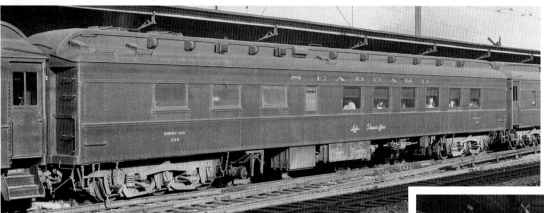

LOWER LEFT: Fine dining Seaboard style was available to patrons of the *Orange Blossom Special* on SAL's famous *Lake*-series diners. Here *Lake Panasoffkee* pauses at Manhattan Transfer on the PRR, the day after Christmas 1936.—GEORGE E. VOTAVA. BELOW: Pullman Sun Room lounges with three compartments and one drawing room like the *Dixieland* operated on the *Orange Blossom Special* in the late 1930's.—SMITHSONIAN INSTITUTION.

TOP: Seaboard's East Coast *Orange Blossom Special* was the haven for a piece of equipment disappearing from recently streamlined luxury trains such as the *20th Century Limited*—the Pullman baggage-club car. Offering Pullman passengers a chance to enjoy good conversation, a choice smoke and refreshing potables, the car was usually a male bastion. Typical of the type was the *Hampton Roads*, pictured here at Manhattan Transfer, N.J., in December 1936. —GEORGE VOTAVA.

BELOW: The public joined SAL in marketing its new streamliner.—HAGLEY MUSEUM COLLECTION.

Seaboard streamliner began to take shape. To rectify this identity crisis and generate a little publicity, SAL conducted a "Name this Train Contest." A whopping 76,366 entries were received and the $500 prize was shared by the 30 winners who suggested the name *Silver Meteor*. On Jan. 25, 1939, the *Silver Meteor* took to the rails for a shakedown cruise, operating over the PRR from the Budd plant in Philadelphia to Downington, Pa., approximately 30 miles, at a top speed of 50 mph. All was in order for the upcoming debut.

Homeward-bound passengers using Philadelphia's Broad Street Station on Jan. 30 were treated to an unusual sight. There on track 9, gleaming like polished silver and tucked in among smoking K4's and tuscan P70 day coaches, was the pride of the Seaboard Air Line. The *Meteor* had been hauled from the Budd plant by steam earlier in the day. The following day the *Meteor* collected nearly 200 invited guests of the Budd Company and whisked them to New York's Pennsylvania Station.

The public was invited to "come and see" the new train in a public exhibition at Penn Station on Feb. 1. From 10 a.m. to 2 p.m., over 9,500 folks took the SAL up on its offer. Visitors to Track 3 found Florida decorations at the concourse gate, and while the palm fronds looked particularly seductive, the star of the show was not to be outshone. As visitors descended the stairs to the platform, they encountered the

Meteor (sans locomotive) stretched out for inspection.

Starting the tour at the head end, the public entered the baggage area of car 6000, a 22-seat baggage-dormitory chair car designated to carry the *Meteor*'s "colored" passengers in this pre-civil rights era. Known as the "green car," it featured blue ceilings, brown walls and blue-and-green-pinstriped chairs. Rubber flooring was common throughout all the coach seating areas of the train, and in this car it was a dark oak color with a stripe pattern in the aisles. Crew accommodations for 12 plus a steward's room were also provided. All of the cars were air-conditioned.

The second car, bright and spacious, with 60 reclining seats, was coach 6200 finished in a scheme featuring a tan, brown and coral ceiling and brown walls. Seats were alternately upholstered in fawn/rust and coral pinstripes. The center aisle was striped in red, gold, black and coral. Spacious ladies' and men's lounges were at opposite ends of the car. Along the

way, visitors were likely to encounter a Budd or Seaboard employee who answered questions and dispensed literature.

Third in line was chair-tavern car 6300 seating 30 coach passengers and providing 30 non-revenue lounge seats. An orchid gray ceiling blended with tuscan rose side walls. On the coach seats, brown pencil-stripe upholstery alternated with patterned chamois. In the middle of the car was the hostess' room where the stewardess, who was also a registered nurse, could tend to her chores. The smartly attired bar area featured a decoratively etched back bar with lighted mirrors. The bar front, reminiscent of SAL's diesel colors, was stainless steel with multicolored stripes of orange, green, yellow and mustard. Red leather upholstery with tan piping covered the seats here, and the oval tables had robin's egg blue tops with a white border. Unlike the coaches, this car was carpeted, with an apple green and brown pattern of diamonds in the card-playing area and ovals in the settee area. Drapery was done in a red and gray stripe.

Next was diner 6100, with its 12 tables decked out in snowy white and striped linens. Olive gray walls sported a three-tone ceiling of sand, stone color and tuscan rose. Beige window curtains blended with gray-and-rose-patterned window drapes. The 48 dining-car chairs bore raisin-color pinstripes with backs of maroon and gray. A rust-colored carpet in a zig-zag pattern led the eye to a walnut veneer buffet at the car end near the all-stainless kitchen.

Behind the diner was 60-seat coach 6201. The "brown car" had an oyster white ceiling, gray walls and brown floral chairs, alternating with others in fawn pinstripes. Another 60-seat coach, the 6202, followed. With seats covered in either blue pinstripe or a blue floral print, this was the "blue car." A lemon cream ceiling complemented the blue walls, and the floors were dark oak.

From here, the visitor left the train with a glimpse through the door of chair-observation 6400. Yellow and turquoise interiors framed coach seats featuring brown or turquoise stripes. The observation area had 17 moveable chairs, three love seats and a writing desk in colors of rose, green or gray. Glass partitions, etched with the likenesses of game fish, separated the coach area from the lounge. A mahogany carpet hosted insets of taupe.

Two more private showings were held between 3 and 9 p.m. at which another 4,565 invited guests of SAL and Budd viewed the new train. Then it was time for a spruce-up and a well-deserved rest before the big day.

As if to remind everyone of the *Silver Meteor*'s purpose, Thursday Feb. 2 dawned cold and dreary. At 10 a.m. the new train, loaded with dignitaries, was coupled to a Long Island third-rail electric DD1 locomotive and hauled from Penn Station under the East River to Flushing Meadows—the site of the Long Island Rail Road station for the New York World's Fair. Here a PRR GG1 electric, leased by Seaboard for the exhibition at a cost of $64, was tacked on to the head end of the new train for appearances.

At 11:45 a.m. the ceremonies commenced at the rear of the train with a WOR radio announcer describing the scene and calling on the gathered officials for short, impromptu speeches. Stephen Vorhees, chairman of the Fair's Board of Design, called the train "a new link between the Fair and the South." Other speakers included L. R. Powell and Henry Anderson, receivers of the SAL, Edward G. Budd and R. F. Evans, vice-president of diesel development for EMD. At the close of remarks, Ruth Frances Schmitt, a fair employee, stepped forward, clad in red cape over black and silver. She tapped the observation end with a wand emitting "audible and visible sparks" saying, "I christen you the *Silver Meteor*, the 'Train of Tomorrow,' and wish you Godspeed on your inaugural trip to Florida." Over the radio, listeners heard the dubbed-in blast of a diesel horn. An era had begun.

Invited guests were loaded onto the train and pulled back to Penn Station while being served a buffet luncheon during the brief trip. At 3:30 p.m., suitably tidied up and in the charge of a sparkling GG1, the *Meteor* eased out of Penn Station on her inaugural run carrying officials and invited guests of the railroads, the manufacturers and enough paying passengers to account for a full house. Emerging from the Hudson tubes and encountering snow mixed with

Seaboard's East Coast *Orange Blossom Special* rockets along southbound somewhere in Florida in March 1939. Note the Pullman heavyweight baggage-club immediately behind the A-B-A set of E4's.—CAL'S CLASSICS, AUTHOR'S COLLECTION.

Early riders on the *Silver Meteor* received this blue-and-silver baggage sticker.—AUTHOR'S COLLECTION VIA HOWARD GRIFFIN.

White flags on the locomotive—indicating a non-scheduled Extra move—and the cadre of photographers at the Hollywood (Fla.) depot may be an indication that this is the inaugural southbound *Meteor* on Feb. 3, 1939. —AUTHOR'S COLLECTION VIA BILL GRIFFIN.

The *Meteor's* coach-observation car played prominent in this folder produced for the new train.—COLLECTION OF WILLIAM F. HOWES JR.

rain, the *Meteor's* passengers experienced one of the great thrills of going to Florida by rail—being tucked snugly into a warm train, impervious to the elements and knowing the next time you stepped outside it would be into 80-degree temperatures and breezes laced with the fragrance of the tropics.

There was plenty to do en route, however. Focal point for the happy dignitaries was the mid-train tavern car where no less than four attendants slaked the thirst of a standing-room-only crowd. Not to be outshone, the dining car was filled with patrons sampling SAL's thrifty 60-cent dinner menu offering a maincourse choice of baked bluefish, fricassee of chicken or beef pot pie. Dessert selections included shortcake and a Florida staple—guava jelly. Suitably wined and dined, passengers could retreat to the observation car for a glimpse at a quickly receding industrial landscape.

At Washington's Union Station, the capable PRR electric was uncoupled from its charge and Seaboard's newest E4 diesel, the 3006, running through over the Richmond, Fredericksburg & Potomac, took the reigns. Built specifically for the *Meteor*, the 2,000-h.p. beauty was an eye popper in its "citrus scheme" of green, orange, yellow and silver. This E4 was identical to

her sisters delivered in 1938 for the *Orange Blossom Special,* save for train-name lettering.

A fast ride over the RF&P put the train in Richmond's venerable Main Street Station (shared with Chesapeake & Ohio). Proud parent SAL took control officially at Hermitage Yard north of the station.

Seaboard's single-track line of predominantly 100-pound rail wound and undulated through the rural Appalachian foothills of Virginia and North and South Carolina. After a pause in Petersburg, Va., the train ran nonstop through the pine belt to Hamlet, N.C. Curiously, it was not until the Sept. 28, 1942, completion of Raleigh's Eugene C. Bagwell Station that the North Carolina capital would become a regular stop for either the *Meteor* or the *Orange Blossom Special.* Prior to that time, lesser SAL trains used Raleigh Union station (shared with Southern and the original Norfolk Southern). Being a stub-end facility, Raleigh Union Station necessitated backup moves and therefore was viewed as too time-consuming a stop for the road's crack speedsters.

Hamlet, reached in the dead of night, was the hub of the Seaboard where its east-west and north-south main lines converged like spokes on a wheel. South from Hamlet, the road chose to operate passenger trains over its more-direct but more-steeply graded line (with ruling grades of 1.3 percent) to Savannah, Ga., via Columbia, S.C. Seaboard's heavier freights were usually diverted onto the flatter line serving Charleston, S.C.

Chances are passengers were just waking up or were busy shaving or preparing for the day in the oversized washrooms and lounges in each coach as the *Meteor* backed into Savannah Union Station. Next came the wonderful experience of breakfast in the dining car. Crisp linens, able waiters and the heavenly

smell of fresh brewed coffee were all part of the scene. For 50 cents, the diner had a choice of ham and scrambled eggs, corned beef hash with eggs, or cereal. Another traditional Florida delicacy—fresh orange or grapefruit marmalade—was offered as, of course, were all manner of citrus fruits, juiced and whole.

At Jacksonville Terminal, reporters from the Jacksonville, Palm Beach and Miami press joined their brethren from Columbia and Savannah for the ride south. From Jacksonville south, the tracks were lined with the curious as Florida welcomed its first streamliner. *The Miami Herald* estimated crowds at West Palm Beach to number a thousand, and two thousand more people turned out at Fort Lauderdale. Even rural grade crossings were festooned with knots of onlookers.

Boarding the train at West Palm Beach was General Motors Vice President Charles Kettering, designer of the diesel engine within the SAL E4. Kettering rode the cab with SAL receivers Powell and Anderson while Seaboard engineer W. L. Leighton, a 36-year veteran of the road, took the train into Miami under clear skies and 76-degree temperatures.

SAL's pink stucco station had never seen such a hubbub as it did on that Feb. 3, 1939. Assembled to greet the arriving dignitaries were City Manager C. A. Fuller, the Miami Drum & Bugle Corps and 7,500 other Miamians. Addressing the crowd and listeners of radio station WQAM, Kettering spoke of the progressiveness of American railroads and of the Seaboard in particular. Edward G. Budd summed it up concisely, saying "The *Silver Meteor* speaks for itself."

The following morning, the *Meteor* departed Miami for New York. Arriving there on Feb. 5, the train was turned, serviced and readied for its next trip south the same day. On its original carding, the *Meteor* served both coasts of Florida, so this next trip south was the train's first scheduled run to Tampa and St. Petersburg. The *Meteor* followed the same route as far as Coleman, Fla., just south of the crew-change point of Wildwood, where it veered southwesterly toward Tampa.

On the *Silver Meteor*'s Feb. 6 arrival at St. Petersburg, informal festivities took place with a short radio broadcast commencing at 4:20 p.m., five minutes after arrival. Again the *Meteor* was mobbed by admiring crowds. Departure for New York took place the following morning at 11 a.m. This alternating schedule—one round trip to Miami followed by a round trip to St. Pete—continued until early June.

Would the new train justify Seaboard's investment? To answer this, consider the following three points. First, could the *Silver Meteor* focus attention on underdog Seaboard and away from competitor ACL? Clearly the answer was yes. SAL ran its first ad for the new train in the Jan. 15, 1939, *New York Times*. Within 48 hours, the railroad received 2,500 inquiries about travel on the new train which had a capacity of 280 seats. Four trips were completely sold out by Jan. 18!

Second, could the train attract riders away from other forms of transportation? To answer this question, SAL circulated a survey among *Meteor* passengers. The form, obliquely entitled "Are You Enjoying Your Trip?," asked "What form of transportation would you have used for your trip if you had not chosen the *Silver Meteor*?" Early numbers culled from riders indicated that a remarkable 40.3 percent of the passengers *wouldn't* have traveled by rail had the *Meteor* not been available.

ABOVE: Florida's first streamliner was certainly cause for celebration at Miami, where the first *Silver Meteor* is scutinized by crowds. The *Meteor* would serve Seaboard's Miami depot for nearly 40 more years.—BOMBARDIER CORPORATION.

ABOVE: Upon opening your *New York Herald Tribune* on Jan. 31, 1939, you would have been greeted by this public invitation to see the new *Silver Meteor* at Pennsylvania Station.—HAGLEY MUSEUM COLLECTION.

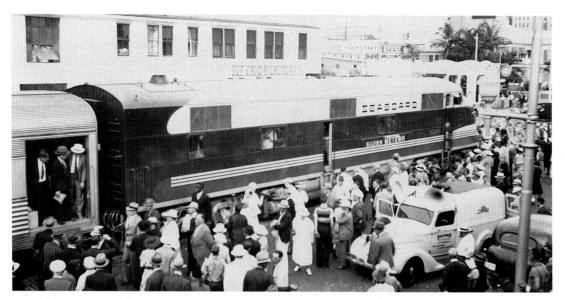

handled a New York-St. Petersburg coach as well as sleepers to St. Petersburg, Venice and Port Boca Grande. A Boston-St. Petersburg 10-1-2 also was included. Steam hauled the West Coast *Blossom* on RF&P and SAL while Seaboard diesels operated on the East Coast section through to Washington.

The *Southern States Special* offered air-conditioned, heavyweight coaches and sleepers from New York to both coasts of the Sunshine State on a one-night-out basis. A 10-section lounge rode from Washington to Miami. When the seasonal East Coast *Orange Blossom* ceased operation for the season in April 1939, her diesels went to the *Southern States* for the summer, allowing for schedule improvements of up to 2 hours and 50 minutes, which boosted revenues on that train.

Not to be forgotten was Seaboard's accommodation train on the New York-Florida run, the *New York-Florida Limited*. Carrying air-conditioned coaches between New York and Miami and Washington and St. Petersburg, the train also featured sleepers between New York and St. Petersburg, Miami, Venice and Port Boca Grande on a leisurely two-night-out schedule.

Despite these other heavyweight alternatives, the clamor for a seat on the *Meteor* continued. In an effort to give passengers more of a good thing, Seaboard decided to abandon the concept of running the *Meteor* as a seven-car train alternating round trips to Miami and St. Petersburg by reducing capacity and increasing frequency to both cities. Commencing June 5, 1939, southbound and June 7 northbound, the *Meteor* was split into two trains at Wildwood. The St. Petersburg section included:

Dancing in the streets: The initial *Silver Meteor* arrival at St. Petersburg on Feb. 6, 1939, has drawn quite a crowd, including the Boardwalk Sound & Amplification truck parked adjacent to E4 3006. Everyone appears dressed for the occasion.—G. W. PETTENGILL JR. VIA WARREN CALLOWAY.

Third, would the new train earn money? An independent examination of the *Meteor*'s earnings for the period Feb. 2, 1939, through June, 30, 1939, showed a healthy net revenue of $1.98 per train-mile. Undoubtedly, the *Silver Meteor* was a drawing card, and it didn't hurt that extra-low coach fares of 1½ cent per mile were in effect on the Southeastern roads.

As discussed earlier, a principal benefit of dieselized, lightweight trains was speed. In pre-diesel 1937, SAL's fastest New York-Miami carding had been 29 hours for the *Orange Blossom Special*. The new *Meteor* cut that time to 26½ hours and would cut it further still to meet competition. With minor exceptions, these numbers reflected the early successes of most of the new streamliners of the prewar period.

The *Meteor*'s principal running mates during its inaugural season included the incomparable *Orange Blossom Special* (in sections), the *Southern States Special* and the *New York-Florida Limited*. One section of the "Twin Blossoms" linked New York to the East Coast of Florida with air-conditioned heavyweight sleepers, diners, a Pullman club-buffet-recreation car and a 6-compartment observation. Two sleepers—a 10-1-2 and a 6-3—operated through to Boston. To the West Coast of Florida a separate *Orange Blossom*

Between June 1939 and May 1940, after the *Silver Meteor* began being split at Wildwood, Fla., for daily service to Miami and St. Petersburg, it was not uncommon to see EMC motorcar No. 2028 hauling the three-car Wildwood-St. Pete section. The 2028 and its twin sister, No. 2027, were built by St. Louis Car Company in 1936. For *Silver Meteor* service, the 2028 received the citrus scheme and a train name board. An aluminum-painted combine trails the 2028 at St. Petersburg on this October day in 1939.—G. W. PETTENGILL JR. VIA TOM KING.

Line No.	Car No.	Car type	Endpoints
1-W	285-288	52-seat baggage-coach	WWD-STP*
2-W	6200	60 seat (Budd) coach	NYP-STP
3-W	6300	30 seat coach-tavern	NYP-STP

*According to railroad notes, this car handled across-the-platform train changes by black passengers with West Coast Florida destinations who had ridden down to Wildwood in car 1-E (below).

Power between Wildwood and St. Petersburg for this diminutive consist was often provided by SAL motor car 2028. And at least one of the Osgood-Bradley-built "American Flyer" combines (so nicknamed in later years after noted toy train manufacturer A. C. Gilbert Company of New Haven, Conn., offered models of Osgood-Bradley Pullman-Standard streamlined cars), Nos. 285-288, was painted aluminum for this prestigious assignment. By late May 1940, SAL Pacifics would be assigned to this run.

The Miami section of the train, usually handled by E4 3006, was:

Line No.	Car No.	Type	Endpoints
1-E	6000	22-seat bag-dorm-coach	NYP-MIA
—	6100	48-seat diner	NYP-MIA
4-E	6201	60-seat coach	NYP-MIA
5-E	6202	60-seat coach	NYP-MIA
6-E	6400	48-seat observation	NYP-MIA

Via this new arrangement, SAL provided service every third day to both Miami and St. Petersburg.

With the *Silver Meteor* quickly repaying the investment, and with competitors Florida East Coast and Atlantic Coast Line stirring from their slumber and finalizing plans in late June for a streamliner of their own, SAL moved to meet the competition.

At a July 7, 1939, conference with PRR, SAL and the northern giant hammered out an expanded *Meteor* concept. Seaboard would purchase two nearly identical additional consists to the original *Silver Meteor*.

To improve current equalization arrangements, PRR would provide three new Budd-built coaches for the *Meteor*. Daily service would be provided to Miami effective Dec. 1, 1939, and two coaches and a diner would serve Tampa/St. Petersburg every third day.

Again the *Silver Meteor* showed its stuff to the general public. No doubt the intention was to steal some thunder from arch rival ACL's new *Champion* streamliner going into service the same day with daily service to Miami. Again, Pennsylvania Station in New York was bedecked in typical Florida trim, and visitors to Track 3 found a sparkling *Silver Meteor* consist, staffed by Seaboard employees eager to field visitors' questions.

The last guest off at 2 p.m., PRR detached coach 6202, sent it back to Sunnyside Yard and spruced up the rest of the six-car train for its entry into revenue service. With a touch of class and diplomacy, PRR dispatched the *Meteor* as a separate section of train 155 on this, its inaugural of daily service. Ordinarily the train was combined with PRR 155, a New York-Washington run.

In like manner, the rival *Champion* was inaugurated temporarily as a separate consist on the same day due to a problem with the New York-Washington train, PRR No. 125, it operated on. Hence, for a day, both the new *Champion* and the *Silver Meteor* ran separate from their ordinary Pennsy host trains. This practice happened on occasion.

ABOVE: Seaboard E4 3013 is shown at Ivy City terminal in Washington, D.C. The 3013 was one of a group of seven E4A's (3007-3013) delivered in November and December 1939 to power SAL trains including the expanded *Silver Meteor*. It remains somewhat of a mystery as to why Seaboard's first batch of E-series passenger diesels were designated model E4. Delivery of the first E4's actually preceded EMC's first production E3, and the two models were nearly identical. Perhaps it was the fact that Seaboard's units were equipped with a retractable nose door which facilitated passage between the locomotive and an adjacent passenger car when the unit was trailing.—CALIFORNIA STATE RAILROAD MUSEUM, GERALD M. BEST. ABOVE RIGHT: When Seaboard expanded the *Meteor* in December 1940 to provide daily service to both coasts of Florida, the road streamlined three Pacifics to handle the Wildwood-St. Pete section. Nos. 865-868 were shrouded and painted in a modified citrus scheme. The 868 is at St. Petersrburg.—JAMES BOWIE VIA JIM SCRIBBINS.

The assignment of equipment for the expanded *Silver Meteor* service was, from New York City, on Dec. 1:

Line No.	Car No.	Type	Endpoints
1-E	SAL 6001	Baggage-dorm-coach	NYP-MIA
3-E	SAL 6302	Tavern-coach	NYP-MIA
—	SAL 6102	Diner	NYP-MIA
4-E	SAL 6206	Coach	NYP-MIA
5-E	SAL 6207	Coach	NYP-MIA
6-E	SAL 6402	Coach-observation	NYP-MIA

From New York, Dec. 2, 1939:

Line No.	Car No.	Type	Endpoints
1-E	SAL 6002	Bag-dorm-coach	NYP-MIA
7-W	SAL 6204	Coach	NYP-STP
8-W	SAL 6202	Coach	NYP-STP
—	SAL 6103	Diner	NYP-STP
2-E	PRR 4014	Coach	NYP-MIA
3-E	SAL 6301	Tavern-coach	NYP-MIA
—	SAL 6101	Diner	NYP-MIA
4-E	SAL 6203	Coach	NYP-MIA
5-E	SAL 6205	Coach	NYP-MIA
6-E	SAL 6401	Coach-observation	NYP-MIA

From New York, Dec. 3, 1939:

Line No.	Car No.	Type	Endpoints
1-E	SAL 6000	Bag-dorm-coach	NYP-MIA
3-E	SAL 6300	Tavern-coach	NYP-MIA
—	SAL 6100	Diner	NYP-MIA
4-E	SAL 6200	Coach	NYP-MIA
5-E	SAL 6201	Coach	NYP-MIA
6-E	SAL 6400	Coach-observation	NYP-MIA

Note that on two out of every three days, the consists was comprised of only six cars. PRR's three new Budd coaches (Nos. 4015-4017) ordered for *Silver Meteor* service would not be delivered until Dec. 29-31. To fill the void, PRR 4014, a 66-seat Budd coach displayed at the New York World's Fair, was placed in the *Meteor* pool, making it the first PRR car to operate on the train. By the end of December, the *Meteor* was carrying its full complement of assigned cars. The 4014 remained in Florida service, however, shifting to a New York-St. Petersburg routing, making an 11-car train on days when the St. Petersburg section ran.

How did folks like these new trains? A glimpse at

Coach-baggage-dormitory 6004, with 18-seat coach seats, was delivered with sister cars 6003 and 6005 in November 1940 to expand the *Meteor* to a daily dual-destination train.—GEORGE VOTAVA.

Coach 6207 and four sisters were delivered in November 1939 to allow for daily New York-Miami and every-third-day New York-St. Petersburg *Meteor* service. The nearly spotless car is pictured at PRR's Sunnyside Yard on Long Island; note the full-width diaphragms. —GEORGE VOTAVA.

Diner 6104, also a member of the *Meteor* expansion program, was built in November 1940. It is shown at North Philadelphia in April 1946.—O. H. BORSUM.

Coach-observation 6401 arrived in November 1939 with twin 6402. The car is shown on Jan. 31, 1940, shortly after its delivery. Note that cars in this second order of observation cars from Budd did not have the rear coupler covered.—O. H. BORSUM.

ABOVE: In 1940, the *Meteor* reached its first milestone: a million miles of service. The train glided through this banner erected at Milepost 1023 north of Hollywood to commemorate the occasion.—BOMBARDIER CORPORATION. ABOVE RIGHT: This questionnaire, handed out to *Meteor* passengers, helped SAL make improvements to expanded operation.—COLLECTION OF WILLIAM GRIFFIN JR.

SAL customer responses for January 1940 indicates that 95 percent or more of the passengers enjoyed the ride, the amenities and the service. Consistent suggestions for improvement almost always concerned the need for more space—more leg room, bigger washrooms and more observation space—which was odd given the fact that these trains were some of the roomiest in the country. It was as if the passengers couldn't get enough of a good thing!

For all intents and purposes they couldn't. The *Silver Meteor* had been sold out nearly every day to both coasts in its first season. A Seaboard survey predicted even greater demand in the coming winter of 1940-41. The West Coast *Orange Blossom Special* had had more requests for Pullman space than it could fill as well. Consequently, two coaches and a combine were withdrawn from the *Blossom* in favor of more Pullmans, reverting the train to all-Pullman status when it reappeared in December 1940.

In mid 1940, Seaboard decided to double the consist of the *Meteor* to 14 cars. Eight cars would operate to Miami and six would split off to St. Petersburg at Wildwood daily in an arrangement like this:

2 EMD diesels	WAS-MIA
SAL 4-6-2 steam locomotive	WWD-STP
1 baggage-dorm-coach	NYP-STP
1 baggage-dorm-coach	NYP-MIA
2 coaches	NYP-MIA
1 diner	NYP-MIA
3 coaches	NYP-MIA
Coach-buffet-obs (sq. end)	NYP-MIA
1 tavern-coach	NYP-STP
1 diner	NYP-STP
2 coaches	NYP-STP
1 coach-observation (round end)	NYP-STP

All told, 18 new cars were ordered from the Budd Company to cover the expanded service, and they reflected the improvements suggested by the customers —more room and more observation space. For the

Seaboard, the new order included the following cars:

Nos.	Qty.	Type
6003-6005	3	18-seat baggage-dorm-coach
6208-6214	7	56-seat chair cars
6104, 6105	2	48-seat diners
6500-6502	3	30-seat chair-buffet-observations (square end)

The new buffet-observation cars had blunt ends so as to better blend with the trains' profiles—one operated mid-train on each consist between New York and Wildwood, at which point it became the tail-end observation of the Miami section after the St. Pete section was cut away.

PRR contributed three more Budd-built coaches for the service, all finished in stainless steel like their predecessors. Coach 4018, like the 4014, was a demonstrator that had been on display at the World's Fair. Cars 4024 and 4025 were constructed expressly for *Silver Meteor* service.

This newly expanded *Meteor* entered service on Dec. 1, 1940. Faced with a shortage of diesels, SAL added streamlined shrouding to three of its 4-6-2's, use of which was necessary to haul the heavier six-car St. Petersburg section out of Wildwood. Steam power wasn't new to the *Meteor;* steam had subbed for diesels (or motor car 2028) on the *Meteor*'s Wildwood-St. Petersburg runs as early as May 28, 1940.

Earlier in 1940, the *Meteor* had reached a milestone, marking its millionth mile of operation. The railroad's principal concern for the train was now a happy one: how to meet demand.

Through the winter season of 1940-41, the *Silver Meteor* and her running mates operated at near capacity. War in Europe had stimulated all manner of preparation at home—not the least of which involved travel. As the heavy winter travel season wound down and the seasonal *Orange Blossom Special* went into hibernation for the summer, SAL was determined to add

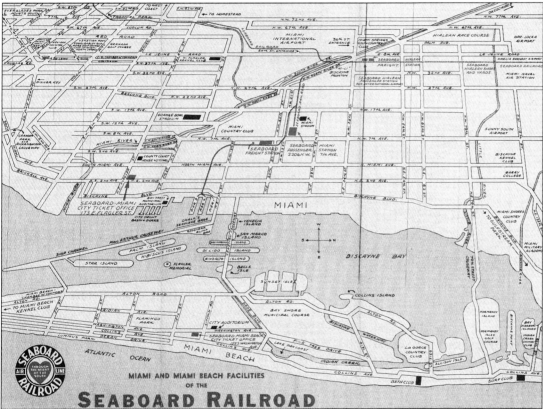

MIAMI AND MIAMI BEACH FACILITIES
OF THE
SEABOARD RAILROAD

LEFT: Seaboard's Miami depot at 2206 N.W. 7th Avenue is shown in 1940. The pink stucco building included commercial shops, such as the Great Atlantic & Pacific Tea Co. store on the nearer corner. Milk was going for 5 cents; the watermelons, 19 cents. The building was hardly an architectural masterpiece, but the neon depot sign was impressive.—MIAMI DADE PUBLIC LIBRARY, ROMER COLLECTION. CENTER LEFT: A brochure dating circa 1950 included this foldout showing Seaboard's Miami facilities and how they related to downtown Miami and Miami Beach. The depot was actually quite a distance from Miami's central business district. Note the location of the Dade County Court House, which was near rival Florida East Coast's Miami station, right downtown.— AUTHOR'S COLLECTION VIA HOWARD GRIFFIN. BELOW: Here is how Seaboard's city ticket office at 173 East Flagler Street (also shown on map at left) looked in downtown Miami in 1940. Reflected in the glass, along with the image of the photographer, is the marquee of a movie theater across the street where "Knute Rockne All American" was playing.— MIAMI-DADE PUBLIC LIBRARY, ROMER COLLECTION.

sleeping cars to the *Meteor* in an effort to meet demand for faster Pullman schedules to Florida.

As of April 28, 1941, the *Meteor* began handling a 10-section, 1-drawing room, 2-compartment car from New York to Miami and two 10-1-2's to St. Petersburg. These heavyweight cars were attired in standard Pullman green and filled in while Pullman shopped another series of cars specifically for *Meteor* service. For the new assignment, this second batch of heavyweight cars would receive what Pullman termed "special streamlined colors," applied as the sleepers were shopped between June 6 and July 15, 1941.

For Seaboard service, this would be a solid aluminum-colored body and roof with black lettering simply reading PULLMAN on the letterboard and a similarly styled car name below the windows. The cars were *not* shadowlined, despite rumors to the contrary. That technique, by which painters mimicked

fluting by means of gradiated bands painted on the cars, would make its debut sometime later on Santa Fe's *Sweewater Valley*, a lightweight 6-6-4 used in transcontinental service in conjunction with B&O.

The Pullman cars specifically painted for and assigned to the *Meteor* at this time were:

Car name	Car type
Miltonvale	10-1-2
Mount Gretna	10-1-2
Mount Joy	10-1-2
Poplar Brook	6-6
Poplar Castle	6-6
Poplar City	6-6
Giotto's Tower	8-1-3
Siebers Tower	8-1-3
Weeper's Tower	8-1-3

Beginning June 9, 1941, southbound and June 11 northbound, the *Meteor*'s assigned Pullman complement would include one 8-1-3 (NYP-MIA), one 6-6 (NYP-STP) and one 10-1-2 (NYP-STP). To handle the expanded 17-car consist, a third diesel was added between Richmond and Jacksonville.

No stranger to publicity and fanfare, Seaboard and its *Silver Meteor* occasionally hosted the great and near-great on their migrations to and from America's playground. Arguably, the most prestigious passengers the train ever carried were the Duke and Duchess of Windsor, "Edward and Wallie." On Sept. 24, 1941, the Duke and his wife—the former Wallis Warfield Simpson—rode the *Meteor* over the SAL, a railroad built in part by her uncle, Baltimore banker Solomon Davies Warfield. En route to Washington, the restless Duke soon indicated an interest in riding the head end. At the next stop he was escorted into the cab of an E4 where engineer Harry Aiken casually showed a former King of England the ropes of the first diesel the Duke had ever seen.

The *Silver Meteor* rocketed northward that day oblivious to clouds of a different kind on the horizon. December 1941 brought numerous changes to the country as a nation adjusted to the shock of being drawn into war. Despite the attack on Pearl Harbor a week before the official start of the winter travel season, the Seaboard was operating business as usual. The venerable *Southern States Special* had been renamed *Sun Queen*, and the *New York-Florida Limited* had been relabeled as the *Palmland*, still operating on a two-nights-out carding. The seasonal *Orange Blossom Special*, however, was

running as one train to Wildwood, splitting there for St. Petersburg and Miami. Meanwhile, sleeping-car service on the *Silver Meteor* had been expanded. Southbound, for the winter season only, it added a Boston-Miami 10-1-2 and 6-3 and a Boston-St. Petersburg 10-1-2. Northward the same car lines were carried in the *Orange Blossom Special*.

In a blizzard of hyphenization, the route was advertised as "The Fastest Ever - One-Night-Out New England-Florida sleeping car service." Both the *Meteor* and the *Blossom* were burning up the rails. Indeed, the all-heavyweight *Blossom* was operated on a blistering 24-hour New York-Miami schedule, one hour faster than the *Meteor*!

The actual makeup for the *Silver Meteor* provided in Consist of Note 1-A shows a typical make-up of the train and provides a rare glimpse at typical operations during the busy spring of 1942.

By 1942 the strain of war was showing on the country and its railroads. On the Seaboard, numerous war-related facilities (factories and training camps) had been springing up nearly overnight. The military and civilian traffic created by the necessities of conflict brought the highest freight and passenger traffic and revenues in the history of the railroad—but sometimes at a price. On June 14, 1942, while stopped to pick up train orders, the southbound *Silver Meteor* was rear-ended by a following freight near Kittrell, N.C. Eight passengers in observation 6400 were killed. The increased frequency and intensity of freight and passenger operations were partly to blame for the tragedy.

In Late 1942, the Office of Defense Transportation, a government agency overseeing the railroads, took steps to deal with the unprecedented demand on the Florida carriers. On SAL, the changes were dramatic. The *Orange Blossom Special* was discontinued for the rest of the war—a victim of its seasonal status. The *Silver Meteor* was expanded to two sections. Commencing Dec. 6, 1942 the *Advance Silver Meteor* began operation from New York to Miami with the following consist:

Heavyweight coaches
Heavyweight dining car
Three 6-compartment, 3-drawing-room sleepers
Two 8-section, 1-drawing room, 3-double-bedroom sleepers
One 6-section, 6-double-bedroom sleeper
One 8-section, 5-double-bedroom sleeper
One 6-compartment buffet-lounge

The regular *Silver Meteor* carried:

Baggage-dorm-coach	NYP-STP
10-1-2 sleeper	NYP-SRA-VEN
10-1-2 sleeper	NYP-STP
6-6 sleeper	NYP-STP
8-1-3 sleeper	NYP-STP
Diner	NYP-STP
Coaches (3)	NYP-STP
Coach-buffet-obs	NYP-STP
Coach-tavern-lounge	NYP-MIA
Coaches (3)	NYP-MIA
Coach-observation	NYP-MIA

This was the first time the *Meteor* carried a car for Sarasota and Venice. The *Advance Silver Meteor* bypassed Savannah Union Station and further bettered

its running time by skirting Jacksonville via the Gross-Baldwin cutoff. The regular train continued to make both of these stops. Between Wildwood and Miami the advance section was combined with the regular *Meteor*'s Miami cars making for a 20-car train. In addition the consist changes detailed above, SAL and its competitors were lengthening schedules to lessen wear and tear on vitally important track and equipment.

To say the railroads were overworked would have been an understatement. In 1942 the government alone was moving a million men every month. Add to this the increase in business traffic, those riding the rails to conserve their irreplaceable auto tires and the still-impressive seasonal Florida tourist trade and you can imagine the demand faced by Seaboard. The railroad sold everything, including lounge seats, as revenue space. Even then the traveler without priority as a military man or a defense contractor made do with what was available or sometimes nothing at all.

On May 23, 1943, the *Silver Meteor*'s operation was split geographically into an East Coast train for Miami and a West Coast section for St. Petersburg, both carrying sleepers and coach accommodations:

Silver Meteor (East Coast)

Coaches	NYP-MIA
Dining car	NYP-MIA
Coach-tavern-lounge	NYP-MIA
6-section, 6-double bedroom sleeper	NYP-MIA
8-section, 1-drawing room, 3-double bedroom sleeper	NYP-MIA
10-section,1-drawing room, 2-compartment sleeper	NYP-MIA
8-section, 5-double bedroom sleeper	NYP-MIA

Silver Meteor (West Coast)

Coaches	NYP-STP
Dining car	NYP-STP
8-section, 1-drawing room, 3-double bedroom sleeper	NYP-STP
6-section, 6-double bedroom sleeper	NYP-STP
10-section, 1-drawing room, 2 compartment sleeper	NYP-STP
8-section,1-drawing room, 3-double bedroom sleeper	NYP-STP

A 27-hour, 10-minute schedule was in effect between New York and Miami. Although diesels had been hauling the East Coast *Meteor* on the Seaboard to Miami, the West Coast section had been getting them only as far as Jacksonville. Here, capable Mountains took over for the run to Tampa/St. Petersburg in a practice that would continue until at least 1946.

SAL passenger service to Florida changed little in 1944 as compared with the previous year. Revenues and loadings again reached record highs, and if Seaboard moved the masses in unprecedented volumes, it also handled individuals vital to the war effort. An obscure memo from the PRR files indicates, for example, that on Feb. 25, 1944, the southbound *Meteor* carried a Messrs. Sloan, Firestone and Marchev all in car SA-27, a New York-Miami stateroom car. They were, respectively, the presidents of General Motors, Firestone Tire and Republic Aviation.

Through the war years, SAL's wise investment paid off. The initial commitment to lightweight streamlining had been a calculated risk. Despite a thorough study of lightweight operations in the West, SAL moved into uncharted territory when it decided to introduce streamliners to the radically different cyclical Florida travel market. Happily, public demand for the *Silver Meteor* seemed insatiable. As the railroad added more sections of the train, ridership—spurred in part by wartime necessity—filled those sections. For 1940, the *Silver Meteor* earned a very respectable $1,097,703 after expenses. In 1944, its most-successful year, the train *cleared* an astonishing $8 million, or nearly the amount the entire railroad had lost in 1933—one of its worst years.

In 1945, a year when the world had finally quenched the fires of a terrible war, Seaboard Air Line would lay the groundwork for what seemed a boundless future.

The exact date of this photo is unknown (probably mid-to-late 1940's) as the *Silver Meteor* pauses at Jacksonville. Chair-buffet-observation car 6500 on the rear is being stocked by the attendant through the small door in the fluting. Heavyweights abound throughout the rest of the consist.—JACKSONVILLE CHAPTER-NRHS.

CONSIST OF NOTE 2-A
PRR train 114, northbound *Silver Meteor*
Wednesday, March 25, 1942

Car	Type
PRR 4836	GG1 (locomotive)
SAL 6004	Baggage-dorm-coach
Point Paloway	10-section, 2-drawing-room sleeper
Ransom	10-section, 1-drwg.-room, 2-comp. sleeper
Glen Grove	6-comp., 3-drawing-room sleeper
Lake Borgne	10 section,1-drwg.-room, 2-comp. sleeper
SAL 101	Diner
PRR 4015	Coach
SAL 6209	Coach
SAL 6502	Coach-buffet-observation (square end)
PRR 4017	Coach
SAL 6200	Coach
SAL 6213	Coach
SAL 6302	Coach-tavern-lounge
SAL 6100	Diner
SAL 6210	Coach
SAL 6205	Coach
SAL 6401	Coach-observation (round end)

3 WINNERS AND CHAMPIONS
Atlantic Coast Line/ Florida East Coast: 1939–1945

To say that the Atlantic Coast Line of the 1930's was an enigma as a passenger carrier would have been an understatement. On the one hand, the railroad was very progressive in its marketing. In 1932, for example, it introduced innovative passenger excursion packages offering savings up to 45 percent over the price of a regular ticket. In 1934, systemwide "experimental" passenger rates as low as 1½ cents per mile went into effect, and air-conditioned diners appeared on the summer runs of the *Havana Special* and the *Tamiami*. By the following year, all regularly assigned Pullmans, diners, lounges and long-distance coaches had received air-conditioning, the single greatest invention of the day—short of streamlining—for boosting ridership.

As with other carriers, the improvements were made with an eye toward recapturing the passenger trade that had been devastated by the Depression.

An examination of ACL's equipment and motive-power purchases for the same period, however, would make you think you were looking at a completely different railroad. Coast Line's buying habits were conservative with a capital "C." In 1938, a year when the road's bankrupt upstart competitor, Seaboard Air Line, was buying state-of-the-art E4 passenger diesels, solvent ACL was acquiring 12 new Baldwin 4-8-4 steam locomotives, Nos. 1800-1811. The behemoths, introduced on the road's year-round *Havana Special*, were at the time the largest steam engines in the South.

Things weren't much different on the equipment front either. While the Seaboard was planning a radi-

many intrastate stops. An address by then-ACL Vice President Champion Davis was also interesting. In it, Davis highlighted passenger improvements, including the carrier's new program to convert conventional all-steel coaches to air-conditioned deluxe cars. The speech was most significant, however, for what it *didn't* say. Nary a word about lightweight streamliners was ever mentioned.

It wasn't as if the road didn't care about coach passengers. The aforementioned changes would disprove that. Further, the nitpickers could point out that it was Coast Line—not SAL—which had introduced the first deluxe coach operation to Florida with the Dec. 15, 1938, inauguration of the heavyweight *Vacationer* between New York and both coasts of Florida. It was just that Coast Line wasn't willing to commit to lightweight, dieselized trains.

In this respect, ACL was not alone. No less an august firm than the venerable Baltimore & Ohio had already replaced its first lightweight train, the *Royal Blue*, with a streamstyled heavyweight in 1937. It was a watershed era when radicals like the Burlington and Seaboard happily abandoned the past while conservatives like Coast Line and Southern hunkered down and hoped the fad would pass.

It didn't. Instead, streamlined, lightweight trains began capturing the public's imagination, drawing them back to the rails like a magnet. Despite ACL's attempts at wooing passengers with its heavyweight *Vacationer*, the road's efforts were completely overshadowed by Seaboard's introduction, less than two months later, of the *Silver Meteor*. And it hurt. One example: On the day of the *Meteor*'s inauguration, Pennsy had, due to the festivities, parked the streamliner in Penn Station hours earlier than normal—next to a train carrying ACL's heavyweight *Vacationer* coaches.

Riders in ACL's staid accommodations were afforded a good, long look at the sparkling new celebrity across the platform and apparently liked what they saw. Infuriated, ACL President Lyman Delano took the extreme step of accusing the Pennsy of placing the new streamliner next to his train in a deliberate put down. In point of fact, the whole thing had been an oversight, but Delano's reaction underscored Coast Line's sensitivity to the competition.

ACL had good reason to be concerned. Early returns on the *Meteor*'s ridership figures indicated that Seaboard's radical new streamliner was generating

cally new lightweight streamliner in 1938, ACL was taking delivery of 15 heavyweight passenger coaches from Bethlehem Steel. Although equipped with reclining, rotating seats and air-conditioning, the 78-ton monsters, Nos. 1116-1130, were among the heaviest day coaches ever built.

If there were any doubts as to ACL's conservative philosophy, its actions in 1938 dispelled them. ACL responded to the *Miami Daily News'* upbeat editorial campaign to bring streamliners to Florida, not with open arms but with reasons why diesel-hauled streamliners *wouldn't* work for a market with so

FACING PAGE: For the *Champion*'s first trip to Miami, Florida East Coast arranged for the nearly identical *Henry M. Flagler* trainset to accompany the *Champion* south of Fort Lauderdale, side by side, by using the northbound main.—FEC VIA THE ASSOCIATION OF AMERICAN RAILROADS. **LEFT:** FEC tavern-observation-lounge *Bay Biscayne* poses at Budd's Hunting Park (Philadelphia) plant before delivery. Ahead was a period of undreamt fame. The name on the blue glass drumhead was destined to become a household word. This car would survive FEC's departure from interstate passenger operations to become Seaboard Air Line 6607 in 1965, then Seaboard Coast Line 5841 and finally Amtrak 3339. Budd built things to last.—BOMBARDIER CORP., AUTHOR'S COLLECTION.

ABOVE: Following the launch of Seaboard's highly successful *Silver Meteor*, ACL quickly decided to join the ranks of streamliner owners. Less than a year after the *Meteor* debuted, ACL and partner FEC's *Champion*s hit the rails. Here, Betty Creighton, who named the train, christens the *Champion* at Washington, D.C. Yes, that's really an FEC E3 (No. 1002), cosmetically altered with an ACL herald.—CSX TRANSPORTATION. BELOW LEFT: *Champion* exhibition promotions included a jab aimed at single-track Seaboard. BELOW RIGHT: Shortly after ACL and FEC ordered their streamliners, promotions began, even though the trains had not yet been named, much less built. Photos—heavily retouched (although not enough to hide AT&SF's famous "warbonnet" scheme)—of Santa Fe's new all-coach *El Capitan* pinch hit for the *Champion* in preview ads released during the summer of 1939.—BOTH ADS, AUTHOR'S COLLECTION.

more than publicity. A comparison of passenger revenues for the SAL and ACL for a two-month period before and after the introduction of the *Silver Meteor* shows clearly that Coast Line was in trouble:

SAL	June	July
1938	$278,766	$266,571
1939	$385,412	$393,918 (*Silver Meteor* in service)
Increase	$106,646	$127,347

ACL		
1938	$336,193	$347,147
1939	$312,600	$327,992
Decrease	$23,593	$19,155

It is unlikely that ACL had access to SAL's earnings as outlined above, but it certainly had a handle on its own—and they were decreasing. One didn't have to look too far to see where those dollars were going—across the platform in Penn Station.

Although Coast Line could be faulted for its conservatism, it had the rare quality found in great companies of being able to recognize its own shortcomings. Acting decisively to counter the Seaboard, ACL

shed its conservative attitude and went to Budd on June 30, 1939, with an order for two seven-car coach streamliners. Florida East Coast, ACL's partner in New York-Miami service (south of Jacksonville), purchased two other seven-car sets. One would be FEC's contribution to New York-Florida service and the other a Jacksonville-Miami train, the *Henry M. Flagler*.

All four trainsets were nearly identical. EMD would provide two E3A diesels to ACL and two to FEC, a single diesel being sufficient to handle each consist. The ACL/FEC trains had many structural similarities to Seaboard's *Meteor*. Externally, the material and construction techniques were identical. Mechanically, the principal difference was ACL's use of steam-ejector air-conditioning, SAL having opted for electro-mechanical.

In making the inevitable comparisons, the major differences between the ACL/FEC trains and Seaboard's *Meteor* involved interiors and seating arrangements. Whereas Seaboard had provided two cars which were half coach, half lounge, ACL and FEC provided a full tavern-lounge-observation car with no revenue seating. This concentration of tavern and observation space allowed the ACL/FEC train to field an additional full coach which also contained a hostess' room.

As the new trains were assembled and outfitted by Budd, ACL and FEC conducted a publicity campaign to name the streamliners. Over 101,000 people submitted suggestions in a hope of nabbing the top prize of $300—a hefty sum by 1939 standards. The winner, first of eight people to submit the same name, was Miss Betty Creighton of Pittsburgh, Pa. She suggested an appellation which would eventually become a household name in Northeast-Florida travel: the *Champion*.

Fretted over by Budd designers and rolled, folded and shotwelded by Budd construction crews, the three new *Champion* trainsets were accepted by ACL and FEC in Philadelphia and moved to Penn Coach

Yard at 30th Street Station there. The arrangement of cars in the new trains was:

Owner	Car No./name	Type
ACL	101	22-seat coach-baggage-dorm
ACL	201	60-seat coach
ACL	203	60-seat coach
ACL	*Philadelphia*	Diner
ACL	205	60-seat coach
ACL	207	52-seat hostess coach
ACL	251	Tavern-observation
ACL	100	22-seat coach-baggage-dorm
ACL	200	60-seat coach
ACL	202	60-seat coach
ACL	*New York*	Diner
ACL	204	60-seat coach
ACL	206	52-seat hostess coach
ACL	250	Tavern-observation
FEC	*New Smyrna*	22-seat coach baggage-dorm
FEC	*Cocoa-Rockledge*	60-seat coach
FEC	*Pompano*	60-seat coach
FEC	*Fort Pierce*	Diner
FEC	*Boca Raton*	60-seat coach
FEC	*Vero Beach*	52-seat hostess coach
FEC	*Bay Biscayne*	Tavern-observation

At Pennsylvania Station in Manhattan on Dec. 1, the Florida East Coast trainset was exhibited to the public. Between 8 a.m. and 11 a.m., visitors had an opportunity to soak in the ambience of the new *Champion* before its inaugural run the same day. Ferns and Poinsettas lent an air of the tropics to the dingy subterranean platform, and as loudspeakers blared information about the train outside, uniformed passenger representatives quietly pointed out the details inside.

First in line was *New Smyrna,* which had the jack-of-all-trades designation of mail-storage-dormitory-coach. As part of its dormitory function, the car provided overnight quarters for a crew of 12 and a separate compartment for the dining-car steward. Beyond this was the passenger compartment which featured reclining seats for 22. Traditionally, cars of this type were used to accommodate a train's black clientele since none of the new New York-Florida streamliners featured full-length coaches with divided passenger sections to meet the "Jim Crow" restrictions of the various Southern states the trains traversed. *New Smyrna*'s interior sported dark blue walls and a rose/tan ceiling. Seat upholstery mirrored the scheme.

Next came two 60-seat chair cars which featured reclining seats which swiveled in pairs. Walls of red-brown contrasted with a muted pink ceiling highlighted by light green stripes. Seating was finished in warm brown. Spacious men's and women's restroom/lounges were provided at opposite ends of the cars.

Behind these cars was diner *Fort Pierce* with a dozen four-place tables covered in snowy linen hosting china and flatware, all gleaming under a new innovation: fluorescent lighting. Gray-brown walls supported a pink ceiling. Chairs were blue.

Fifth in line was another 60-seat coach with gray-green walls, yellow-and-white ceiling and green upholstery. Following this was a 52-seat coach which included a compartment for the train hostess/maid where she dispensed such duties as watching the children of passengers while they dined. Brown walls faded to a gray-white ceiling with amber-rose upholstery.

The crown jewel in the *Champion* consist was the tavern-lounge-observation, in this case *Bay Biscayne*. With a floorplan given over entirely to entertainment, the car seated 57 passengers in two distinct areas separated by a bar. In the forward end, 36 travelers could be accommodated in curving divans or in booths. In this end of the car, the walls had a deep blue wainscotting, upper side walls of light tan and a deep tan ceiling. The bar featured a marine motif backed by an etched mirror and glass shelving for glassware. The observation lounge was an oval-shaped room, with one end formed by the tear-drop-shaped end of the car and the other by a lowered oval ceiling. Large windows, comfortable single and sofa seating and a writing desk forward were all part and parcel of the new philosophy of catering to the coach passenger. Fluorescent lighting provided a bright, modern look.

After a brief dedication ceremony, the FEC trainset departed Penn Station behind a PRR GG1 at 12:30 p.m. as the inaugural revenue run of the joint ACL-FEC *Champion* (from noon to 10 p.m. that day, ACL's odd-numbered *Champion* set would assume ex-

hibition duties). On board the sell-out run were numerous dignitaries including Edward G. Budd, Betty Creighton and ACL's Champion McDowell Davis.

At Washington (D.C.) Union Station at 4:25 p.m., the GG1—which had barely broken a sweat hauling the seven-car lightweight—gave up the reigns to Florida East Coast E3A No. 1002. The striking slant-nosed cab unit, attired in red and yellow, trimmed in silver and black and lettered THE CHAMPION, would haul the new train south over the Richmond, Fredericksburg & Potomac to Richmond and from there ever sunward via Atlantic Coast Line and FEC into Florida. The matters of a christening were handled at the nation's capital as Miss Creighton broke the obligatory champagne bottle over the 1002's nose, which, curiously, had been adorned with a temporary ACL herald.

The train's tight 25-hour schedule dictated that the Washington ceremonies be brief. They were, and within 15 minutes the consist was on its way south. Exiting Washington, riders glimpsed the Capitol dome and other landmarks in the gathering twilight, and upon arrival at Richmond's Broad Street Station, many were perhaps enjoying the finishing touches of a thrifty 60-cent dinner. At Richmond, ACL operating crews took over for the fast, nonstop (for passengers) run to Jacksonville.

Ripping south over ACL's double-track north-south main line—the pride of the 5,000-mile ACL system—the *Champion* offered nightcaps (non-alchoholic in Virginia) to its passengers in the new tavern-lounge where one might have found such luminaries as Davis and Budd holding forth in the social center of the moving city they'd helped create. Presumably, rest came easily for those passengers who returned to their comfortable coach seats, softly silhouetted by blue night lights.

Jacksonville Terminal, Florida's rail gateway, wel-

To Our Colored Friends:

Coast Line is glad to serve its colored friends, and is pleased that so many of them ride with us.

Coast Line hopes that you will continue to use its trains, and that you will tell others that Coast Line welcomes its colored friends and is seeking to provide accommodations and service which make travel on the Coast Line a pleasure.

C. McD. DAVIS, President

ABOVE: The modern, streamlined era was at hand in the late 1930's, but civil rights in the U.S. lagged far behind any advances in rail transportation technology, as evidenced by this notice, albeit issued with good itentions by ACL. It was still a case of "separate but equal."—COLLECTION OF MIKE SCHAFER. BELOW: Palm trees line the platform of Boca Raton station as the *Champion* pauses on Jan. 4, 1940.— ROMER COLLECTION, MIAMI-DADE PUBLIC LIBRARY.

RIGHT: Somewhere between Jensen Beach and Melbourne on the Florida East Coast, the *Champion* parallels the Indian River very early in its career. The trainset is one of two built for ACL, as evidenced by the purple letterboard wrapped around the observation car.—DE-GOYLER LIBRARY, SOUTHERN METHODIST UNIVERSITY

ABOVE: Sausage curls were in fashion for little girls when this interior of the *Champion's* diner was photographed in 1939. The china pattern does not appear to be that of FEC or ACL, which may mean that this scene was posed at the Budd Company plant before the cars were released to their respective owners.—HENRY M. FLAGLER MUSEUM. ABOVE LEFT: An FEC breakfast menu dating from May 1943.—WILLIAM F. HOWES JR. COLLECTION.

comed the train at dawn. Following a 15-minute stop, the new streamliner pulled out at 7 a.m. for points south, with the 1002 now cruising home rails. Knots of well-wishers greeted the train at various stops including St. Augustine, Daytona Beach and West Palm Beach.

Florida East Coast knew how to throw a party. At Fort Lauderdale, FEC's other E3, the 1001, and its *Henry M Flagler* streamliner joined the nearly identical *Champion*. In a spectacular one-time stunt, the *Flagler* and the *Champion* then paraded south side by side down FEC's double-track main line (the *Flagler* riding what was normally the northbound main). The two trains' arrival at Miami at 1:30 p.m. was a spectacle worthy of the occasion. Buzzed by a squadron of smoke-trailing biplanes, serenaded by the Miami University band and welcomed by the mayor and 5,000 others, the "Magic City" spared no effort in its greeting.

Keynote speaker upon arrival at FEC's modest depot just west of the Miami business district was Edward G. Budd who, in rather roundabout fashion, summed up the reason for all the hullabaloo, "Few people realize it, but 30 million persons reside in the eastern section radiant from New York. Only two percent of them have ever come to Florida. We feel that with the advent of streamlined service into Florida, at least nine more persons will be added to that two out of every hundred to come to this state every winter."

He wasn't far off. By all accounts, the 1939 season to Florida would be one of the busiest travel seasons thus far. The war in Europe had shocked Americans into staying on home soil, and Coast Line was well-positioned to take advantage of the increased potential for domestic travel. Twenty extra all-room heavyweight sleepers had been secured from Pullman for Coast Line customers that winter. A new West Coast section of the venerable all-Pullman *Florida Special* was placed in service in December 1939, and the *Vacationer* was re-equipped for its second winter season,

going into service on Dec. 15, 1939.

Despite the fact that it was second fiddle to the *Champion*, this version of the *Vacationer* featured an impressive consist. Typically it carried six air-conditioned reclining-seat coaches rebuilt from heavyweights. A diner was joined by a completely new tavern-lounge rebuilt from heavyweight coaches at ACL's shops in Rocky Mount, N.C. This lounge featured modern aluminum-framed furnishings, radio entertainment, a writing desk and a bar. The same personal service and economy afforded *Champion* passengers were available on the *Vacationer*. Passenger representatives, coach attendants and train maid were available, as well as economical 60-cent dinners. For 1939, the steam-hauled *Vacationer* schedule was speeded up by two hours, giving it a competitive 26 1/2-hour carding on the New York-Miami run.

This one-two marketing punch was typical of Coast Line. Not only did it now field a duo of luxury coach operations to Florida, it also offered, in addition to its crack *Florida Special*, a second all-Pullman train to Miami—the winter-season *Miamian*. There was more. This was still the era of trains operating in multiple sections to accommodate high demand. ACL was so confident of such demands that it published the consists of extra sections in its timetables.

And extra sections there were. For the period Dec. 16 through Jan. 12, the *East Coast Florida Special* operated in two sections—one originating in New York, the other in Washington, D.C. Effective in mid-January 1940, the East Coast train operated in two sections, both originating and terminating in New York, with the first or *Advance East Coast Florida Special* carrying a deluxe coach as well as sleepers.

Maid-of-all work, summer and winter, was the *Havana Special*, which took 24 hours just to reach Jacksonville and a leisurely nine more to achieve Miami on its two-night-out schedule. The train was timed to provide connections to both the P&O overnight steamship run to Havana and Pan Am *Clipper* service out of Miami to Havana and Nassau, in the Bahamas.

Finally, there was Coast Line's venerable year-round *Florida Mail*, which carried coaches between Washington and all points south, and sleepers between selected intermediate points. Its importance, as suggested by its name, was as a mail carrier, but the *Florida Mail* also served as a Jacksonville-Gulf Coast connection to several prime Midwest-Florida trains.

Florida service was largely still seasonal, and the summer schedule of 1940 reflected this with only four trains connecting the Northeast to the Sunshine State. Among these was something odd for Florida—a

summer-season train, the *Tamiami*. On a one-night-out basis, this train offered heavyweight sleepers and "Super de Luxe" heavy-weight coaches to both coasts in addition to a 3-compartment, 1-drawing room lounge between New York and Miami. The year-round *Champion*, *Havana Special* and *Florida Mail* rounded out the schedule. Gone come spring were the crowds—and the *Vacationer,* the *Miamian* and the *Florida Special*.

As things were slowing down for summer tourism in the humid South, they were gearing up in temperate Maine. Beginning June 21, 1940, the *Champion* offered connections (but not through cars) to the summer-season *East Wind* operating between Washington, D.C., and Portland and Bangor, Maine, over the PRR, New Haven and Boston & Maine.

Because the *East Wind* was a daylight operation, its northbound morning departure from Washington fit nicely with the northbound *Champion*'s 6:25 a.m. arrival in the capital, thus affording one-night-out service between Florida and Maine. ACL provided more than just a connection for this *East Wind*. For the summer of 1940, the tavern-lounge cars from its idled winter-only *Vacationer* were used as lounge space on the Yankee speedster.

Simultaneous with rival Seaboard's order to Budd to double the size of its now-daily *Silver Meteor*, Atlantic Coast Line placed an order with the same Philadelphia manufacturer to increase its daily *Champion*

to 14 cars as well. The move came, not just in response to competition, but because of demand. Between December 1939 and December 1940, the *Champion* had handled 151,000 passengers, or—more to the point—had averaged close to 200 passengers per trip at a respectable revenue-per-train-mile figure of $2.60. That meant that each "Champ" run had collected an average of $3,600—or $7,200 per day (considering that one *Champion* was operated in each direction every day). The only thing standing in the way of even greater success was a lack of equipment.

The investment had showed immediate dividends. In the five months immediately after the *Champion* was expanded to a 14-car train, between January and May 1941, the larger consist averaged 362 passengers per trip at a revenue-per-train-mile of $5.34, a clear indication that demand for the service was extremely high and that an expanded consist was a much more economical way to operate the train.

The new cars which swelled the consists were:

14-seat baggage-dormitories (ACL series 102-104)
56-seat coaches (ACL series 208-215)
60-seat coaches (PRR series 4026-4029)
48-seat diners (ACL *Baltimore, Boston, Newark*)
57-seat tavern-lounge-obs' (blunt end) (ACL series 252-254)

All of the new cars, including PRR's coaches—the first contribution that road had made to the pool—

ABOVE: It is doubtful that photographer Pettengill thought of this as anything more than a pretty good shot of the *Florida Special* leaving St. Petersburg in March 1941. Take a closer look and you will see that this photo says a whole lot more. The vintage autos, the neat, tile-roofed depot bordered by trimmed hedges and palm trees, and local businesses like Harry's Place all convey the essence of St. Petersburg in 1941. Likewise, the picture sums up big-time railroading ACL style. P5-b Pacific 1746 prepares to get its train underway as the brakeman nonchalantly reviews paperwork on the front step. Behind the 4-6-2, in the "super deluxe" coach or Pullmans, passengers are settling down for the ride north, their Florida vacation already a memory. Thank you, Mr. Pettengill.—G. W. PETTENGILL JR. VIA KEN MARSH JRR. ABOVE LEFT: An ad from ACL's 1940-41 winter season timetable heralds the coming of the new E6 fleet.—AUTHOR'S COLLECTION.

carried the color scheme of the original ACL *Champion*: stainless-steel exterior with a purple letterboard and aluminum lettering and numbering. With the exception of the Pennsy, which stuck with 60-seaters, the 56-seat coaches featured more leg room than their original *Champion* counterparts. Some of these new cars had not arrived in time for the expanded train's debut on Dec. 20, 1940, but, by January 1941, all of the new equipment was on the property. The three *Champion*s then looked like this:

FEC CONSIST

FEC *New Smyrna*	22-seat coach-baggage-dorm
ACL 102	14-seat coach-baggage-dorm
FEC *Cocoa-Rockledge*	60-seat coach
FEC *Pompano*	60-seat coach
FEC *Fort Pierce*	Diner
FEC *Boca Raton*	60-seat coach
ACL 208	56-seat coach
ACL 252	Tavern-lounge-obs (square end)
FEC *Vero Beach*	52-seat coach
ACL 209	56-seat-coach
ACL *Newark*	Diner
ACL 210	56-seat coach
ACL 211	56-seat coach
FEC *Bay Biscayne*	Tavern-lounge-obs (round end)

ACL "Uneven" CONSIST

ACL 101	22-seat coach-baggage-dorm
ACL 103	14-seat coach-baggage-dorm
ACL 201	60-seat coach
ACL 203	60-seat coach
ACL *Philadelphia*	Diner
ACL 205	60-seat coach
ACL 213	56-seat coach
ACL 253	Tavern-lounge-obs (square end)
ACL 207	52-seat coach
PRR 4029	60-seat coach
ACL *Baltimore*	Diner
PRR 4027	60-seat coach
ACL 215	56-seat coach
ACL 251	Tavern-lounge-obs (round end)

ACL "Even" CONSIST

ACL 100	22-seat coach-baggage-dorm
ACL 104	14-seat coach-baggage-dorm
ACL 200	60-seat coach
ACL 202	60-seat coach
ACL *New York*	Diner
ACL 204	60-seat coach
ACL 212	56-seat coach
ACL 254	Tavern-lounge-obs (square end)
ACL 206	52-seat coach
PRR 4028	60-seat coach
ACL *Boston*	Diner
PRR 4026	60-seat coach
ACL 214	56-seat coach
ACL 250	Tavern-lounge-obs (round end)

The short period of "experimental" seven-car streamliners was over. In its place had come an era of prolonged demand—a demand met by the expanded *Champion* and no less than six other through ACL/FEC New York-Florida trains during the winter of 1940-41. Backstopping the *Champion* again was the fast, multi-feature *Vacationer*. The deluxe heavyweight coach train had changed little from the previous season, with one important exception—diesels. Twenty-two Electro-Motive E6A units and five E6B units were being delivered to ACL between 1940 and 1942, and four more to FEC. The happy result for *Vacationer* passengers was a 1¼-hour speed up in running time.

ABOVE: The *Champion*'s capacity expansion was advertised in ACL's 1940-41 winter season timetable.—AUTHOR'S COLLECTION. **FACING PAGE:** Circa 1941, the expanded *Champion*'s FEC consist is en route through Stuart, Fla., on the Florida East Coast.—FEC VIA THE ASSOCIATION OF AMERICAN RAILROADS.

Also included in the parade were:

❀Trains 87-88, the *Florida Special*—now diesel-hauled, with heavyweight Pullmans between New York/Boston and Miami, recreation car, Pullman-lounge and dining car between New York and Miami.

❀Trains 187-188, the *Advance Florida Special*, daily effective Jan. 9, 1941, and now also diesel-powered; featuring dining car, recreation car, Pullman and Pullman-lounge-observation between New York/Washington and Miami.

❀Trains 287-288 to the West Coast of Florida, the *West Coast Florida Special,* with dining, recreation car, Pullmans and Pullman-lounges not to mention a heavyweight deluxe coach between the Northeast and Gulf coast destinations.

❀The *Miamian*, ACL's all-Pullman "Train of Society," with a Pullman 3-compartment, 2-drawing-room lounge, observation, dining car and several Pullmans between New York/Washington and Miami. Also handled was an oddball New York-Thomasville (Ga.) 10-1-2 Pullman which transferred to the northbound Miami-Chicago *Florida Arrow* (FEC-ACL-CofG-NC&StL-L&N-PRR) at Jacksonville for the ride to South central Georgia.

❀Still steam-hauled, the year-round *Havana Special* continued to provide reliable accommodations on its 32-hour, two-night-out journey to sunshine.

Handling all of this seasonal demand would have been impossible without Pullman's pool of sleeping and lounge cars. Through the peak years of Florida travel in the 1920's and into the 1930's, this huge roving fleet of hotels on wheels had answered the call. Now in the early 1940's, the phenomenon continued. Like the swallows returning to Capistrano in spring,

each winter thousands of travelers flocked to the familiar comfort of standard Pullmans as a means of escaping winter.

Pullman enjoyed a virtual monopoly in the U.S. sleeping-car business during the first half of the 20th Century, when few U.S. railroads operated their own sleepers. Controlling a nationwide fleet and operating its cars under contracts with the railroads, Pullman was able to shift sleepers from locations and roads experiencing reduced seasonal traffic to those whose demand was on the upswing. In summer the call would be for cars to handle the still-booming New England and Western trade. In the winter, to a degree unparalleled anywhere else, it was Florida.

At this time, 1940-41, summer demand on Coast Line's Northeast-Florida trains required approximately 27 cars; by January the number might exceed 200. Happily, the requirements were somewhat predictable. As summer traffic waned, Pullman would direct cars with the specific floorplans requested by the Florida roads to the principal gathering point—Sunnyside Yard of the Pennsylvania Railroad at Long Island. Here the new arrivals would hobnob with cars regularly assigned to the Florida routes.

Heavyweight sleepers, permanently in the pool or temporarily released to it from other roads, did yeoman duty accommodating the waves of travelers to Florida. Tuscan red PRR-assigned heavyweights were common but, in general, the overall scheme for most of the fleet was dark green—the term "Pullman green" not quite being definitive, as over the years several shades of the color were employed. Indeed, despite the proliferation of streamlined equipment, the vast majority of cars railroad-owned or otherwise operating to Florida during this era sported variations of this traditional color.

Defining which of those predominantly green heavyweight cars most often comprised the Florida pool in the 1930's, '40's and '50's would be a monumental task. With little exaggeration, it might be easier to determine which Pullman pool cars *didn't* operate to Florida. Nevertheless, some types did find themselves habitually in Florida service. Among them were the omnipresent *Lake*-series 10-section, 1-drawing room, 2-compartment cars—a type which was unpopular with some patrons because it squeezed two additional sections into its floorplan at the expense of washroom space. Also prominent were rebuilds with more private-room space, like the *Tower* series with 8-sections, 1-drawing room and 3 double bedrooms. *Poplar*-series car with their 6 sections and 6 double bedrooms, and *Clover*-series cars with 8 sections and 5 double bedrooms dotted consists, too.

Florida trade meant stateroom cars—lots of them; in fact, the largest concentration of them anywhere. Bumped from the consists of recently streamlined trains like New York Central's *20th Century Limited* and PRR's *Broadway Limited*,

CONSIST OF NOTE 3-A

ACL train 71, southbound *Miamian*

Charleston, S.C.
March 4, 1940

Car	Type
[ACL 1807]	[4-8-4 steam locomotive]
ACL 700	Baggage-mail
RF&P 164	Baggage-express
ACL 573	Baggage-express
Red Lick	12 section, 1-drawing-room sleeper
Poplar Summit	6-section, 6-double-bedroom sleeper
Lake Poygan	10-section, 1-drwg. room, 2-cmpt. sleeper
Point Shirley	10-section, 2-drawing room sleeper
Daggett	10-section, 1 drwg. room, 2-cmpt. sleeper
Field	6-compartment, 3-drawing-room sleeper
FEC *Breakers*	Diner
CB&Q 175	Diner
Camp Cody	10-section, 1-drwg.-room, 2-cmpt. sleeper
Ranston	12-section, 1-drawing-room sleeper
Central Park	3-cmpt., 2-drwg.-room lounge-observation

RIGHT: The southbound *Havana Special* pauses at Fayetteville, N.C., on May 28, 1939. White-jacketed porters are out in force enjoying the air, and a train crewman stands on the ballast waiting to give the highball. Meanwhile the tower operator has lined the home signal for a northbound movement across the Atlantic & Yadkin crossing in the foreground.—BARRIGER COLLECTION, ST. LOUIS MERCANTILE MUSEUM.

ABOVE: Double-headed FEC Mountains with the second section of the *Miamian* in March 1939.—CAL'S CLASSICS. ABOVE RIGHT: Double-headed Pacifics get underway with the second section of train 73, the southbound *Gulf Coast Limited*, at Savannah, Ga., in March 1939 during its last season of operation.—HUGH M. COMER.

CONSIST OF NOTE 3-B

FEC train 34, northbound *Tamiami*

Miami, Fla.
Oct. 25, 1940

Car	Type
[FEC 802]	[4-8-2 steam locomotive]
Glen Stockdale	6-cmpt., 3-drwg. room sleeper (deadhead)
Clover Gate	8-section, 5-d.bdr. sleeper (deadhead)
FEC 458	Baggage-express
FEC 454	Baggage-express
RF&P 182	Baggage-express (mail storage)
FEC 462	Baggage-express
FEC 141	Coach
ACL 1122	Coach
FEC *Miami*	Diner
Fort Amador	10-sect., 1-drwg.-room, 2-cmpt. sleeper
Clover Bloom	8-section, 5-double-bedroom sleeper
Dixie Springs	3-cmpt., 1-drwg. room lounge-observation

the Florida trains were home to these aristocrats whose solid blocks of compartments and drawing rooms appealed to the kind of folks who wintered in Florida. Chief among this car type was the *Glen* series. These 6-compartment, 3-drawing room cars were Florida regulars from the 1920's onward. Amazingly, as late as the 1960's, it was not uncommon to still find a *Glen* car in the consist of the *Florida Special*.

In lounges, the Florida trains of the immediate prewar period leaned toward classy hand-me-downs. There were *Central*-series 3-compartment, 2-drawing-room observations, such as the *Central Park* and *Central Plateau*, once the pride of the *20th Century*, now carrying the marker lamps of the *Miamian*. High-windowed *Valley*-series observations, hallmarks of the *Century* as well, made a brief appearance on the *Florida Special* in 1936 and 1937, the *Oswego Valley* and *Portage Valley* being regulars. Midtrain it might be "Sun Room" lounges like the 3-compartment, 1-drawing room *Palm* series. The *Sun* series—*Sunshine*, *Sunburst*, etc.—with their 2 compartments

and 1 drawing room, displaced from the Missouri Pacific-Texas & Pacific *Sunshine Special*, also found a home here. *Dixie*-series Sun Room cars like *Dixie Springs*, originally built for the *Dixie Flyer*, a Chicago-Florida train jointly operated by Chicago & Eastern Illinois, the Nashville, Chattanooga & St. Louis, the Louisville & Nashville, ACL and FEC, and bearing the same floorplan as the *Palm* cars, were regulars too. In the early 1940's, the Pullman baggage-club car, once a regular component of many now-streamlined trains and shrinking in popularity, survived on competitor SAL's *Orange Blossom Special* until the train was suspended in 1942.

Less obvious but equally challenging was the aspect of feeding all of the hungry passengers in those pool cars. No other railroad in North America (including Seaboard) had to deal with such a tremendous seasonal expansion and contraction of its dining-car department as did ACL. Emphasizing the challenge, remember that there no longer existed a dining-car equivalent of the Pullman pool to accommodate the demand. Consider this: In the summer lull of 1940, ACL needed only 17 diners to cover its trains. Six months later, at the peak of the winter season, a total of 68 diners and their crews were in service. Of these, 33 were ACL-owned, 17 came from partners FEC and RF&P and 18 more were leased from off-line roads such as Burlington and PRR.

Crew requirements were no less daunting. At the height of the same winter season, 917 people worked in the ACL dining department. Of these, more than

700 were employed for the winter only. Even into the 1960's, when traffic levels were nowhere near those of the early 1940's, it was common for off-line dining crews, such as those of the B&O, to work the Florida trains in winter. Little known, too, is the fact that enginemen from Northern roads such as New Haven and Boston & Maine were permitted to work winters on the FEC and, perhaps, other roads, as well.

The crush that affected the railroad also impacted the passenger. So popular were the new Florida streamliners that ticket scalping of return seats became common practice among Florida hotel employees. Folks who needed to change their return date often found the trains sold out well in advance. To accommodate this problem, a black market sprang up. A passenger needing to change dates was encouraged to surrender his or her useless return ticket in exchange for a ticket for a new date of travel—previously given up by a passenger in a similar predicament. For this service, hotel employees would extract a "fee" of up to $5. Considering that the New York-Miami one-way coach fare of that period was $22.40, that fee was a steep premium.

As the winter season wound down in the spring of 1941, ACL made a significant change. In an effort to provide faster summertime Pullman service to both coasts of Florida, the summer-season heavyweight *Tamiami* was discontinued. In turn, effective May 2, 1941, southbound and May 4 northbound, the *Champion* assumed a new identity, becoming the *Tamiami Champion*, operating in two sections. Numbers 1 and 2 ran to the East Coast of Florida while Nos. 91 and 92 served the West Coast. It was more than just a name change. On the same date, the new train began handling heavyweight sleepers along with the regular lightweight cars of the former *Champion*.

In keeping with the train's premier status, a program was initiated to finish regularly assigned *Tamiami Champion* Pullmans in what was termed "special streamlined colors." Between June 6 and July 15, 1941, 17 heavyweight Pullmans were released from the Pullman shops for Coast Line service in a unique

---

CONSIST OF NOTE 3-D
FEC train 87, southbound *Florida Special*

Jacksonville, Fla.
Jan. 10, 1942

Car	Type
ACL 1969	Dormitory
ACL 517	Express car
Point Emmons	10-section, 2-drawing room sleeper
New Yama	14-section sleeper
Port Rowan	14-section sleeper
Clover Bloom	8-section, 5-double-bedroom sleeper
Glen Rae	6-compartment, 3-drawing-room sleeper
Palm City	3-cmpt., 1-drwg. room buffet-lounge
ACL *Dothan*	Diner
ACL *Lakeland*	Diner
Topaz	Parlor car (serving as recreation car)
Glen Esk	6-compartment, 3-drawing-room sleeper
Glen Tana	6-compartment, 3-drawing-room sleeper
Corot	6-compartment, 3-drawing-room sleeper
Chimes Tower	8-section, 1-drwg. room, 3-d.br. sleeper
Mountain Top	10-section sleeper lounge
Nightwatch	14-single-bedroom sleeper

---

scheme. No definitive information on this scheme has yet surfaced, but this was thought to be overall solid aluminum, black trucks, purple letterboards and gold PULLMAN lettering. Between May 2 and the shoppings, other standard green heavyweight Pullmans had served the new train.

The specific cars assigned to the *Tamiami Champion* and repainted in this rare special scheme were:

Car Type	Car Name
10-1-2	*Fort Amador*
10-1-2	*Fort Dodge*
10-1-2	*Cape Cod*
10-1-2	*Cape Ferello*
10-1-2	*Cape Fortunas*
10-1-2	*Cape Lookout*
10-1-2	*Cape Sable*
6-6	*Poplar Summit*
6-6	*Poplar Trail*
6-6	*Poplar Valley*
10-2-1	*Southern College*
10-2-1	*Rollins College*
10-2-1	*Vassar College*
10-2-1	*Washington College*
8-5	*Clover Bank*
8-5	*Clover Bloom*
8-5	*Clover Creek*

The cars were assigned in the following manner:

Trains 1/2		Trains 91/92	
Tamiami Champion		*Tamiami Champion*	
(East Coast)		(West Coast)	
6-6	NYP-MIA	10-1-2	NYP-STP
8-5	NYP-MIA	10-2-1	NYP-TPA
10-1-2	WAS-MIA		

Bigger plans were on the drawing board for the coming winter of 1941-42. The *Tamiami Champion* was to drop the Tamiami prefix and its sleepers, pick up two new cars and operate as a 16-car New York-Miami coaches-only streamliner. An eight-car West Coast section was to operate as a separate entity carrying six cars to Tampa and two for St. Petersburg in the following manner:

1	Coach-baggage-dorm	NYP-TPA
1	Diner	NYP-TPA
3	Coaches	NYP-TPA
1	Tavern-lounge	NYP-TPA
2	Coaches	NYP-STP

Plans of another kind, however, were being formulated across the Pacific, dooming the proposed ex-

pansion. Delayed at first, the additional 30-car order needed to make the above consists a reality was quietly suspended in the spring of 1942. Wartime concerns took precedence. The *Champion* would drop the Tamiami part of its name and its sleepers as planned, but it would run as a 14-car New York-Miami streamliner for the winter of 1941-42 with no new cars or destination.

On Dec. 12, 1941, just five days after the attack on Pearl Harbor, ACL's Florida winter travel season commenced with no other visible impact on schedules. The *Florida Special* (East Coast) was back for its 55th consecutive season. New Electro-Motive E6's ensured the all-Pullman *Special* would make the New York-Miami run in a scorching 24 hours—one hour faster than the lightweight *Champion*! This year the *Florida Special* was carrying two 14-section sleepers and a 14-single-bedroom sleeper. Boston passengers for the venerable *Special* had their own section this year with through Pullmans between the "Hub City" and Miami, Tampa, Sarasota and St. Petersburg. This operation also handled coaches between Boston and Washington where coach passengers could transfer to the *Vacationer* for the East Coast or the *Florida Special* (West Coast) for Gulf Coast points.

Still steam-hauled, the hard-working *West Coast Florida Special* operated daily over the ACL behind brutish 1800-class 4-8-4's. At Jacksonville north or southbound, it picked up or delivered the West Coast Pullmans of the *Florida Special*'s Boston section. Through heavyweight coaches with reserved, reclining seats worked between New York and the West Coast. A coach connection as well was provided between Nahunta and Brunswick, Ga., for those wishing to visit coastal Georgia resorts such as St. Simon's Island.

The *Miamian* was back, all Pullman and sporting for the first time a recreation car with musicians and game tables. The *Miamian* continued to offer its obscure New York-Thomasville 10-1-2 car. Back, too, was the *Vacationer,* attesting to the popularity of the

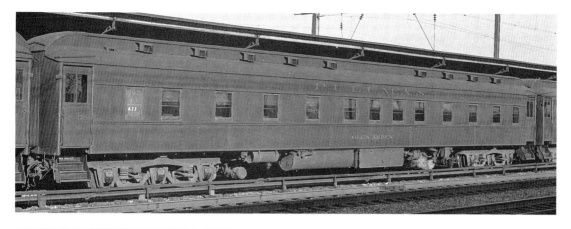

LEFT: Stateroom cars, offering compartments and drawing rooms, were common on the Florida trains. Among the regulars were the *Glen*-series with 6 compartments and 3 drawing rooms. *Glen Arden* is at Manhattan Transfer, N.J., in January 1937.—GEORGE E. VOTAVA.

LEFT: Its waiters at attention, heavyweight diner *Florence* also pauses at Manhattan Transfer in the consist of a Florida train. The car typifies the appearance of the heavyweight diners in operation between New York and Florida in ACL service from the late teens to the early 1940's.—GEORGE E. VOTAVA.

BELOW: A leased Chicago, Burlington & Quincy diner is just ahead of 3-2 observation car *Central Plateau* at far right on what is probably the *Miamian* circa 1940. Despite the flashy new Florida streamliners, most trains to Florida before and during World War II were comprised of these veterans, but eventually streamlining would nearly erase scenes like this of solid heavyweight trains.—ACL VIA THE ASSOCIATION OF AMERICAN RAILROADS. LEFT: Dining in the heavyweight diners assigned to the Florida fleet in the 1930's and early 1940's was typical of the experience that had been offered to patrons since time immemorial. Save for the fashions, this shot taken in the late 1930's could have been recorded any time in the 1920's.—FEC.

all-coach train concept with roughly the same complement it had fielded before. The diesel-hauled speedster now made the Gotham-Miami run in 25⅓ hours.

The year-round *Havana Special* offered extra through sleeping cars between New York and West Palm Beach and St. Petersburg this year. A new 8-section buffet-lounge ran between Jacksonville and Clewiston, Fla., on the shores of Lake Okeechobee.

It was at this time that Jacksonville Terminal revived its reputation as one of the busiest in the country. Here, a great shuffling of cars to and from the Northeast and Midwest occurred daily. The conservative, Doric-columned station, completed in 1919, looked slightly out of place as a gateway to the tropics, contrasting as it did with the royal palms which lined its driveway. But there was no getting around its purpose. When it came to handling the crowds, Jacksonville Terminal was all business. ACL Pacifics, 4-8-4's and diesels handed over consists to FEC Mountains and E-units which whisked the cars down the road's East Coast speedway. Opponent Seaboard came to call, too, as did the Southern Railway, which dipped its toes in the tropics here and interchanged trains and cars to FEC. All of this activity had been at its height in the Florida boom of the 1920's, had tapered off in the Depression Thirties and was now climbing again.

Largely, it was the Midwestern trains which under-

TWIN FLORIDA TRAINS

TAMIAMI CHAMPION
(EAST COAST)

Between New York and Miami. A daily "2-in-1" train. Reclining chair cars (all seats reserved) and diner for coach passengers. Pullman sleeping cars and diner. Diesel powered.

CONDENSED DAILY SCHEDULE		
Read Down Nos. 105-1	(Eastern Standard Time)	Read Up Nos. 2-104
a 3 55 PM	Lv New York (Penna. Sta.)..........(P.R.R.) Ar	10 00 AM
a 4 09 PM	Lv Newark.....................................'' Ar	a 9 42 AM
a 5 30 PM	Lv Philadelphia (Penna.Sta.30th St.) '' Ar	a 8 14 AM
a 7 13 PM	Lv Baltimore.................................'' Ar	a 6 40 AM
8 15 PM	Lv Washington.........................(R.F.& P.) Ar	5 45 AM
10 45 PM	Lv Richmond...............................(A.C.L.) Ar	3 15 AM
3 45 AM	Ar Florence..................................'' Lv	10 00 PM
c 5 25 AM	Ar Charleston (North Sta.)..............'' Lv	c 8 20 PM
7 25 AM	Ar Savannah.................................'' Lv	4 36 PM
de 8 56 AM	Ar Nahunta...................................'' Lv	d 4 47 PM
10 10 AM	Ar Jacksonville.............................'' Lv	2 46 PM
11 00 AM	Ar St. Augustine........................(F.E.C.) Lv	1 55 PM
11 53 AM	Ar Daytona Beach.........................'' Lv	12 55 PM
3 25 PM	Ar West Palm Beach.....................'' Lv	10 25 AM
4 17 PM	Ar Fort Lauderdale........................'' Lv	9 32 AM
4 29 PM	Ar Hollywood...............................'' Lv	9 21 AM
4 55 PM	Ar Miami....................................'' Lv	9 00 AM

a—Stops to take or let off passengers to or from south of Washington.
c—Passengers must arrange own transportation between Charleston (North Station) and Charleston (Union Station).
d—Stops to let off or take passengers from or for Richmond and beyond.
e—Connects with train arriving at Brunswick 10.10 a.m.

TAMIAMI CHAMPION
(WEST COAST)

Between New York and Tampa (via Orlando), New York and St. Petersburg (via Ocala)—another "2-in-1" train. Reclining chair cars (all seats reserved) for coach passengers. Pullman sleeping cars and diner. Diesel powered.

CONDENSED DAILY SCHEDULE		
Read Down Nos. 127-91	(Eastern Standard Time)	Read Up Nos. 92-1st. 174
a12 50 PM	Lv New York (Penna. Sta.)..........(P.R.R.) Ar	1 50 PM
a 1 05 PM	Lv Newark.....................................'' Ar	a 1 32 PM
a 2 29 PM	Lv Philadelphia (Penna.Sta.30th St.) '' Ar	a12 12 PM
a 3 59 PM	Lv Baltimore.................................'' Ar	a10 41 AM
5 10 PM	Lv Washington.........................(R.F.& P.) Ar	9 25 AM
7 50 PM	Lv Richmond...............................(A.C.L.) Ar	6 45 AM
11 30 PM	Ar Fayetteville..............................'' Lv	b 2 51 AM
* 2 39 AM	Ar Charleston (North Sta.).............'' Lv	* 1145 PM
4 40 AM	Ar Savannah.................................'' Lv	9 50 PM
7 25 AM	Ar Jacksonville.............................'' Lv	6 55 PM
8 00 AM	Lv Jacksonville............................'' Ar	6 25 PM
11.08 AM	Ar Orlando...................................'' Lv	2 50 PM
1 00 PM	Ar Tampa.....................................'' Lv	1 00 PM
8 35 AM	Lv Jacksonville.........................(A.C.L.) Ar	6 20 PM
11 40 AM	Ar Ocala......................................'' Lv	2 10 PM
3 16 PM	Ar Clearwater...............................'' Lv	10 26 AM
4 00 PM	Ar St. Petersburg..........................'' Lv	9 55 AM

a—Stops to take or let off passengers to or from south of Washington.
b—Stops to let off passengers from Florence, south, or take for Richmond, Norfolk, beyond.
*—Passengers must make own transportation arrangements between Charleston (North Station) and Charleston (Union Station).

ATLANTIC COAST LINE RAILROAD
"the only" DOUBLE TRACK ROUTE BETWEEN THE EAST AND FLORIDA"

ABOVE LEFT: It's Sunday evening March 28, 1943, and the *Tamiami Champion* East Coast section has just arrived at Miami behind E3A 1002 and E6A 1003. Note the 1003's different livery, with the red swooping down toward the back of the locomotive and giving way to aluminum color. The 1003 was delivered in 1940 and lettered for the Chicago-Florida *Dixie Flagler*.—BOB MALINOSKI. **LEFT:** ACL's summer-season timetable for 1942 announced the *Tamiami Champion* twin trains, which ran about three hours apart.—AUTHOR'S COLLECTION. **BELOW:** Twin E6's hurtle through Nahunta, Ga., with the southbound *Tamiami Champ* during the summer of 1941. Note that the lead locomotive has been lettered for the short-lived name.—HUGH M. COMER.

LEFT AND BELOW: When ACL released this handsome three-color brochure on its impending new *Champion* streamliner in 1939, it probably had no idea the little seven-car speedsters would grow into a major train operation that would become a standard for rail passenger service all up and down the Atlantic coast. The jousting knight theme perhaps signaled ACL's new-found aggressiveness in the streamliner era. —CSX CORPORATION.

went complicated dissection at Jacksonville. As an example, in winter 1941-42, the *Havana Special* picked up the Chicago-Miami and Chicago-St. Petersburg sleepers of the *Floridan, Dixiana* or the *Florida Arrow,* a series of trains running on alternate days. Miami-bound coach passengers on the *Seminole, Dixie Flyer* or *Southland* found themselves tacked onto the high-speed *Vacationer.* Southbound Pullman passengers on the same trains were picked up at Jacksonville by the Boston/Washington section of the *Florida Special,* as were patrons en route to Miami from Kansas City on Frisco/Southern's *Kansas City-Florida Special.*

Bound for the Gulf Coast over the ACL, the humble *Coast Line Florida Mail* found itself receiving a Chicago-Tampa heavyweight sleeper off a trio of all-Pullman runs operating on alternate days: the *Sunchaser, Jacksonian* or the *Dixieland.* These trains' Chicago-Miami cars would continue down the East Coast in FEC's Jacksonville-Miami local, the *Gulf Stream.*

Expert switching, performed by JT crews in their 0-6-0 steam switchers and Electro-Motive NW2 diesels, was necessary, as many of those cars were occupied while being shifted. If the delicate switching ballet wasn't enough to impress, the volume was. While the passenger from Dayton in Upper 3 might have benefitted from what he didn't notice about Jacksonville Terminal, anyone with more than a passing interest in trains was sure to notice the station's incredibly busy routine. Each winter day, at this time, over 75 trains came to call. In addition to human cargo, they brought with them, in a typical December, 9,000 express cars carrying citrus, flowers, produce, fish and other perishables headed for Northern markets. At its all-time busiest in 1944, the terminal would handle nearly 10 million passengers.

Typical of the trains that plied the railroad in the busy winter of 1941-42 was the makeup of the *Champion* shown in Consist of Note 3-E. The presence of two baggage-dormitory coaches in this consist is not a fluke. The first car, reservation line CH-1, was used for black passengers and the second car was added for "overflow white" travel as demand necessitated.

The start of the 1942 summer season saw the chameleon-like *Champion* regaining its *Tamiami Champion* label and its sleeping cars and running as

CONSIST OF NOTE 3-E
PRR train 104, *Champion*
Sunnyside Yard, N.Y.
March 17, 1942

Car	Type
[PRR 4850]	[GG1 electric locomotive]
FEC *New Smyrna*	Baggage-dorm-coach
ACL 102	Baggage-dorm-coach
FEC *Cocoa-Rockledge*	Coach
FEC *Pompano*	Coach
FEC *Boca Raton*	Coach
ACL 208	Coach
ACL 252	Tavern-lounge (blunt end)
FEC *Fort Pierce*	Diner
ACL *Newark*	Diner
FEC *Vero Beach*	Coach
ACL 209	Coach
ACL 212	Coach
ACL 211	Coach
FEC *Bay Biscayne*	Tavern-lounge-obs (round end)

RIGHT: Florida East Coast's *Champion* tavern-observation *Bay Biscayne* is pictured at Miami in April 1944. Note that the roof has been painted black as a concession against road grime. —HAROLD K. VOLLRATH. BELOW RIGHT: In the summer of 1943, ACL *Champion* observation car No. 250 was wrecked. This scene graphically illustrates what can happen when an EMD E6A meets a passenger car at high speed.—HUGH H. COMER COLLECTION.

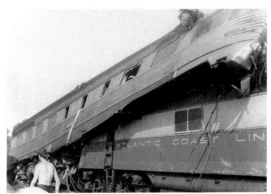

With connecting service between Boston and the Sunshine State, "Florida" and "Deep South" became unlikely key words for the cover of this New Haven Railroad timetable from 1943.—VIA W. CONNOLLY.

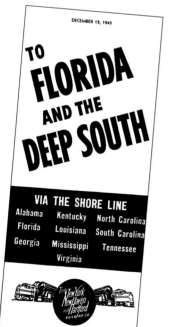

two separate trains to both coasts. Consists looked like this:

West Coast *Tamiami Champion*

Car type	Line No.	Endpoints
14-seat bag.-coach	CW-6	WAS-TAM
20-seat bag.-coach	CW-12	WAS-TAM
52-seat coach	CW-11	WAS-TAM
56-seat coach	CW-7	WAS-TAM
56-seat coach	CW-8	NYC-TAM
60-seat coach	CW-9	NYC-TAM
56-seat coach	CW-10	NYC-STP
Coach	CW-15	WAS-TAM
Diner		????
10-2-1 sleeper	CL-64	NYC-STP
10-1-2 sleeper	CL-63	NYC-TAM
10-2-1 sleeper	CL-65	NYC-TAM
8-br. sleeper lounge?	CL-66	NYC-JAX

NOTE: 8-bedroom lounge substituted by 6-bedroom car every third day)

East Coast *Tamiami Champion*

Car type	Line No.	Endpoints
14-seat bag.-coach	CE-1	NYC-MIA
60-seat coach	CE-2	NYC-MIA
52-seat coach	CE-3	NYC-MIA
60-seat coach	CE-4	NYC-MIA
60-seat coach	CE-5	NYC-MIA
Coach	CE-8	NYC-MIA
Diner		
10-section sleeper	CL-67	NYC-MIA
6-6 sleeper	CL-68	NYC-MIA
8-5 sleeper	CL-69	NYC-MIA
10-2-1 sleeper	R-61	WAS-MIA

Although a business-as-usual atmosphere pervaded the schedules in this first year of the war, ACL was hunkering down for the rush it could see coming. Its timetables admonished travelers to "use transportation wisely," exhorting them to buy tickets early. Troop traffic continued to mount as did civilian travel due to gas and tire rationing as well as the increase in wartime industry. A quirk of geography ensured that Coast Line, its allies and its competitors would be even busier than the average railroad—a quirk known as Washington, D.C.

Already this formerly sleepy Southern town was being transformed overnight, by dint of war, into the bustling capital of the Free World. The war effort drew secretaries, bureaucrats, diplomats, spies, officers of flag rank and soldiers in record numbers from all corners of the globe. Hefty numbers of these travelers arrived at Washington Union Station via rail, many having traveled at least a portion of their journey via Coast Line.

The increase in war traffic was about to butt heads with the normal seasonal increase of Florida winter travel. Adding fuel to the flames was the newly created Office of Defense Transportation—seen by the railroads as a necessary evil to mediate the vast wartime requirements on the nation's railroads. Run by the respected Joseph Eastman, a New England lawyer and three-time chairman of the Interstate Commerce Commission, the "Office" was viewed as an improvement over the totalitarian United States Railroad Administration (USRA) necessitated by World War I.

Despite the even-handed approach of Eastman, the Office of Defense Transportation forced hard changes on the Florida roads in the winter of 1942-43. In the early autumn of 1942, the Office "froze" passenger service, prohibiting the addition of new trains or sections of existing ones. This was an effort to manage the crush the railroads and Pullman were facing as a result of the necessities of war.

No one was more threatened by this move than the Florida roads, whose service traditionally expand-

ed enormously in the winter. All but swamped through the normally quiet summer season of '42, Coast Line was suddenly faced with the fact that multiple sections of the *Florida Special*, *Miamian* and *Vacationer*—the backbone of its winter service—would not be permitted to run. All ACL could offer was an East and West Coast (coach and Pullman) section of the *Tamiami Champion* as well as the *Havana Special*. Pressure, protest and pleading by the railroads and the formidable Florida tourism industry brought a minor conciliation: A second all-coach section of the *Tamiami Champion* to the East Coast of Florida would be permitted. All else fell on deaf ears. There was a good reason for what would seem, at first glance, a rash act. Cars of the Pullman pool, which had heretofore carried the Florida winter season mobs, were now busily engaged in moving troops.

In the midst of chaos came an event which would impart direction. On Oct. 15, 1942, Champion McDowell Davis was named president of ACL. More than any other executive before or since, his name would come to *mean* Atlantic Coast Line (despite his unique first name, it had not been an influence in the selection of labels for the road's first streamliner).

Starting as a messenger with ACL predecessor Wilmington & Weldon in 1893, Davis had moved through the ranks, spending most of his time as a traffic man. The hard-driving Episcopalian served a stint with the USRA between 1918 and 1920 before returning to ACL. In 1928 he became vice president of

traffic, then executive vice president in 1940. Viewed by some as an autocrat, Davis would prove up to the task of focusing the railroad on handling the burdens of war while keeping a weather eye on the future.

Evidence of ACL's ability to deal with the present was the rebuilding, in only 11 weeks between November 1942 and January 1943, of six diners from heavy-weight coaches. Completed at Emerson Shops, the *New Bern*, *Hartsville*, *Orangeburg*, *Troy*, *Gainesville* and *Bradenton* were immediately pressed into service. Two other diners, the *Kinston* and the *Valdosta*, were acquired from Pullman. They were sorely needed, as other railroads from whom ACL had leased diners on a seasonal basis now had a year-round need for every car they could muster. Consist of Note 3-F shows a war-era *Havana Special* with one of the Pullman diners.

Ever mindful of the future and now convinced of the merits of streamlining, Davis was meeting with PRR president Martin Clement to

---

CONSIST OF NOTE 3-F
ACL train First 76, northbound
Havana Special
Rocky Mount, N.C.
Oct. 17, 1943

Car	Type
[ACL 1565]	[4-6-2 steam locomotive]
ACL 1627	Express car
C&O 685	Coach
PRR 860	Coach
PRR 1898	Coach
PRR 1179	Coach
PRR 1433	Coach
PRR 2137	Coach
PRR 1165	Coach
ACL *Kinston*	Diner
Pullman 2208	13-section tourist sleeper
Rubens	6-compartment, 3-drawing-room sleeper
Glen Willow	6-compartment, 3-drawing-room sleeper
USA 89021	U.S. Army hospital car

ABOVE: FEC E3A 1002 strikes a classic pose with the original FEC *Champion* consist in 1939.—FEC PHOTO BY HARRY WOLFE, VIA SETH BRAMSON. Hallmark of the modest seven-car streamliners were their tavern-lounge-observation cars, one of whose interiors (RIGHT) was photographed by a New York-based company specializing in color photography and engraving.—CSX CORPORATION, POWERS REPRODUCTION CORPORATION.

propose joint completion of more lightweight equipment as soon as the wartime prohibitions on new construction were lifted. While the planning went on, something no one planned on happened in a sleepy Southern hamlet.

In the early morning of Dec. 16, 1943, ACL train 91, the southbound *Tamiami Champion* (West Coast), screeched to a halt in the frigid darkness of Buie, N.C. Snow covered the ground and, reportedly, the night was the coldest in the county in 60 years.

The apparent cause of the stop was a break in the train line. The conductor and trainmen proceeded back along the 18-car consist and hadn't gone far when they discovered the suspected problem—a broken coupler knuckle and disconnected air hose between the second and third cars. On this section of double-track main line, block signaling and Automatic Train Stop protected the route. Nevertheless, manual flag protection was the rule, and a brakeman proceeded toward the rear.

Unknown to the crew at the head end, the cause of the stop was not just the break in the train line near the front of the train, but the derailment and uncoupling of the last three cars of the train, caused by a transverse fissure in a rail. These last three cars—two Pullmans and a diner—jolted along the ties for 1,300 feet before coming to rest more than half a mile from the rest of the train and leaning heavily over the northbound tracks.

No serious injuries had occurred and the derailed cars were prudently evacuated, leaving passengers standing in the cold night on an embankment overlooking the scene. However, in this pre-radio age, the seriousness of the problem remained unknown to the head-end crew. Forward flag protection was provided by the train's fireman. Carrying a single fusee and red and white lanterns, this crewman had stationed himself a mere 100 feet in front of his own train. While the crew at the head end assumed they were dealing with a minor problem, crew members at the rear end assumed that adequate flag protection at the head end was protecting the derailment. Forty minutes later and apparently having just been made aware of his train's derailed cars, the half-frozen fireman saw to his horror the fast-approaching headlight of No. 8, the New York-bound East Coast *Tamiami Champion*.

On the long tangent, No. 8's engineer, Frank Belknap, had had a clear view of the stopped southbound's headlight for over four miles but observed no warning signals. Upon seeing the onrushing train, the fireman on the ground ran forward, attempting to light his fusee, but slipped and broke the flare. He was reduced to frantically waving his red lantern as the northbound train screamed by him at 85 mph with no acknowledgement. Engineer Belknap's first observed warning came when a passenger waved a marker lamp taken from the disabled rear car. The speed of the oncoming train had barely been reduced to 80 mph when it collided with the derailed cars. Miraculously, No. 8's three diesels escaped major damage, but the second and third cars of the northbound train were demolished.

Seventy-one passengers died—two thirds of them soldiers. Only one passenger of the derailed train perished. It would prove to be the worst wreck ever of a Florida streamliner and one of the worst American rail passenger disasters of the century.

Despite the tragedy, the work of moving people continued unabated. For the winter season of 1943-44, the railroad offered much the same lineup as the previous season: an all-coach East Coast *Tamiami Champion* along with a coach/sleeper version to Miami; a West Coast *Tamiami Champion* with coaches and sleepers to the Gulf Coast; the *Havana Special* in two sections, a Washington-Miami section and its regular New York section with coaches and sleepers for both coasts. One change, perhaps as a result of the wreck at Buie, went into effect in the spring of 1944: The *Tamiami* prefix would never be used again.

Consists, destinations and timings remained largely static through 1944 and 1945. However, the railroads were selling every seat they had, including lounge seats, as reserved space. In some ways, this may have been the U.S. railroads' finest hour, for their Herculean effort played an instrumental role in the war effort. The down side was that, through sheer traffic volume, operating performance was hardly optimum.

The *Champion*s and the *Silver Meteor* sometimes ran so far off the advertised that northbound trains were terminated at Washington to allow enough time to turn the consist for its southbound run the same day. Meanwhile, passengers destined for points north of Washington had to transfer to the next-available PRR train headed for New York.

The previously high travel period of August 1943, when close to one million troops alone traveled the nation's rails, was expected to be surpassed in the fall and winter of 1945 as troops were redeployed to fight a Pacific war. Japan's quick surrender in September 1945 meant this westward movement would be largely unnecessary. Nevertheless, the end of hostilities presented what may have been an even bigger logistical problem—getting everybody home. Troops rode to mustering-out points in everything that could be put on a track—including baggage cars. The nation's all-time high for passenger rail traffic would come, after all, in the Christmas season of 1945 but for a happier reason than had been originally envisioned.

With the uncertainty of war behind it, the Coast Line and partners FEC, PRR and RF&P reiterated their order for new cars with Budd. The original request had been for 30 cars, but by the end of the war the order had been beefed up to 59 lightweights. It was understood that the cars would be completed as soon as materials and labor became available and the swamped car manufacturer could complete the order.

The recent storm had been weathered and the future seemed to hold much promise. ACL and its partners had, by their early change of heart and commitment to streamlining and dieselization, survived the crush of wartime travel. Moreover they had laid the groundwork for an improved service for decades to come.

While the war drew to a conclusion and as the Florida railroads were planning for that bright future, a little-remarked event with far-reaching impact took place in Washington, D.C. Concerned about future defense needs, the federal government authorized the development of a "defense highway" system. The interstate had been conceived and the future of American railroads altered forever.

ABOVE: ACL's summer season 1942 timetable correctly predicted—if unknowingly—the outcome of the war that would forever transform America and its railroads. BELOW: From its modest beginning in 1939, the *Champion* was destined to become the spine of ACL's New York-Florida services, one that would quickly shed the constraints offered by the initial seven-car consists. ACL E3A 500 poses with the new *Champion* near Lake Worth, Fla., in December 1939.—FEC PHOTO BY HARRY WOLFE, JONATHAN S. NELSON COLLECTION.

THE KEYSTONE IN FLORIDA

Pennsylvania Railroad: The Cold

All journeys must have a beginning and an end. For many a winter-weary passenger seeking a temporary home in the sun, the journey to Florida began with a taxi ride through a dreary urbanized landscape of slush and snow. Deposited at the doorstep of, say, New York's Pennsylvania Station, the traveler would weave through a well-bundled crowd, safe in the knowledge that most of those encountered were bound for less-exotic destinations.

Descending the stairway to a subterranean platform and hearing a muffled rumble, the first hint of anticipation washed over the pensive voyager. Confirmed by the glow of a distant headlight, the sense of expectancy was brought to crescendo with the thunderous, bell-clanging arrival of a massive GG1 electric locomotive and its train—a Florida train. Eighteen cars gleamed in the artificial light as vestibule doors swung open nearly in unison. The inviting glow of car windows beckoned and soon, with passengers hanging up coats they'd no longer need, you were on your way.

WHETHER IT WAS the standard Pullman elegance of the *Orange Blossom Special* or the sparkling finery of the streamlined *Champion*, for travelers between the Northeast and Florida, the first part of a journey

south to sunshine always included a fast ride "under wire" (catenary charged with 11,000 volts) on the Pennsylvania Railroad.

Although the Florida trains were just another part of the daily parade of name trains to the mighty PRR, the Pennsylvania Railroad was an integral part of Florida-train operations. Along its relatively short 227 route-miles lay opportunity. New York, Philadelphia, Baltimore, Washington and their environs—the most populous area in the nation—was the market. Sunshine was the product. Pennsy was the broker.

At the time of the *Silver Meteor*'s inaugural in 1939, better than 30 million people lived within reach of the PRR and the Florida trains. The railroads' aim was to convince as many of those folks as possible to visit Florida by rail. They were remarkably successful.

Pennsylvania's rich contributions to the success of the Florida trains dated to at least 1884 when the railroad began carrying a Jersey City-Jacksonville sleeper for the Atlantic Coast Line. Within a few short years, the Pennsylvania, thanks to electrification, had expanded into the heart of Manhattan itself with an aggressive program of tunnel-building and electrification under the Hudson River and the 1910 opening of Pennsylvania Station in Manhattan.

SERVICE
Climate Anchor

ABOVE: Just nine days old, the *Champion* is southbound behind Pennsylvania Railroad GG1 No. 4847 at Elizabeth, N.J. In its original incarnation, the seven-car streamliner usually operated attached to PRR New York-Washington trains, which makes this scene a rarity among photos of the original *Champion.*—GEORGE E. VOTAVA. **LEFT:** Also shortly after its inaugural, the original *Silver Meteor,* pauses at Elizabeth in February 1939 as a completely separate train on the PRR. Like its *Champion* rival, the original *Meteor* usually was combined with PRR trains north of Washington, D.C., partly due to PRR's concern over train lengths.—CAL'S CLASSICS.

ABOVE: Autumn's colors are just seeping into the trees surrounding the busy PRR main line at Metuchen, N.J., as a well-weathered GG1 strides along with the southbound *Silver Meteor* in 1963. Although PRR initially operated the *Meteor* and the *Champion* attached to regular PRR consists, the New York-Florida streamliners grew to be so popular—and therefore so large—that they soon commanded their own motive power and separate schedule between New York and Washington.
—JOHN DZIOBKO JR.

Overhead electrification of the PRR linking metro New York and Washington was completed by 1935. In that year, too, the greatest straight-electric locomotive ever built—the GG1—began hauling the Florida fleet, supplanting, then replacing P5 box-cab electrics. Heavyweight consists such as the *Orange Blossom Special* and *Florida Special* were child's play for the brutish new electrics, and when the Florida streamliners arrived in 1939, the sleek GG1's blended beautifully with the new equipment.

The fun-seeking Florida trains worked side by side with Pennsy's renowned fleet, which included such household names as the *Congressional* and the *Broadway Limited*. In addition to name trains, the busy PRR New York-Washington main line handled dozens of others, from the celebrated New York-Philadelphia "Clockers" to the ubiquitous MP54-class electric multiple-unit commuter cars scuttling to and fro on their more-mundane assignments.

To a much lesser degree, Pennsy served as a bridge route, too, forwarding Florida cars to New England and even Canada via the New Haven and other roads. Trains like the *Orange Blossom Special*, *Florida Special* and *Havana Special* often carried Boston sleepers in their consists. For a few seasons in the early-to-mid

1950's, Atlantic Coast Line's winter-season *Vacationer* operated as a through consist from Boston to Florida via the PRR until the train's termination in the spring of 1955.

In deference to the important markets Pennsy helped them reach and mindful of the enormous amount of traffic it handled, both Seaboard and Atlantic Coast Line treated the PRR with kid gloves. Case in point: Before Seaboard finalized its order with Budd for the very first *Silver Meteor* on Oct. 12, 1938, it sought and received the Pennsylvania's approval of the venture—despite the fact that PRR contributed not a single car to the original streamliner. Two more times within the year, PRR would flex its muscles and make decisions which would affect the operation of the *Silver Meteor*.

As the *Silver Meteor* was being constructed, SAL and PRR tried to reach an agreement on how to operate the new streamliner over the Pennsy's busy four-track New York-Washington main line. Seaboard, it seems, had jumped the gun, announcing that the new train would operate as a separate consist between New York and Miami/St. Petersburg. In its original September 1938 conference with PRR, Seaboard had indicated that the "entire plan" for introducing the

LEFT: Regal in its gold-pinstripe livery, another PRR GG1 sweeps through the reverse curves at Elizabeth with the southbound *Champion*, bathed in the late evening sun of Oct. 13, 1952.—JOHN DZIOBKO JR. BELOW: Early electric motive power for PRR trains in and out of Pennsylvania Station were the P5-class motors. P5a 4730 hums into Manhattan Transfer, N.J., on Feb. 11, 1933, with the incomparable *Orange Blossom Special*. The electrification has not yet been installed all the way to the nation's capital, so the low-roof 2-C-2 motor is about be exchanged for PRR steam.—GEORGE E. VOTAVA.

Meteor was predicated upon PRR's handling it separate from its New York to Washington local service, thus affording the speedster a cachet of elegance it would otherwise lack tied to the rear of a work-a-day New York-Washington consist.

Pennsy lent a sympathetic ear to the request, but its operating people were adamantly opposed to a separate operation. By the time the roads met again in October, SAL's demand had been whittled down to a "request" to run the *Silver Meteor* separately for 90 days. On Nov. 4, 1938, PRR responded with its final offer: 30 days operation as a separate train and thereafter the *Meteor* was to be combined with PRR train 155 the *Constitution*, a heavyweight New York-Washington train leaving New York at 3:30 p.m. Northbound, the new streamliner was to be tacked onto PRR 124, the *Potomac*, departing

Washington at 8 a.m. for New York.

In a letter which explained Pennsy's operating philosophy on the New York-Washington main, PRR's J. F. Deasy summed up the reasons for declining the Seaboard request: "The principle reason why we [PRR] spent a large sum of money electrifying our line between New

Bird's-eye View of the P. R. R. Depot, New York.

Almost all Northeast-Florida trains terminated at Pennsylvania Station in Manhattan, which opened in 1910. The granite-and-glass masterpiece was patterned after the Roman baths of Caracalla and the Basilica of Constantine. In its early years, Penn Station stood in contrast with relatively subdued surroundings, for the area was largely still residential, as this colorized postcard illustrates. But, as Manhattan boomed, Pennsylvania Station became a contrast in reverse—by being a low-storied complex surrounded by skyscrapers that had sprung upon the bedrock. Tragically, the station succumbed to money interests and was leveled in 1965.—AUTHOR'S COLLECTION.

ABOVE: Strange bedfellows. A Pennsy 2-8-2 has a grip on a GG1 and the *Champion* on Aug. 13, 1947. The whole assortment is way off course at Bound Brook, N.J., on the Lehigh Valley Railroad. The cause of the detour is a derailment on the PRR at South Elizabeth, N.J. —H. H. HARWOOD JR. RIGHT: Its gold pinstripes gleaming in the sunshine, nearly new Brunswick green PRR GG1 4813 majestically leans into the curve at Elizabeth on March 29, 1936, with the southbound *Florida Special*.—GEORGE E. VOTAVA.

York and Washington was to enable us to haul . . .18 cars of normal weight behind one of our electric locomotives and maintain a speed of 90 mph. To project a seven car lightweight . . . into this kind of operation [would be] . . . an extravagance PRR can ill afford." By 1940, the entire issue would be a moot point. Seaboard's *Silver Meteor*, wildly popular, would be expanded to a 14-car consist and operated as a separate train.

A second confrontation between Pennsy and Seaboard, shortly after the *Meteor*'s successful introduction, would have far greater impact on the future of the train. Secure in the knowledge that its gamble on streamlining was paying off, Seaboard turned toward another market and another adversary—Birmingham and Atlanta and the Southern Railway. Like Atlantic Coast Line, Southern had resisted streamlining in favor of conventional, steam-hauled trains.

It isn't clear whether SAL had intentions of mod-

ernizing its Atlanta/Birmingham route all along, but in describing the forthcoming *Silver Meteor* in its 1938 Annual Report, the road stated, ". . . the points between which this train may be operated can be varied if conditions warrant." They were not talking about Miami and St. Petersburg, as those end points had already been established. Clearly, those "conditions" must have warranted, for on Feb. 20, 1939—a scant 18 days after the *Meteor*'s inaugural—SAL approached the PRR for its thoughts on operating the *Silver Meteor* to Birmingham and Atlanta on a rotating basis with the Florida destinations.

To avoid alienating the Southern and in an attempt to limit through coach operations into its crowded New York terminal facilities, the Pennsylvania declined to participate in the idea. In 1939, the New York-Florida route was the only route south of Washington on which through coaches operated to and from New York (through Pullman sleepers of

TOP: *Silver Meteor* contemporary *Orange Blossom Special* (East Coast) is shown in full heavyweight glory behind GG1 4863 in March 1939.—CAL'S CLASSICS. LEFT AND BELOW: With a wave from the engineer, the southbound *Meteor* winds through the reverse curves at Elizabeth in May 1967. A smoothside PRR 10-6 sleeper is tucked in behind the dorm, "blemishing" an otherwise all-stainless consist. Trailing the train that day was tavern-lounge-observation 6603 (destined to soon be rebuilt by Seaboard Coast Line for mid-train service). Ahead of the obs is a former Florida East Coast coach which Seaboard had purchased from FEC after a strike halted that road's participation in New York-Florida service.—BOTH PHOTOS, J. C. SMITH JR.

ABOVE: "G" 4907 on the northbound *West Coast Champion* wears Pennsy's rare Tuscan red single-stripe scheme on a spring morning in 1964 at Washington, D.C.—JOHN DZIOBKO JR. BELOW: During World War II, delays were carefully explained.—AUTHOR'S COLLECTION

course, were another matter). Pennsy was acutely aware that if it offered a through coach route to Atlanta to Seaboard it would also have to do so for the Southern. In addition, PRR felt the move would open up the floodgates to the requests of other southern-region carriers like Chesapeake & Ohio.

The idea was dropped quietly. In 1941 Southern introduced its streamlined *Southerner* on this route; it would be 1947 before Seaboard countered with its first lightweight train to Birmingham and Atlanta, the *Silver Comet*.

The whole issue was indicative of how serious PRR was about traffic on its vital New York-Washington artery. For many years to come, the Pennsylvania would continue to exercise a control over its connecting partners to the South that was out of proportion to its New York-Florida route mileage . . . but completely in-step with the importance of the market it helped the Florida roads reach.

In addition to its importance as a partner, Pennsy also provided a home away from home for both ACL and SAL's Florida fleet. At PRR's vast Sunnyside Yard complex on Long Island, reached via the tunnel under the East River from Manhattan, the Florida trains found rest and replen-

ishment amidst the Pennsy's Blue Ribbon fleet and the heavyweight P70 coaches. Simply put, no other passenger car yard in North America could rival Sunnyside for size and complexity.

At its zenith, the facility handled over 100 trains every day. Over 1,200 cars crowded its 44-mile, 75-track network, daily. Eleven switching crews and their distinctive B1 electric switchers dissected and reassembled trains as a veritable army of over 3,200 people tended the cars, performing chores which ran the gamut from cleaning to laundry to electrical repair. The Pullman Company maintained a separate force of over 600 people in place to repair and replenish its fleet of sleepers and, likewise, the Sunnyside Commissary catered to the huge fleet of Pennsy dining cars as well as off-road diners arriving from the South on the likes of the *Crescent Limited* and the Florida trains.

By the 1940's the relationship between PRR and the Florida roads had settled into a comfortable operating partnership. Still, on most issues, Pennsy got its way. When the time came to re-equip the Florida trains after World War II, PRR limited its contributions to the Florida fleet to revenue-producing cars such as coaches and sleepers. The northern giant was very firm in stipulating that, in its relations with the Southern roads, it would not contribute rolling stock which it considered "specialty" cars such as diners and lounges. Pennsy's aim was to maximize the revenue capacity of trains serving its own markets, and it occasionally would berate connecting roads whose cars it handled for operating equipment over the PRR with low capacity. It was crooked logic. While Pennsy was busy scolding ACL for running low-capacity, 46-seat, coaches on its *Champions*, for example, the Pennsy east-west fleet—which in part utilized the New York-Washington main line—was almost exclusively comprised of 44-seat coaches.

Snow—the bane of Northerners driven to Florida climes—brought havoc to the Northeast-Florida fleet in February 1958 when a rare form of the precipitation known as "diamond snow" hit New Jersey and Pennsylvania coastal areas. Diamond snow has a very fine crystalization structure that occurs at about five feet above ground level—coincidentally the height of air-intake vents on GG1 electrics. The result: Frozen armatures and an almost entirely disabled GG1 fleet. Havoc resulted as Pennsy scrambled to find other motive power to keep its lines fluid. P5 electrics, whose air intakes were much higher than the G's, were unaffected and therefore could be used to protect schedules of important PRR runs, while diesels filled in elsewhere. In the case of the Florida fleet, the Southeastern operators had to send their diesel power through from Richmond and Washington to keep traffic moving. ABOVE: A pristine RF&P E8A&B set leaves Newark Penn Station on Feb. 22, 1958, with the southbound *Silver Star*. BELOW: One of the few operating GG1's has just brought combined PRR train 121, the *Representative*, and the southbound *Miamian* out of New York Pennsylvania Station to Hudson Tower outside east of Newark Penn Station. In short order, the G is exchanged for a stunning A-B-A set of Atlantic Coast Line E7's, all wearing the celebrated purple-and-silver scheme. The storm prompted PRR to experiment with a special epoxy/resin coating developed by Altoona (Pa.) Shops and intended for all 1,668 armatures in PRR's 139 GG1's. PRR also mounted special filters on GG1 air-intake grids to alleviate the problem, which apparently never happened again.—ALL PHOTOS, JOHN DZIOBKO JR.

Mechanically, too, PRR dictated its own terms. Although Pennsy cars ordered for Florida service generally matched the livery of the intended road, be it purple letterboard for ACL or black on stainless for Seaboard assignment, many times PRR specified different mechanical components than those on their sister cars.

As time wore on into the 1960's and passenger revenues declined, the gulf in operating philosophies between the Florida roads and the PRR widened. By this time, the Pennsylvania, strapped with unprofitable runs, generally saw the long-haul passenger train as something to be grudgingly tolerated, while the Florida roads maintained an upbeat attitude about the service. As revenues declined further and the roads went through their respective mergers—ACL and SAL becoming Seaboard Coast Line and PRR and New York Central becoming the Penn Central in February 1968—the differences flared into outright hostility.

Penn Central attempted to convince SCL to abandon its association with Pullman, announced its intention of not handling sleeping cars into New York

and attempted to block the return of the legendary *Florida Special*—SCL's flagship. Happily, in two out of three of its efforts, the bumbling Northeast giant failed. In a third, the Pullman issue, PC hastened Pullman's demise despite SCL's continued loyalty.

Through it all, the Florida trains survived, outliving Penn Central (not to mention ACL, SAL and SCL). Today, Amtrak's operation of the Northeast-Florida market is the only long-distance route the carrier has that features double-daily (or more) service in each direction. All of this is a tribute to the strength of the appeal that Florida trains have long had.

The entire turn of events was more than a bit ironic, for had the Pennsylvania Railroad not been there to provide access to lucrative northern markets, the entire concept of train travel to Florida might well have remained a regional effort doomed to failure by low ridership. Instead, through the foresight of the Florida roads and the PRR back in 1939, one of the greatest passenger operations in American history—the Florida streamliner—was launched. And, for that, fans of the Florida fleet owe an undying debt of gratitude to the great Pennsylvania Railroad.

LEFT: PRR 4029 was one of four 60-seat coaches (4026-4029) owned by the "P Company" for ACL operations. They were delivered in December 1940, with purple letterboards, for expanded *Champion* service.—CSX CORPORATION. BELOW: The *Silver Meteor* departs Sunnyside Yard, Queens, N.Y., for a short trip under the East River into Pennsylvania Station in Manhattan to be positioned for its trip south. It's May 1954 and the train has drawn a GG1 with the rare keystone emblem on the nose instead of the usual numbered one.—H. H. HARWOOD JR.

LEFT: Concurrent with the use of roomette cars in Budget Room Coach service, ACL refrained from offering standard roomette/bedroom cars in the *East Coast Champion*. In place of the 10-6's, the *East Coast Champion* in the summer of 1966 offered Pennsy 12-duplex-roomette, 4-double-bedroom cars *Cabin Creek* typifies the class.—D. T. HAYWARD, PETER TILP COLLECTION. LOWER LEFT: PRR contributed two ACF-built 14-2 sleepers to the *Champion/ Florida Special* pool. *Anacostia River* was one, *Hackensack River* was the other.—ACF INDUSTRIES VIA GEORGE VOTAVA.

LEFT: Broad Street Station in Richmond catered to Florida travelers until the mid-1970's when a new Richmond station opened in an industrial area on the north side of the city. This view shows the stately building as it appeared in 1965. Above the right portico is the inscription RICHMOND, FREDERICKSBURG AND POTOMAC COMPANY CHARTERED 1834; a similar inscription for ACL appeared over the left portico. Seaboard was not one of the original tenants. BELOW: Minutes away from Washington Union Station, an RF&P FP7 and an E8B roll a northbound Florida train past Potomac Yard at Alexandria, Va., in the spring of 1964.—BOTH PHOTOS, JOHN DZIOBKO JR.

The Relay Between North and South

RICHMOND, FREDERICKSBURG &

*I*f the Pennsylvania Railroad played an important role in helping the Florida trains tap northern markets, the Richmond, Fredericksburg & Potomac was equally critical in connecting them to the PRR.

Chartered in Virginia in 1834, the RF&P had evolved into a key bridge line connecting railroads to the south of Richmond (RF&P's southern terminus) with the Pennsylvania Railroad to the north at Washington, D.C., via a connection with a PRR subsidiary, the Washington-Southern, at Quantico, Va. Virtually every Florida train bound for the Northeast used RF&P's 117-mile, double-tracked main line to reach the PRR. The relationship dated to the beginning of Northeast-Florida service.

By the late 1800's, RF&P's status as a vital freight

link had been ensured with the introduction, in 1888, of the "Atlantic Coast Dispatch," forerunner to the Fruit Growers Express Company. Southern growers found quick access to northern markets via this through freight service and thousands of tons of perishable fruits and vegetables found their way to northern tables courtesy of the RF&P.

Likewise, the Old Dominion carrier played a long-standing and vital role in passenger operations to Florida. When the *Florida Special* began service in January 1888, it did so over the RF&P, "Atlantic Coast Line" having gained control of the bridge line in 1885. In July 1900, after a protracted legal battle which even embroiled the Virginia State Legislature, upstart Seaboard Air Line began interchanging cars to

POTOMAC RAILROAD

P O T O M A C   R A I L R O A D

RF&P train 21, the southbound *Silver Star*, is posed for a company photograph on the Rappahannock River bridge at Fredericksburg, Va., in this late 1940's view. Motive power is provided by hefty 4-8-4 No. 621, the *Governor Richard Henry Lee*. Several non-streamlined cars in the consist had been airbrushed by the photography studio to better match the stainless-steel *Star* cars.—A. L. DEMENTI PHOTOGRAPH, WILLIAM E. GRIFFIN JR. COLLECTION.

and from the north via the RF&P as well.

To allow for an equitable traffic arrangement between the RF&P and Seaboard, it was important to remove total control of the company from the hands of Seaboard competitor ACL. In July 1901, by way of an agreement, six railroads which served Richmond or depended on the RF&P—PRR, ACL, Seaboard, Southern, Baltimore & Ohio and Chesapeake & Ohio—gained control of the RF&P and Washington-Southern, forming the Richmond-Washington Line. In February 1920, RF&P and W-S formally merged, becoming simply the Richmond, Fredericksburg & Potomac Railroad.

Seaboard trains entering Richmond paused at Main Street Station on the southeast end of Rich-

mond's business district. Motive power was exchanged north of Main Street at Hermitage Yard. Main Street was a French Revival-style facility shared with the C&O, whose trains, such as the *George Washington*, also stopped at the Virginia capital. For a time, Southern called here as well.

Atlantic Coast Line trains serving Richmond interchanged with the RF&P at Broad Street Station, which opened in 1919. A classic, Doric-columned beauty constructed of Indiana limestone, the domed station was designed by John Russell Pope, whose impressive list of accomplishments included the Jefferson Memorial—to which Broad Street Station bears a family resemblance.

Although Broad Street Station was a considerable

distance from downtown Richmond (and in the opposite direction from Main Street Station), it was located on an important vehicular artery and better positioned for access by trains of RF&P and ACL. On Nov. 21, 1958, Seaboard Air Line acquired one-third ownership of the Richmond Terminal Company and abandoned operation into Main Street Station in favor of Broad Street.

Getting into Broad Street by rail may well have been the most unique thing about the facility. The depot itself was located off the RF&P main line on a special loop track belonging to RTC. The track arrangement was such that all trains, regardless of being northbound or southbound, pulled through the station in the same direction. This setup allowed engine-servicing facilities to all be at one end of the platforms. The one-direction flow through the station tracks worked fine for trains off the ACL and RF&P mains, but when Seaboard entered the fray in 1958, a seesaw back-up move was required for its trains before entering and after leaving the Broad Street station loop.

RF&P contributed more than just track to Northeast-Florida operations. It provided top-notch handling of the Florida fleet. Whether behind RF&P's sleek 4-8-4 steam engines in the *Governor*, *General* or *Statesman* class (so called for the names each locomotive carried) or, later, behind distinctive blue-and-gray E-units, Florida passengers were assured a fast ride over the RF&P.

Until the late 1930's, steam ruled uncontested on

the RF&P. Later, when EMD diesels began appearing on the head end of both SAL and ACL/FEC trains in 1939, these roads negotiated "run-through" agreements to allow diesel power on their crack streamliners—the *Silver Meteor* and the *Champion*—as well as other diesel-hauled trains to operate through to Washington. At first, this was done for marketing purposes—ACL, FEC and SAL being particularly concerned about deriving the maximum publicity from their sleek new motive power. An additional concern was speed. The new diesels had allowed the railroads to slice hours (not minutes) off their trains' schedules.

As World War II engulfed the nation, diesel run-throughs were used as a time saver and as a way to handle increased demand for motive power due to the appearance of added sections of regularly scheduled trains and "Extras" (non-scheduled trains). Seaboard run-throughs over the RF&P appear to have lasted until Sept. 30, 1942, after which RF&P steam locomotives took over the chores on passenger trains.

Run-throughs of Coast Line and Florida East Coast motive power on the *Champion*s over the RF&P began the day the trains were inaugurated and appear to have continued nearly unabated until May 1945 when RF&P steam took over the reigns again. When the *Florida Special* received diesel units, the roads also operated these diesels through as well. In May 1946, diesel run-throughs commenced again on virtually all of ACL's top trains with the exception of the *Havana Special*. Thereafter, the practice continued sporadically until the arrival of RF&P's own diesels

Dreary skies greet passengers aboard the northbound *Miamian* cruising along the RF&P behind FP7 1203 early in the 1950's. Note the rake of heavyweight sleepers trailing the string of purple-letterboard stainless-steel cars.—S. K. BOLTON JR., COLLECTION OF WILLIAM F. HOWES JR.

put steam permanently out to pasture.

Interestingly, while at first the through operation of diesels over the RF&P was done at the request of the ACL/FEC, in 1942, perhaps because of concerns over traffic and schedule adherence, RF&P turned the tides, requesting that ACL and FEC continue to run their diesels through over the RF&P.

For a short time after World War II, then, RF&P's 4-8-4's had returned to or continued at the head end of the Florida trains, handling the streamliners as well as secondary runs. But, in late 1949, RF&P took delivery of the first of 15 EMD E8A's and five E8B's, the first diesel passenger units owned by the Virginia carrier. In November 1950, the road would add three dual freight/passenger FP7A locomotives. Internal combustion was here to stay. By 1952, RF&P had abandoned steam completely.

In addition to providing motive power for the Florida fleet, RF&P passenger equipment was routinely operated in the Florida trains. In the heavyweight era, for example, RF&P diners often graced ACL route trains, filling a vital need for equipment during the peak winter travel season. Curiously, when the *Silver Meteor* and *Champion*s arrived and were expanded in the prewar period, RF&P was the only one of the participating railroads which did not contribute equipment to the pool. This oversight would be rectified shortly after World War II when the partners in Florida service heavily reequipped their fleets. RF&P would contribute equipment to both the Seaboard pool and the Atlantic Coast Line fleet.

The process was known as "equalization." Railroads were to contribute equipment to an operating pool in percentages roughly equal to the amount of the route-miles they carried the trains. Notes from one series of negotiations regarding equalization and the future ACL fleet revealed that not everything was as equal as it may have seemed.

In February 1946 as meetings took place between PRR, RF&P ACL and FEC to mediate the composition and ownership of cars to reequip the postwar *Champion*s, Pennsylvania Railroad President Martin Clement expressed a desire *not* to contribute "feature" cars to the fleet. The railroad's argument was a simple one. Based on mileage, PRR, with only 227 one-way Florida route-miles, wasn't one of the principal contributors to Coast Line operations. It should therefore be allowed to defer purchase of less-utilitarian diners and sleeper-lounges in favor of more-useful sleepers and coaches. ACL, which was taking the lead on the fleet purchase, acquiesced, allowing Pennsy off the hook.

This argument sounded pretty good to RF&P President Norman Call, too. After all, the Old Dominion railroad carried the Florida trains a mere 117 miles, 110 fewer than PRR. To make matters worse, RF&P could see no earthly use for the sleeper-lounge or full diner, it was committed to providing, in local service between New York and Richmond should they be released from Florida service.

Call brought up the issue with Coast Line President Champion McDowell Davis who politely but firmly refused to let RF&P off the hook. In doing so, Davis gently pointed out that RF&P's concerns about using the equipment elsewhere were largely unfounded as the Florida trains would always be RF&P's heaviest-traveled passenger operation. And until RF&P disappeared into CSX Corporation nearly a half century later, that turned out to be true.

Like the faithful partner it was, RF&P stuck with the Florida roads through thick and thin. As revenues dropped and the bottom line got tougher to meet, RF&P's short route-miles and smaller expenditures for passenger service became an advantage in the battle against the mounting deficit. Right up until the advent of Amtrak and beyond, the little railroad with the big name played a key role in moving passengers from the Northeast to Florida. In the process, RF&P earned a place in history as a vital partner in one of the true triumphs of the streamlined passenger era.

Delivered in April 1947, RF&P 52-seat coach No. 856 (shown in 1948) was one of a large number of cars from Budd which arrived to reequip the *Silver Meteor* and create the *Silver Comet* and *Silver Star*. The RF&P cars of this group were Nos. 850-857. RF&P passenger cars probably had the longest letterboards of any railroad!—GEORGE E. VOTAVA.

5 A STAR IS BORN
AND OTHER TALES
Seaboard Air Line: 1945–1967

ith the world's worst war and its attendant hardships moving to a close in the spring of 1945, Seaboard Air Line surveyed the future of its passenger operations.

The war had brought higher revenues than the road could ever have imagined in those dark days of 1938 when it was begging creditors for enough money to "experiment" with a lightweight streamliner. It all seemed so long ago. Since then, Seaboard and the South itself had been changed forever by the war. During the conflict, industry had discovered the benefits of the temperate "Sun Belt." The result for Seaboard and ACL were undreamed of freight revenues.

The war had been good to the passenger department, too. Net revenues from February 1939 through March 1945 for that "experiment," the *Silver Meteor*, were nearly $23 million. But, to borrow a line from the physicists, "for every action there's an equal and opposite reaction." In the case of SAL and most other American railroads, much of those windfall earnings were offset by a major problem—they had nearly run

LEFT: The northbound Miami section of the *Silver Meteor* sweeps gracefully around a curve at Opa Locka, Fla, in September 1966 behind an A-B set of E7's adorned in Seaboard's new light green and coral scheme. The palm fronds are reminiscent of early Florida train publicity stills. Visible are a postwar Budd-built baggage-dorm, a Pullman-Standard 5-2-2 sleeper, an RF&P-owned P-S 10-6 sleeper, the 5-double-bedroom Sun Lounge, a Budd diner, a SAL 52-seat Budd coach, a P-S 52-seat coach-lounge, an RF&P 52-seat Budd coach and (also from Budd) the tavern-lounge observation. The Sun Lounge (FACING PAGE) was the postwar trademark of Seaboard in its finest hour.— *METEOR* SCENE, DAVID W. SALTER; SUN LOUNGE INTERIOR, PULLMAN TECHNOLOGY. **ABOVE:** An ad from a 1952, SAL public timetable enticed travelers to all parts of the Atlantic seaboard.—AUTHOR'S COLLECTION.

the wheels off their equipment earning them. All over the country, railroad and Pullman car foremen were assessing the damage—and it wasn't pretty. Streamlined cars built and advertised to last 25 years were being demoted to secondary runs after just seven.

To replace them, the railroads placed orders with the major carbuilders. SAL was no exception. In conjunction with partners PRR and RF&P, Seaboard went to Budd in April 1945 with a large order for coaches, diners, baggage-dormitories and observation cars. The order was apportioned by route-miles:

Type	Number	Road	Delivery
Baggage-dormitory	6050-6052	SAL	6/47
52-seat chair car	6215-6226	SAL	1-3/47
52-seat chair car	4058-4067	PRR	3/47
52-seat chair car	850-857	RF&P	4/47
48-seat diner	6106-6114	SAL	5-6/47
Tavern-lounge-obs	6600-6605	SAL	7/47

Wear and tear was one reason for the upgrades, increased competition was another. Removal of wartime restrictions on the use of the private automobile and the resurgence of another pesky adversary, the airliner,

were expected to impact ridership.

Another concern was public relations. Wartime passengers forced to ride the rails due to gas rationing had suffered at the hands of overburdened railroads. Unable to buy tickets or shuffled aboard standing-room-only trains attended by overworked employees, some customers had come away with bad impressions of rail travel. The new cars were a partial remedy.

If the coach rider was in for a treat, so was the Pullman passenger. In late 1945, Seaboard had convinced the Pennsylvania and RF&P to participate in the purchase of 31 sleeping cars—enough to equip the *Silver Meteor*, the *Advance Silver Meteor* and the soon-to-be streamliner *Silver Comet* on the New York-Atlanta-Birmingham route. This marked the first time SAL would purchase sleeping cars direct from the manufacturer. Prior to this, sleeping cars had been built and operated by Pullman, but a recent federal antitrust action against the sleeping-car giant was changing the way the railroads did business.

In July 1940, the U.S. Department of Justice filed a civil antitrust suit against Pullman Inc., its officers

RIGHT: Seaboard 52-seat coach 6221 was part of a series (6215-6226) of chair cars which arrived from Budd between January and March 1947 to re-equip the *Silver Meteor* and help create the *Silver Comet* and *Silver Star*. The car is shown in May 1948 at New York's Sunnyside Yard. RIGHT: Budd-built 48-seat diners 6106-6114 were delivered in May and June 1947 for Silver Fleet service. The full-width diaphragms, common to many early streamliners, would eventually be eliminated for maintenance reasons. The car is shown in the consist of the *Silver Comet* at North Philadelphia on Oct. 12, 1947. —BOTH PHOTOS, GEORGE E. VOTAVA. BELOW: Silver Fleet trains come and go on the cover of this 1951 *Silver Meteor* menu.—COLLECTION OF WILLIAM F. HOWES JR.

and subsidiaries. It was the culmination of a battle that had been waged behind the scenes for five years. In 1935, Chicago, Burlington & Quincy had attempted to purchase sleeping cars from the Budd Company instead of Pullman-Standard, Pullman Company's manufacturing arm. Upon learning of the potential defection of business, Pullman's operating division, which was to staff and operate the cars, put up such a fight that Burlington withdrew its order.

It wasn't the only time the venerable company would throw its weight around. In a like manner two years later, Pullman intimidated Santa Fe into curtailing its orders to Budd for any more sleeping cars beyond the first few in its initial *Super Chief* streamliner. Burlington, Budd and American Car & Foundry—the latter two sensing the danger Pullman's actions posed to their carbuilding business—joined forces in claiming that Pullman enjoyed a monopoly. The feds agreed and so did the courts. In May 1944, Pullman was ordered to divest of either its manufacturing or its operating division. The choice was easy. Pullman retained its manufacturing business, offering to sell the less-lucrative operating division for the court-ordered price of $75 million. There were no takers.

To sweeten the pot, Pullman offered to sell its 600 streamlined cars to the railroads, thus lowering the asking price by $35 million. Still-cautious, the railroads became interested in the purchase only when threatened with an even worse option: one Robert R. Young, flamboyant financier and owner of the Chesapeake & Ohio who had alienated the industry with his blunt advertisements decrying the poor state of rail passenger travel. Now Young began to make noises about purchasing Pullman. That would have put the railroads at Young's mercy for the provision of sleeping-car services.

Not surprisingly, what had once seemed an impasse suddenly resolved itself. Pullman obtained a court order requiring that its operating business be sold to a consortium of railroads, and in March 1947 the Supreme Court finally approved the sale. As a result of the judicial decisions, the railroads were required to directly solicit bids from the various car manufacturers based on the railroad's specifications for the sleeping cars it needed. Seaboard, having the greatest proportion of route mileage among its New York-Florida partners, took the lead in soliciting bids for streamlined sleepers for the fleet.

The result of the process yielded a proposed order that looked like this:

❋From Budd, six 10-roomette, 6-double-bedroom sleepers for PRR and six similar 10-6's for SAL.

❋From P-S, thirteen 16-duplex-single-room, 4-double-bedroom cars for SAL and three 16-4's for RF&P.

❋From AC&F, three 6-double-bedroom bar-lounges for SAL.

The proposed consists were to be:

SAL trains 43-343 and 344-44 (*Silver Meteor*)

1 Baggage-dormitory	NYP-MIA
1 Coach ("colored")	NYP-MIA
1 10-6 sleeper	NYP-MIA
1 16-4 sleeper	NYP-STP
1 16-4 sleeper	NYP-STP
1 Diner	NYP-STP
3 Coaches	NYP-STP
1 Tavern-coach	NYP-MIA
1 Diner	NYP-MIA
2 Coaches	NYP-MIA
1 Coach-observation	NYP-MIA

ABOVE: In the lightweight era, nearly every streamliner deserving of its name carried an observation car. Tavern-lounge observation 6602 on the *Silver Meteor* at Waldo, Fla., on March 12, 1950, flashes past SAL 2-8-2 No. 317, a regular on the Waldo-Sulfur Springs line. These postwar Budd observation cars, with their kitchy interiors featuring marine motifs of carved linoleum (INSET), represented the new order of railroading as the steam era wound down in the 1950's. Indeed, postwar Florida Fleet observation cars would see active duty for some 30 years.—METEOR SCENE, WILLIAM J. HUSA JR.; INTERIOR, SAL.

SAL trains 243-443 and 444-244 (*Advance Silver Meteor*)

1 Coach-baggage-dorm	NYP-MIA
1 10-6 sleeper	NYP-MIA
1 16-4 sleeper	NYP-MIA
1 16-4 sleeper	NYP-STP
1 Diner	NYP-STP
1 Coach-lounge	NYP-STP
3 Coaches	NYP-STP
1 Diner	NYP-MIA
3 Coaches	NYP-MIA
1 Tavern-observation	NYP-MIA

SAL trains 247 and 248 (*Silver Comet*)

1 Coach-bag-dorm	NYP-BHM
1 10-6 sleeper	NYP-BHM
1 16-4 sleeper	NYP-BHM
1 16-4 sleeper	NYP-BHM
1 6 bedroom-lounge	NYP-BHM
1 Diner	NYP-BHM
5 Coaches	NYP-BHM
1 Tavern-observation	NYP-BHM

By August 1946, the interesting order for duplex cars from Pullman would be changed to more of the increasingly popular 10-6 sleepers.

Ordering the equipment was the easy part. Waiting for delivery was nerve-wracking. In its 1946 annual report, Seaboard said it expected all deliveries to happen by early 1948. That date came and went, and although the coach order arrived, the sleeping cars were nowhere in sight. There is little doubt that the enormous strains caused by the sheer volume of postwar orders played into this, but a July 1947 memo from Pullman-Standard Vice President J. C. Snyder to the Seaboard explaining the delay was more definitive.

A principal culprit was the shortage of materials and the engineering changes caused by having to substitute similar, more-available items. A second cause was the lack of standardization and the demand for large numbers of custom cars in small lots. Snyder particularly lamented the appearance of the "innumerable gadgets" being built into the postwar cars and the inevitable shop problems caused by their inclusion.

Breakdowns in supervision, where Snyder was quick to point out the problem had worsened, went hand-in-hand with manpower shortages. Perhaps the most interesting revelation in the letter was Pullman's explanation of its intent to remedy the situation by hiring workers from the Scottish shipbuilding trade—a vast pool of joiners and finishers that Pullman had drawn from in the past. Much of Pullman's top supervision at the time had originally come from the Clydebank builders of such marvels as the *Aquitania* and the *Queen Mary*.

While awaiting its new equipment, Seaboard was using what it had on hand to field a full complement of trains. Wartime restrictions were gone, and, beginning Dec. 12, 1946, the famed *Orange Blossom Special* was back. It had lost its trademark Pullman baggage-club at the head end—several of the type had been purchased from Pullman by Seaboard and remodeled into baggage dormitories—but the rest of the consist was still in the old heavyweight Pullman tradition. No

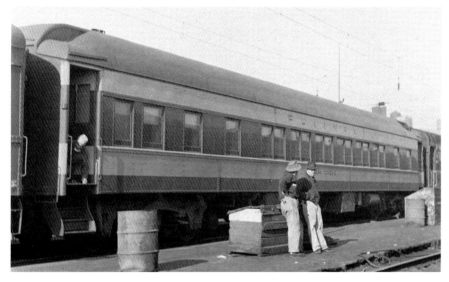

ABOVE: Photos of cars in the short-lived *Orange Blossom Special* scheme of maroon and gray are exceedingly rare. This shot of *Oak Grove* shows the scheme as applied to Pullman-owned cars used in the *Blossom* for the 1951-52 season. Only one other photo, previously published, of an SAL-owned car is known by this author to exist. —JOSEPH FISCHER VIA PETER V. TILP. **UPPER RIGHT:** The newly styled *Blossom* was announced in Seaboard's fall 1951 timetable. —AUTHOR'S COLLECTION. **ABOVE RIGHT:** *Sunburst* was typical of the 2-compartment, 1-drawing-room buffet-lounge Sun Room cars which served on the *Orange Blossom Special*. —O.H. BORSUM VIA FOSTER GUNNISON.

fewer than five compartment and drawing-room cars were included along with two lounges, a 2-compartment, 1-drawing-room car (e.g., *Sunburst*) midtrain for Miami and, on the rear, historic 6-compartment lounges like the *Wayneport, Waldameer* or *Westboro*, all three of which had been veterans of the first all-steel *20th Century Limited* of 1911. As for hungry passengers, they could enjoy traditional Southern meals in one of SAL's remodeled heavyweight diners fussed over by some of the finest waiters in the business.

The *Orange Blossom*'s running mate, the *Silver Meteor*, underwent a change effective with the 1946-47 winter season. The previous summer, the train had been running in East and West Coast sections, both departing in early afternoon. For the winter, it ran with an "advance" section which left in the morning and carried cars for both coasts. In early afternoon, the regular *Silver Meteor* would head south, also with cars for both coasts including a New York-Sarasota-Venice 10-section, 1-drawing room, 2-compartment Pullman. Northbound, the *Advance Silver Meteor* handled the Venice car.

The East and West Coast components of the *Blossom* split and combined at Jacksonville Terminal, but the southbound *Advance Silver Meteor* and the northbound regular *Meteor* made use of the Gross-Baldwin cutoff to avoid Jacksonville and save time.

New diesels were arriving, too. Nineteen E7A's were on the property by the end of 1946, supplementing Seaboard's overworked fleet of E4's which had toiled so hard during the war. Despite their presence, it was not unusual for secondary trains like the

Sun Queen and the *Palmland* to still draw SAL's burly 4-8-2 Mountains. When diesel run-through agreements with RF&P lapsed, the Old Dominion carrier's stately 4-8-4's handled everything from the *Silver Meteor* on down between Washington and Hermitage Yard at Richmond.

Consist of Note 5-A for early 1947 provides a good perspective on the *Silver Meteor*'s typical appearance in the period immediately before the arrival of the new postwar equipment.

The year 1947 was a big one for inaugurals on the Seaboard. On May 18, SAL's Atlanta-Birmingham route saw the arrival of the *Silver Comet*. No less a celebrity than actress Jean Parker was on hand to christen the new streamliner that would fulfill SAL's 1939 dream of rejuvenating the route with a lightweight speedster. The new train was a dead ringer for the partially re-equipped *Silver Meteor*. Indeed, they both would draw equipment from a group of cars just arriving from Budd, many of which were not yet on the property in time for the *Comet*'s inaugural. Also on May 18, the *Sun Queen* was renamed the *Camellia*, picking up the Venice 10-1-2 which had previously been carried on the *Silver Meteor*.

By July 1947, all of the coaches, diners, baggage-dorms and tavern-observations from Budd would be on hand, working hand-in-hand with heavyweight sleepers on the *Meteor* and the *Comet*.

In contrast to the *Silver Comet*, the other new addition to the Silver Fleet was a hand-me-down kid brother to the *Meteor*. The catalyst for the new train's creation was the confusion to passengers caused by

the operation of two versions of the *Silver Meteor*—the regular and the advance section. To alleviate the problem, SAL Passenger Traffic Manager C. E. Bell suggested renaming the *Advance Silver Meteor*, but continuing the "Silver" fleet name. And thus was born the *Silver Star*.

Before making the name official, Bell cleared the idea with the Lehigh Valley, which ran its own *Star* between New York and Buffalo. LV said "no problem," and SAL legitimized the choice of a name with a contest, to which a paltry 1,000 people submitted suggestions. Initially, the *Silver Star* largely used existing prewar streamlined equipment and heavyweight sleepers.

Befitting its status, the train's inaugural featured, not Jean Parker, but a lesser known beauty's induction into the Seminole Indian tribe at the hands of appropriately dressed natives in the unlikely locale of subterranean Penn Station, New York. During the early postwar period, SAL had been showing much interest in the advertising efficacy of Indian lore. Indeed, many of the carved linoleum murals completed by Mary Lawser and decorating SAL's postwar fleet accentuated the theme with such scenes as a Seminole boy leading his pet alligator and Seminole women working. It was reminiscent of Santa Fe's fascination with the Navajo.

Operating on the *Advance Silver Meteor*'s schedule to both coasts of Florida, the new *Silver Star* entered service on Dec. 12, 1947, as a winter-season companion to the *Meteor* with the following cars:

ABOVE: Never streamlined, the *Orange Blossom Special* and its all-heavyweight consist is just getting underway southward from Baldwin, Fla., on March 26, 1949.—DAVID W. SALTER. LEFT: Some of the men who made the *Orange Blossom . . .* special included Steward Walter Roberts (at right in photo) presiding over (from left to right) Chester Jones, Luther Cheatham, H. L. Thomas, L. H. Miller, Julius Frazier and C. F. Hammond. The year is 1947, and the curtain dividers toward the end of the dining room are an indication that segregation was still the law on trains in the South.—CSX CORPORATION.

CONSISTS OF NOTE/5-A
SAL train 182, northbound *Silver Meteor*

Location unknown
Feb. 20, 1947

Car	Type
SAL 182	Baggage-dorm (heavyweight)
Poplar Manor	6-section, 6-double-bedroom sleeper
Chimes Tower	8-section, 1-drwg.-room, 3 compt. sleeper
Glen Meadow	6-compartment, 3-drawing-room sleeper
Penn Square	6-compartment, 3-drawing-room sleeper
Conneaut	7-compartment lounge
SAL*	Diner (lightweight)
Lake Conway	10-section, 1 drwg. room, 2-compt. sleeper
Puerto Rico	10-section, 1 drwg. room, 2-compt. sleeper
Weeper's Tower	8-section, 1-drwg.-room, 3-d.br. sleeper
SAL*	Diner (lightweight)
SAL*	Coach (lightweight)
SAL*	Coach (lightweight)
SAL*	Coach-tavern-lounge (lightweight)
SAL*	Coach (lightweight)
SAL*	Coach (lightweight)
SAL*	Coach (lightweight)
SAL*	Coach-observation (lightweight)

*Number not recorded

Silver Star

SAL baggage-dorm (heavyweight)	NYP-MIA
Pullman 6-6 (heavyweight)	NYP-MIA
Pullman 10-1-2 (heavyweight)	NYP-MIA
Pullman 6-3 (heavyweight)	NYP-MIA
Pullman 10-section lounge (hywt.)	NYP-MIA
Pullman 8-1-3 (heavyweight)	NYP-STP
Pullman 10-1-2 (heavyweight)	NYP-STP
SAL diner	NYP-STP
SAL diner	NYP-MIA
SAL 60-seat coach	NYP-MIA
SAL 60-seat coach	NYP-MIA
SAL 52-seat coach	NYP-MIA
SAL 60-seat coach	NYP-STP
SAL 52-seat coach	NYP-STP
SAL 30-seat coach-tavern	NYP-MIA
SAL 48-seat coach-observation	NYP-MIA

Despite the inauguration of new streamliners, passenger revenues for 1947 dropped by 25 percent. The rather sharp decline was precipitated by a society adjusting to peace time. More people were using their cars, military traffic was down and the airlines were increasing their competition.

ABOVE: Things look a bit tense on the platform at New York's Pennsylvania Station as a young woman is initiated into the Seminole Indian tribe for the inauguration of the *Silver Star* on Dec. 12, 1947. Seaboard enjoyed a fleeting moment of fascination with Indian lore that, in a small way, harkened Santa Fe's affection for the Indians of the Southwest.—CSX CORPORATION. BELOW: A *Silver Star* dinner menu from 1949. —AUTHOR'S COLLECTION.

Things perked up a bit in 1948. On Aug. 1 of that year, the *Silver Star* returned as a year-round New York-Miami operation with service also provided to Tampa and St. Petersburg for the winter season. It was an arrangement that would continue for several years. That December, too, the *Camellia* name disappeared from the timecard for good, as trains 7-8 and 107-108 received the name *Sunland*.

SAL passenger revenues increased marginally (3 percent) that year but a look back showed just how far Seaboard had come.

Overall, the number of passengers carried was up 200 percent over 1940 levels. The train most responsible for that phenomenal increase was in the midst of its postwar re-equipping, and a look at the *Silver Meteor* at this time (Consist of Note 5-B) reveals a train made of something old and new.

A few of the heavyweight Pullmans in that consist and many of their brethren were about to pass into Seaboard ownership. In December 1948, as a result of the Pullman antitrust action, 31 heavyweight sleepers and sleeper-lounges were purchased from Pullman and leased back to that company for operation in SAL service. The cars selected for purchase by Seaboard were:

8-1-3	6-6
Bartlett Tower	*Poplar Brook*
Chimes Tower	*Poplar Castle*
Pinnacle Tower	*Poplar City*
Siebers Tower	*Poplar Creek*
Weeper's Tower	*Poplar Road*
Giotto's Tower	*Poplar Run*
	Poplar Springs

8-5	10-1-2
Clover Harvest	*Hollywood Beach**
Clover Nest	*Lake Alexander*
Clover Pond	*Lake Borgne*
	Lake Chicot
10-section lounge	*Mackay*
Columbia Basin	*Mount Gretna*
Columbia Bluffs	*Mount Joy*
Columbia Bridge	*New Lyme*
Columbia Lake	*New Portage*
	New Waterford
	North Berne
	Renamed Norlina 10/55

These cars would serve side by side with other heavyweights still in Pullman ownership and on assignment to the Seaboard.

In the summer of 1949, the streamlined sleepers which had been on order for more than three years finally arrived (see appendix for complete listing); all

(see appendix for complete listing)

three of Seaboard's premier trains received them. The *Meteor* began handling 10-6 cars as well as the 6-double-bedroom *Mountain*-series sleeper-lounges. This series had originally been ordered for the *Silver Comet* (the geography of the cars' names and SAL's files both support this) but, by the time the cars arrived, priorities had shifted, and the *Meteor* got the spoils.

Sleeper-lounge facilities on the *Star* and the *Comet* were still the province of heavyweights. The assignment usually went to Seaboard's *Columbia*-series lounges or heavyweight, Pullman-owned veterans with six compartments, like the *Wayneport*.

For the winter of 1949-50 the seasonal *Orange Blossom Special*, which had originated in New York since its return to service in 1946, began handling Boston cars again. The bad news for Seaboard was that passenger revenues were still declining. The inroads of the automobile, the airliner and even the ACL were all very noticeable. Indeed, Coast Line and partners were busy introducing a larger fleet of re-equipped streamliners which competed directly with SAL for a slice of pie that was already shrinking for railroads in general.

With an eye toward improving the situation, SAL had, with some success, introduced special round-trip fares which equated to 150 percent of the one-way charge. The results were higher passenger loadings and earnings for the summer of 1950.

While the seesaw battle for earnings continued in 1951, the Civil Aeronautics Board was making things difficult for the railroads. The CAB, forerunner of the Federal Aviation Administration, authorized airlines to lower their rates to be competitive with rail coach fares. At the same time, Pullman was raising its sleeping-car rates 15 percent while Southeastern railroads increased full coach fares 10 percent to cover operating costs.

CONSIST OF NOTE 5-B

SAL train 58, northbound *Silver Meteor*
Raleigh, N.C.
Feb. 27, 1948

Car	Type
[SAL 3014]	[Electro-Motive E6A diesel]
[SAL 3003]	[Electro-Motive E4A diesel]
[SAL 3103]	[Electro-Motive E4B diesel]
SAL 6051	Dormitory
Daleford	10-section, 4-private-section sleeper
Poplar Road	6-section, 6-double-bedroom sleeper
Glen Dochart	6-compartment, 3-drawing-room sleeper
Lake Alexander	10-section, 1-drwg. room, 2-compt sleeper
Lake Tahoe	10-section, 1-drwg. room, 2-compt sleeper
The Citadel	10-section, 1-drwg. room, 2-compt sleeper
SAL 6104	Diner
SAL 6213	Coach
RF&P 830	Coach
SAL 6112	Diner
SAL 6204	Coach
SAL 6214	Coach
PRR 4601	Coach
SAL 6205	Coach
SAL 6605	Tavern-observation

Hemmed in by competition on all sides and facing a newly streamlined rival—ACL's *Florida Special*—the *Blossom* underwent a facelift for its debut for the 1951-52 winter season. Assigned Pullmans and SAL-owned sleepers and diners received distinctive exteriors colors of maroon and gray. Interiors were redecorated, and mechanical appliances were overhauled and modernized. The specific heavyweight sleeping cars which received this unique livery were:

Pullman-owned

6-3

Glen Arbor
Glen Arden
Glen Canyon
Glen Crag
Glen Dale
Glen Dower
Glen Eagles
Glen Elder
Glen Falls
Glen Farm
Glen Grove
Glen Island
Glen Morgan
Glen Ridge
Glen Rogers
Glen Saddell
Glen Sannox
Glen Springs
Glen Sutton
Glen Tay

12-1-4

Oak City
Oak Dome
Oak Grove
Oak Hall

6-4-4

Fir Crest
Fir Forest
Fir Gardens

2-1-buffet lounge

Sunbeam
Sunrise
Sunshine

3-1-buffet lounge

Palm Lane
Grand Canyon
Palisade Canyon

SAL-owned

6-6

Poplar Brook
Poplar Castle
Poplar City
Poplar Creek

8-1-3

Barlett Tower
Giotto's Tower
Siebers Tower
Weeper's Tower

The consist for this very "special" *Orange Blossom* included (all cars heavyweight, not in consist order):

Baggage-dorm	NYP-MIA
Diner	NYP-MIA
Poplar series 6-6	NYP-MIA
Oak series 12-1-4	NYP-MIA
Sun series 2-1-buffet lounge	NYP-MIA
Glen series 6-3	NYP-MIA
Glen series 6-3	NYP-MIA
Glen series 6-3	NYP-MIA
Canyon or *Palm* series 3-1 buffet lounge	NYP-MIA
Glen series 6-3	NYP-MIA
Tower series 8-1-3	BOS-MIA
Diner	WAS-MIA
Fir series 6-1-4	WAS-MIA

If there were any doubts as to the status of the *Blossom*'s loyal clientele, one look at the number of stateroom cars in this consist was enough to dispel them. The *Orange Blossom* was still considered by many to be the finest way to Florida. And, when its wealthy passengers headed north to summer in Bar Harbor, Maine, they would find themselves riding practically the same train. After the completion of the winter season in April 1952, many of these unique cars spent the summer in the pool for the Washington-Bangor *Bar Harbor Express*.

The following winter, the *Orange Blossom* would return, keeping alive a tradition dating from 1925. As the ads put it, "Once again it was Orange Blossom Time." And although the ads ensured travelers they would want to use the *Blossom* again and again, they wouldn't get the chance.

It had started in the winter of 1949-50, the year ACL introduced the *Florida Special*—the *Blossom*'s bitter rival—as a lightweight. Suddenly the Seaboard flagship found itself old news. It was an ironic twist of fate, for it was the same lesson Seaboard had taught the Coast Line in 1939. No matter how hard you tried, a solid heavyweight service could not outdraw a lightweight competitor.

Indeed, the *Orange Blossom*'s true rival in its final years could more accurately be said to be ACL's *Vacationer*. Both fielded Boston cars, both were heavyweight trains and both were all-Pullman. By contrast, the *Florida Special*, despite its paucity of premium room accommodations, was as a lightweight truly in a class by itself. Coast Line highlighted this distinction relentlessly, never missing the opportunity to tout its *Special* as the *only* all-Pullman *streamliner* to Florida. It worked.

The obvious answer for SAL to keep up might have been to streamline the *Blossom*, but it would have meant a very large investment for SAL in a time when passenger earnings were not at their greatest. Part of the problem lay in the size of the rival fleets. Whereas Coast Line fielded more trains and had a pool of 75 streamlined sleepers to draw from, SAL had only 31—too few to equip the *Blossom* and the rest of the Silver Fleet. Any lightweights it needed, SAL would have to purchase itself, for Pullman could

ABOVE: Brand-new *Silver Meteor* look-alike—the New York-Birmingham *Silver Comet*—pauses at North Philadelphia southbound on Oct. 12, 1947. The 11-car consist, pulled by a single GG1, includes three heavyweight sleepers.—GEORGE E. VOTAVA.

Although the *Camellia* ad appearing in a late 1940's timetable implies the train to be a streamliner, heavyweight stalwarts far outnumber the lightweights on the short-live train racing north from Hialeah, Fla., on Sept. 13, 1947. The weathered A-B set of E4's have northbound No. 8 moving at nearly 70 mph. The second car back is a rare SAL Railway Post Office-coach combine.
—DAVID W. SALTER.

not provide lightweight pool support; almost all of its pool sleepers were heavyweights.

Seaboard was backed into a corner. Faced with the option of buying a lot more streamlined sleepers it couldn't hope to employ in the slower summer months and not wishing to divert sleeping-car business from its Silver Fleet, SAL decided to withdraw the *Orange Blossom Special*. The road's intention was to focus on its premier moneymakers, fielding extra sections of the *Silver Meteor* and *Star* when necessary instead of carding a daily *Blossom*. There was common sense in the decision but, emotionally, it hurt. The *Blossom* had been the leader of the fleet and a point of pride for every SAL employee for as long as anybody could remember.

At the close of the winter season on April 26, 1953, the *Orange Blossom Special*, one of the greatest names in the history of U.S. passenger railroading, vanished from the timecard for good, victim of a lesson Seaboard never should have forgotten.

Despite the pending change, it was business as usual for the Silver Fleet, and Consist of Note 5-C shows that, in the winter season, heavyweight sleepers remained an integral part of SAL streamliners. During summer and fall, Seaboard's streamliners were just that, nearly all streamlined—the fleet wasn't spread as thin:

Summer consists, 1953

SAL trains 21 & 22, the *Silver Star*
(lightweight equipment except as noted)

14-seat baggage-dorm-coach	WAS-MIA
52-seat coach	NYP-MIA
52-seat coach	NYP-MIA
52-seat coach	NYP-MIA
24-seat tavern-coach	WAS-MIA
Diner	WAS-MIA
10-6 sleeper	WAS-MIA
10-6 sleeper	NYP-MIA
10-section lounge (heavyweight)	NYP-MIA

SAL trains 57-157 and 58-158, the *Silver Meteor*
(lightweight except as noted)

Baggage-dorm	NYP-MIA
52-seat coach	NYP-MIA
10-6 sleeper	NYP-JAX
6-double-bedroom lounge	NYP-MIA
Baggage-coach (heavyweight)	WWD-STP
10-6 sleeper	NYP-VEN
Coach (light- or heavyweight)	TAM-VEN
10-6-sleeper	NYP-STP
Diner	NYP-STP
52-seat coach	NYP-STP
52-seat coach	NYP-STP
Diner	NYP-MIA
52-seat coach	NYP-MIA
52-seat coach	NYP-MIA
52-seat coach	NYP-MIA
Tavern-observation	NYP-MIA

In spite of streamlined equipment, seductive palm trees and tropical breezes, revenues continued to decline. In 1954 the industry as a whole showed a marked downturn. Seaboard was no exception. Its passenger earnings dropped 13 percent from 1953 levels.

Earnings may have been dropping, but speeds did not. The Florida railroads were traditionally home to some of the fastest trains in the country. Government-mandated signaling improvements in the late 1940's and railroad-instigated track upgrades were part of the reason; old fashioned competition was the other. On the Coast Line, Champ Davis had been spending money on the Richmond-Jacksonville main line with an eye toward achieving sustained running speeds of 100 mph for his streamliners. Seaboard, cursed with a sinuous, undulating route through the Piedmont, strived to keep pace. The road maintained the ICC-prescribed 79-mph speed limit on much of its passenger line despite the geographic handicap.

But if SAL was hindered by hilly terrain farther north, it was blessed with a section of track in Florida made to order for its E-unit-hauled streamliners. Razor straight and flat as a tabletop, the 57 miles of tangent track between Sebring and West Palm Beach saw some of the fastest running in the country. Whether making up time or just making time, the Silver Fleet had screamed over this line for decades. In

1955, for example, stops included, both the *Silver Star* and the *Silver Meteor* had averaged over 70 mph on the line. Head-end crews in the prewar, pre-speed-restriction days, regaled listeners with tales of E4's pushing the upper limits of their 117-mph top speeds. Those days were gone, but, even in 1955, the business end of SAL's tight schedules were still played out daily on this stretch.

Though mindful of the need for speed in competing with ACL and its 24-hour schedules, Seaboard placed most of its emphasis on equipment. It was here that the smaller carrier hoped, once again, to steal a march on its larger rival.

Although Coast Line and its partners had purchased a larger number of sleeping cars than SAL in 1949, their fleet was top heavy with roomettes. In the five years since 1949, passenger space requests had been proving the liability of that decision, as the double bedroom and larger accommodations became the rooms most demanded by Florida travelers—many of whom were couples and families.

Conservative Coast Line was wary of heavy investment in yet more streamlined cars in a business with increasingly discouraging revenues. (Curiously, though, the road had recently participated in the purchase of new cars to fully streamlined one of its lowest money-earners, the *Dixieland*, a Chicago-Florida joint operation with Chicago & Eastern Illinois, Nashville, Chattanooga & St. Louis, Louisville & Nashville and FEC. Within three years, the *Dixieland* would vanish.)

Seaboard, on the other hand, had listened to its passengers. They wanted more-modern, larger sleeping accommodations. Coast Line had largely resisted this trend. In a May 1954 discussion of its passenger operations with *Modern Railroads* magazine, ACL revealed that its plan had been to use heavyweight cars to supplement streamlined equipment in peak season demand. The road lamented the fact that these heavyweights hadn't been accepted by the riding public and theorized that the introduction of streamliners had prematurely obsoleted the older cars in the public mind.

It was the classic case of a company trying to tailor its customer's needs to its own product. That was, in fact, how the railroad business generally operated. Seaboard, however, was an exception. In January and February 1955, SAL and partner RF&P ordered from Pullman-Standard a series of cars to re-equip its *Silver Meteor* and *Silver Star*. It was an abrupt turnabout from SAL's reluctance to purchase equipment just

CONSIST OF NOTE 5-C	

SAL *Silver Star*
Location unknown
March 24, 1953
Lightweight cars except as noted

Car	Type
SAL 182	Baggage-dorm (heavyweight)
PRR *Elberton*	10-6 sleeper
Wonalancet	10-1-2 sleeper (heavyweight)
Wayneport	6-cmpt. buffet-lounge (heavyweight)
NYC *Algonquin Pass*	8-1-2 sleeper (heavyweight)
Glen Trail	6-3 sleeper (heavyweight)
SAL*	Diner
PRR *Bradenton*	10-6
SAL*	Lounge
SAL*	Coach
SAL*	Coach
SAL*	Diner
SAL*	Tavern-coach
SAL*	Coach
SAL*	Coach
SAL*	Coach
SAL*	Coach-observation

*Number not recorded

We're at Florida Junction (Savannah) on March 3, 1949, as Seaboard 4-8-2 No. 252 smokes it up with train 10, the northbound *Palmland*. Note that the second coach is a Seaboard "American Flyer" car.—HUGH M. COMER.

three years earlier. Aside from that, there were several other things which set this order apart. First, like a similar group of cars being built for the Union Pacific at the same time, these cars were some of the last traditional Pullman accommodations ever built.

These SAL and RF&P cars were constructed primarily of stainless steel—a fairly new practice for P-S which, unlike Budd, had usually relied on Cor-Ten steel for most lightweight structural car members, applying stainless steel as cosmetic skirting. Pullman Standard had finally perfected (or at least satisfied itself with) a way of fastening the metal successfully. It didn't have access to Budd's patented "shotwelding" technique, and some of Pullman's previous attempts at working with stainless steel for structural purposes had been less than resounding successes. This included a batch of 1949-built sleepers for SAL which suffered roof warping as a result of poor welding. In March 1954, Pullman had completed a stainless-steel demonstrator car for the Missouri-Kansas-Texas, No. 1202R, the *J. Pinckney Henderson,* a 72-seat coach. The new Seaboard cars, too, would be wrought largely from the corrosion-resistant metal.

Seaboard's 1955 Pullman-Standard order

52 seat coaches	5-double-bedroom, 2-compartment, 2-drawing-room cars
SAL Nos. 6235-6241 RF&P Nos. 861, 862	
	Boca Grande
11-double bedroom cars	*Clearwater*
	Fort Lauderdale
Avon Park	
Hialeah	**5-double-bedroom-buffet Sun Lounges**
Ocala	
Sebring	*Hollywood Beach*
Tallahassee	*Miami Beach*
Venice	*Palm Beach*

The 1955 order included a series of 52-seat coaches with an unusual 10-seat smoking lounge in the center of the car. But it was a series of sleeper-lounges which distinguished this Seaboard order as something special. Faced with a desire to provide its passengers with a dome-car-like experience of sunlit spaciousness but cursed with constricting clearances on the PRR (numerous tunnels and 11,000-volt catenary), SAL turned to Pullman-Standard. The result was the "Sun Lounge," a 5-double-bedroom buffet-lounge with an airy "sun room" created by ten $42 \times 58\,1/2$-inch antiglare side windows and an equal number of smaller panes in the roof, all accomplished at the standard roof height.

Seaboard's advertising summed it up. There was nothing quite like the Sun Lounge. The decor was that of a tropical patio with murals of beach scenes, sand-colored carpet woven in a seashell pattern and driftwood lamps. The featured attraction was the sun itself, which flooded the lounge on sunny days.

One of the first men to work the new sleeper-lounges was James McCants, a Pullman employee since 1927 and a veteran of the heavyweight Pullman parlor-buffet cars on Pennsylvania Railroad's famed "Clockers." In 1956 McCants was reassigned to the Sun Lounges. His interview with historian Peter Tilp provided this retrospective of life aboard the cars:

Peter Tilp: How long did you work on Pennsy's "Clockers?"
James McCants: From 1930 until the railroad took over service on these cars.
PT: Do you mean when Pullman pulled out of parlor cars and their meal service?
JM: Yes.
PT: That was in the fall of 1956. Where were you assigned after that?
JM: I went into Florida service.
PT: And were you a lounge-car man there?
JM: Yes . . . Yes . . . I worked mostly on the Seaboard and handled those new cars with the big windows.
PT: You mean on the *Silver Meteor?*

RIGHT: Modernized Railway Post Office (RPO) cars were regulars at the head end of SAL's trains, including the *Silver Meteor*, which handled cars like this south of Jacksonville. The addition of a "turtleback" roof (covering the more-traditional monitor roof) and aluminum paint helped blend these steam-era cars into streamliner consists. Seaboard RPO 113 is shown at Waycross, Ga., in 1969.—CONNIFF RAILROADIANA COLLECTION.

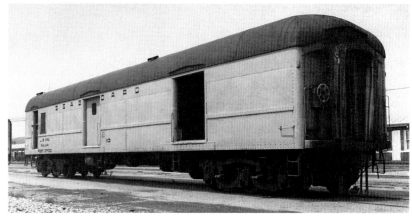

RIGHT: In December 1948 as part of anti-trust judgement, Pullman sold the sleeping cars it had built and operated to the railroads over which they had run. The exception were cars maintained by the company as pool cars. Here we see *Siebers Tower*, an 8-section, 1-drawing-room, 3-double-bedroom car wearing its first Seaboard Air Line paint scheme: dark green and dulux gold lettering. The car is shown at New York's Sunnyside Yard circa 1950.—JOSEPH FISCHER, VIA PETER V. TILP.

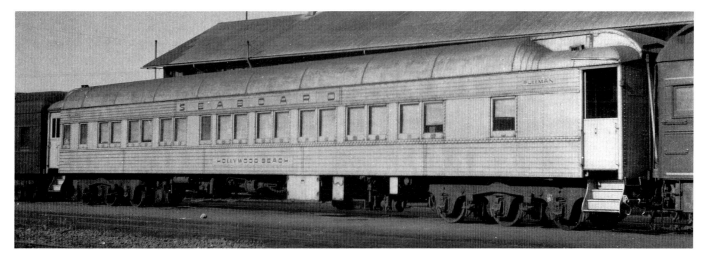

ABOVE: Before lightweight Sun Lounge *Hollywood Beach* arrived in December 1955, the name had belonged to a heavyweight 10-section, 1-drawing-room, 2-compartment car. The original *Hollywood Beach* is pictured at New Orleans in July 1951. Shadowlining was applied in the early 1950's to match heavyweights to lightweight cars. The car was renamed *Norlina* in October 1955.—JOSEPH FISCHER. UPPER LEFT: *Clover Harvest* with 8 sections and 5 double bedrooms was one of three *Clover* cars owned by SAL; others were *Clover Nest* and *Clover Pond*. The car displays a paint scheme common on the cars from the early 1950's through their retirement.—DEGOYLER LIBRARY, SOUTHERN METHODIST UNIVERSITY. LEFT: *Columbia*-series 10-section observation lounges had been regulars in Florida service for years. In 1948, SAL purchased *Columbia Basin, Bluffs, Bridge* and *Lake. Columbia Lake* is shown in the early 1950's when it operated on either the *Silver Star* or the *Silver Comet*.—JOSEPH FISCHER.

JM: Yes.

PT: They were named *Miami Beach, Hollywood Beach* and *Palm Beach*.

JM: Uh huh—they were the most beautiful cars we had.

PT: They had five double bedrooms. Didn't you have a problem with them? Or did they have another man on the car? [Mr. McCants had a bad back.]

JM: No, no. They were one-man cars. The beds were easy to make—not like in the old green Pullmans.

PT: I bet they kept you busy—I mean between the rooms and the lounge service.

JM: Only sometimes. The trip was overnight and we had plenty of time to do our work—out of New York in the afternoon was the busiest. I'd serve drinks all afternoon and the evening. Then my passengers would go to the dining car, and I had time to make up the rooms and clean up the lounge. After 11 o'clock there wasn't much business. The Florida people weren't big drinkers.

PT: You told me once that coming out of Miami was different.

JM: Yes. We left in the morning . . . rode all day through Florida. There wasn't much for me to do . . . oh, once in a while we served lunch from the dining car in one of the rooms.

PT: But that was usually brought in by a waiter from the dining car?

JM: When they were busy, I picked up the meal check and served and cleaned up.

PT: Tell us about the big windows.

JM: Out of Miami in the morning—sometimes when it was sunny—I had to keep the big blinds drawn to let the air conditioner work—else the car got too hot.

PT: What did you serve out of the buffet?

JM: Mostly drinks—highballs, beer, soda, Coke, 7-Up.

PT: Any meal service?

JM: No. These weren't food cars. We only had little cans of peanuts for snacks.

PT: These were among the last Pullmans built. How were they?

JM: Beautiful . . . they were beautiful cars. And if anything went wrong, we'd wire ahead, and they'd fix it in the next station. They took good care of my car. Breakdowns weren't often. It was a nice service . . . very nice . . .

The new Sun Lounges replaced the 1949-built *Mountain*-series cars as first-class lounge space on the *Silver Meteor* on Jan. 4, 1956. The *Mountain* cars then went to the *Silver Star*, bumping a heavyweight 3-compartment, 1-drawing-room buffet-lounge. Again, the kid brother got the hand-me-downs.

Another new series of stainless-steel sleepers arrived from Budd in November 1955. Hedging its bets against the future need for sections (by late 1955, only the *Silver Comet* and secondary trains still offered them), Seaboard took delivery of six cars from Budd—the *Bay Pines, Camden, Cedartown, Henderson, Pinehurst* and *Southern Pines*—with an unusual floorplan: 5 double bedrooms, 1 compartment, 4 roomettes and 4 sections. In floorplan, the cars mirrored a colossal order of 42 sleepers, also built by Budd, delivered to Canadian Pacific for its *Canadian* and *Dominion* streamliners earlier in the year.

On the Seaboard, this series of cars made its debut on the *Silver Star*, holding down a New York-St. Petersburg assignment and also replacing a heavyweight *Elm*-series 12-roomette, 2-single-bedroom, 3-drawing-room car on a New York-Miami carding as of early January 1956.

The rejuvenated Silver Fleet looked like this:

SAL Nos. 21-121, *Silver Star*, Jan. 1, 1956

Baggage	WWD-STP
Baggage-dorm	NYP-MIA
10-6 sleeper	WAS-MIA
5-1-4-4 sleeper	NYP-MIA
5-2-2 sleeper	NYP-MIA
10-6 sleeper	NYP-MIA
6-bedroom buffet-lounge	NYP-MIA
10-6 sleeper	NYP-PBG
Coach (unreserved)	TPA-PBG
Diner	NYP-STP
5-1-4-4 sleeper	NYP-STP
52-seat coach	NYP-STP
Diner	NYP-MIA
52-seat coach	NYP-MIA
52-seat coach	NYP-MIA
52-seat coach	NYP-MIA
52-seat coach	NYP-MIA
52-seat coach	NYP-MIA
Tavern-observation	NYP-MIA

(Note that the *Silver Star* got the premium 5-2-2 sleepers and inherited the postwar-built tavern-observation from the *Silver Comet*.)

SAL Nos. 57-157 and 58-158, *Silver Meteor*, January 1956

Baggage-dorm	NYP-MIA
Combine (unreserved)	WWD-STP
52-seat coach	NYP-MIA
10-6 sleeper	NYP-MIA
10-6 sleeper	NYP-MIA
11-double bedroom sleeper	NYP-MIA
5-double-bedroom Sun Lounge	NYP-MIA
10-6 sleeper	NYP-VEN
Coach	TPA-VEN
Diner	NYP-STP
10-6 sleeper	NYP-STP
11-double-bedroom sleeper	NYP-STP
52-seat coach	NYP-STP
52-seat coach	NYP-STP
Diner	NYP-MIA
52-seat coach	NYP-MIA
52-seat coach	NYP-MIA
52-seat coach	NYP-MIA
Tavern-observation	NYP-MIA

Despite the new equipment, trains like the *Palmland* and *Sunland* were still almost completely heavyweight affairs. The *Palmland* was offering, in addition to a full diner, a recently remodeled grill-coach between Hamlet and Jacksonville.

As profound as the equipment upgrades had been,

BELOW: Seaboard Air Line's *Red Mountain* and mates *Stone Mountain* and *Kennesaw Mountain* with 6 double bedrooms and a buffet-lounge arrived from ACF in August 1949. Originally intended for *Silver Comet* service (the names are from mountains on or near the *Silver Comet* route), they wound up instead in *Silver Meteor* service when they arrived.—ACF INDUSTRIES.

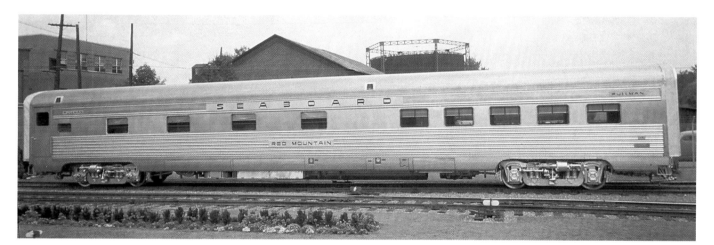

ABOVE: Interior of a *Red Mountain* bedroom. Pastel walls were in vogue; dark blue corduroy upholstery provided a contrast. RIGHT: Clean-lined decor was *de riguer* for postwar modernism.—BOTH PHOTOS, ACF INDUSTRIES.

ABOVE: Not quite a dome and certainly not quite a standard car, Seaboard's Sun Lounge sleepers were the perfect solution to constricting clearance problems on the PRR. Ample windows top and sides let sunlight flood the lounges, making these cars among the cheeriest on rails. They were a fixture on the *Silver Meteor* from January 1956 through Amtrak. *Hollywood Beach* is shown fresh out of the Pullman-Standard plant in Chicago. Ads for the new cars (BELOW) extolled the cars' "setting of relaxation and gay companionship." Meanwhile, members of the Sun Lounge Club received an attractive leather baggage tag (LEFT).—PULLMAN TECHNOLOGY

NOTHING QUITE LIKE THE

SUN LOUNGE!

When you travel to Florida by Seaboard this winter, you'll be greeted by NEW Pullman and coach equipment *representing the most advanced concepts of luxuriously modern rail transportation.* Among the many delightful innovations is the SUN LOUNGE for Pullman passengers on the Silver Meteor. SUN LOUNGE decor and facilities offer a patio-like atmosphere *unlike anything on the rails at the present time.* Glare-proof, glass paneled roofs and extra-large windows give the impression of out-door spaciousness; chairs and divans are arranged in small, informal groups; carpets simulate Florida's sand beaches, and realistic murals of beach scenes glimpsed through jalousies add to the resort effect, as do the specially selected decorative fabrics and soft lighting.
A buffet for your favorite refreshment completes the picture of a delight-ful, well-appointed club, as you travel swiftly between North and South in the SUN LOUNGE setting of relaxa-tion and gay companionship.

FOR MORE DETAILS OF SEABOARD'S N E W EQUIPMENT PLEASE SEE THE FOLLOWING PAGES

SEABOARD RAILROAD

THE ROUTE OF COURTEOUS SERVICE

another social improvement would far outweigh in significance anything wrought in stainless steel. On Jan. 10, 1956, by order of the Interstate Commerce Commission, all interstate passenger trains were to no longer carry their passengers separated by race. It was the beginning of the end for a practice as old as American passenger railroading itself.

Curiously, the concept of separating railroad passengers by race had its strongest origins in the North—not the South. In a pioneering look at American railroads of the early 1800's, Austrian engineer F. A. Ritter Von Gerstner reported that, although many Southern roads provided half-fare seating areas in the baggage car for blacks, blacks were also permitted to ride in coach next to whites. The only requirement was the payment of a full fare. Von Gerstner pointed out that this practice differed from railroads in the North where blacks were required to ride in separate cars.

By the 1850's, the custom of separating the races, including freedmen, was general practice in both the North and the South. After the Civil War, separation of the races on trains ended in the North but continued in the South where it was mandated by state law.

In American slang this segregation had a name— "Jim Crow." Coaches and combines alike were partitioned to separate the races. On the Seaboard, the practice had continued as mandated into the streamlined era. The original *Silver Meteor* had, in keeping with custom initiated a century earlier, a baggage-dormitory-coach specifically earmarked for "colored" (a then-commonly used term that has since become dated) passengers. So did its rival, the *Champion*. Seat identification coupons for the *Silver Meteor*, in addition to destination, were to be punched "White," "Colored," "Male" or "Female."

Little by little though, the practice was shrinking. In 1941, the Supreme Court interpreted the Interstate Commerce Act as requiring the Pullman Company to provide equal accommodations for blacks (Mitchell vs. U.S.A.). It was a victory, but far from a complete one.

Nowhere was the assault on the dignity of the black passenger more obvious than in the dining car. Following a Supreme Court decision in 1949-50, President Truman directed the Interstate Commerce Commission to issue an order abolishing segregation in dining cars. These instructions from a Seaboard Air Line dining car department manual of April 1944, predating the decision, illustrate the nature of the problem:

"SERVING MEALS TO COLORED PERSONS"

Portieres are to be hung between stations "One" and "Two" at all times between 6 a.m. and 10 p.m. These curtains are to be pushed back against the wall until occasion arises for use of same.

You are provided with a "Reserved" placard, which is to be placed on the two stations nearest the buffet at the beginning of each meal. These two tables are to be reserved for colored passengers until all other seats in the dining room have been occupied. If no colored passengers have presented themselves, the "Reserved" cards may be removed and the tables used for white passengers.

No white passengers are to be allowed in the space reserved while colored passengers are being served therein. This also means that no white persons will be seated in this space while colored persons are waiting to be assigned seats therein.

If while the first two tables are occupied by white passengers, a colored person should present himself and request service, he is to be informed that he will be called as soon as seats reserved for use of colored passengers are vacated. When such seats are vacated, the colored persons will be called and served in the space set apart for them. No white persons are to be allowed in such space while colored persons are being served therein.

If colored passengers present themselves while this reserved space is occupied, the steward will also offer to serve them in the coach or the Pullman, as the case may be, promptly, in event they do not wish to wait until the space which has been reserved for them is available.

Colored nurses accompanying white families may be seated in the dining car at the table with such white families for the purpose of taking care of children, such nurses to be allowed to have their own meals at the same time. It is understood that in such cases, no other person (other than the family the nurse is accompanying) are to be seated at the table with the colored nurse.

The irony, of course, was that the crews responsible for the enforcement of these regulations during this period in history were comprised predominantly of blacks themselves.

WHETHER DUE TO EQUIPMENT IMPROVEMENTS or not, passenger revenues for 1956 increased 9.1 percent over the previous year. The uptrend was to continue in 1957 with nearly another 2 percent jump in earnings.

The gains of the mid-1950's were partially negated in 1958, a recessionary year for the U.S. economy and railroads in general and the Florida roads in particular. A double whammy was dealt in the form of an unusual cold snap in early 1958 all the way into Florida, which discouraged travel to the Sunshine State.

Things picked up a bit in 1959, and 1960 was a banner year with revenues up 8.5 percent over 1959—the highest earnings since 1952. Seaboard was particularly proud of the increase in summertime travel, which was at its highest level since 1947. Some of the credit for leveling the nagging disparity between summer and winter travel had to go to aggressive marketing. For years the Florida railroads and the tourist industry had suffered at the hands of migratory business, heavy in winter and light in summer, which made a nightmare out of operating their business. For Seaboard (and ACL) the answer had been to implement "package vacations," thrifty combinations of reduced-price rail and hotel accommodations aimed at middle-class travelers. It worked.

In the 1960's, the summer tourist trade, much of it catered to in coach, would become the backbone of Seaboard's business. But there were plenty of traditions still in place. One of them was the heavy migration of Pullman travelers in the winter season, as Consist of Note 5-D proves for the Miami section of the *Silver Meteor*.

Another tradition which persisted was complete dining-car service. Dining on Seaboard rails in the 1950's and early 1960's was, for the most part, like taking part in a historic ritual. The service had changed little since the 1900's.

Passengers dined at tables set with linens, china and polished silver. They were served in full

LEFT: Miss Patricia Powell, senior registered nurse on the Seaboard, helps Miami Mayor King High (at left in photo) cut a birthday cake in celebration of the 20th anniversary of the *Silver Meteor* when it arrived in Miami on Feb. 4, 1959. At right is Wesley J. Ficht, general passenger agent for SAL in Miami.—SAL.

CONSIST OF NOTE 5-D
SAL train 57, southbound *Silver Meteor*

Fort Lauderdale, Fla.
Feb. 27, 1960
All cars, lightweight, New York-Miami

Car	Type
SAL 6052	Baggage-dormitory
SAL *Lake Wales*	10-roomette, 6-d.br. sleeper
PRR *Imperial Terrace*	4-cmpt., 4-d.br., 2-drwg. rm. sleeper
SAL *Winter Haven*	10-roomette, 6-d.br. sleeper
RF&P *Lancaster*	10-roomette, 6-d.br. sleeper
SAL *Fort Lauderdale*	5-d.br., 2-cmpt., 2-drwg. rm. sleeper
SAL *Petersburg*	10-roomette, 6-d.br. sleeper
SAL *Hollywood Beach*	5-double bedroom Sun Lounge
SAL 6104	Diner
RF&P 853	Coach
SAL 6224	Coach
SAL 6605	Tavern-observation

Route of the *Silver Fleet*
POWERED BY GENERAL MOTORS DIESEL LOCOMOTIVES

dining cars by a staff of white-jacketed waiters presided over by a steward. The world of the dining car in mid-century America spoke of a formality then still present on railroads and ocean liners but fading fast elsewhere in society. It was a world in which SAL waiters were expected to stand at attention at each major stop along the way when not serving guests, lest a passerby on the platform form the wrong impression.

The tableware was nearly as impressive. Seaboard's original plaid table linens of the the first *Silver Meteor* had by now given way to white table clothes and napkins. The heavy china was usually "Desert Tan"—a tan body color with darker stripes of brown and tan on the border, with no railroad logo visible. Flatware was in SAL's "Century" pattern.

The food itself, rooted in Southern cooking styles, was still available in great diversity, although things here had changed since the 1920' when selections—and presumably waistlines—had been gargantuan. It was still possible in 1960 to select from a Silver Fleet breakfast menu offering no less than eight different combination plates, including kippered herring. In keeping with the ways of a fine restaurant, SAL menus stated "It will be a pleasure to serve any dish not listed if available." It was no idle promise. An amazing assortment of victuals, along with four cooks, were crammed into the cramped quarters of the diners' 7-foot-wide kitchens.

Fish in all its forms was a staple on Seaboard menus: Bass, halibut, swordfish and shrimp were regulars. And, if you knew where to look, there were hints of the deep South on the menu, too. Guava Jelly, a Florida staple but virtually unknown outside the Sunshine State, was a regular part of the Seaboard breakfast larder as was peanut soup—another hint of the deep South. Wisely, hominy grits, almost universally despised by Northerners, would be available on request-only or as part of the "Deep South Breakfast" selection.

SAL maintained a General Superintendent and Superintendent of Dining Car Services in offices in Washington, D.C., as well as a superintendent at Jacksonville and an assistant at Miami. It also had a representative at Sunnyside Yard in New York—for good reason. Dining cars and crews on the *Silver Star* and *Silver Meteor* usually ran through to New York. Here, immediately upon arrival from the south, the SAL steward would contact the PRR dining-car agent at Pennsylvania Station. Requisitions for the return run southbound would be phoned ahead to the Sunnyside commissary and the entire train would then proceed to that vast yard. The huge catering facility at Sunnyside was there principally to provision PRR's far-flung fleet of dining cars, but, armed with advance copies of menus for the Florida trains, it also stocked Seaboard's pantries with most of the items needed—including crockery and kitchenware. Each month a more thorough equipment requisition would be made to SAL's Washington office.

Many diner patrons to which the crews catered represented a new breed of Florida traveler. Prior to the introduction of streamliners, the general profile of the Florida traveler was wealthy, traveling in Pullman in winter; by 1960 it read "cost conscious, traveling in coach in summer."

This gradual shift in the market had been taking place nationwide as airlines and the auto continued to skim the cream of the trade away from the railroads. It was particularly vexing for roads not positioned to handle the change. Southern Pacific's formerly all-Pullman *Lark* between Los Angeles and San Francisco—mortally wounded by airlines which could move its business clientele ten times faster for almost the same price—was struggling to survive. Likewise, the greatest first-class operation in history, New York Central's *20th Century Limited*, was downgraded to a coach/sleeper operation in April 1958. By the onset of the 1960's, some roads, like Lehigh Valley, had abandoned passenger service altogether. But through all this pessimism, the Florida trade held its own.

Depending on how you viewed the situation, this

was either because of the Florida road's optimistic attitude or the cause for optimism in the first place. While other roads were taking a critical look at their passenger operations and slashing service, SAL and rival ACL maintained an upbeat if cautious attitude. Their trains were positioned to handle the changing clientele. On the Florida trains in the 1950's and early 1960's, there was no downgrading of service, no Automat cars, no deferred maintenance. Instead there were package vacations, auto-rail packages, new passenger stations and aggressive advertising.

The positive attitude was rewarded. Seaboard's passenger revenues began an upward turn in 1955 following a post-Korean War slide. Revenues continued to increase through most of the late 1950's while ACL struggled. For SAL, the 1960's began on an even more promising note. Passenger revenues for 1960 were up 9 percent over 1959 and for 1962 were the highest in ten years. The peak travel period that year was not winter but the summer months of July and August. Like a dancer deftly trading partners in mid tune, Seaboard was now embracing tourist class instead of first class.

The trend had been unfolding for years. Shrinking Pullman patronage had led to the demise of the *Orange Blossom Special* in 1953. But, putting everything in perspective, the Florida roads were still carrying a large number of first-class passengers, too, in addition to an increase in coach travel compared to railroads elsewhere. Note the preponderance of sleeping cars in the following winter-season consists from December 1963. The number of sleepers in the *Meteor* was larger than the amount typically included in the *20th Century Limited* at this time:

TOP AND MIDDLE: In a blur of silver, the northbound *Silver Meteor* sweeps through the Florida countryside south of Ocala in April 1964. The E4 leading the pack has traded its Art Deco color scheme for the more-austere light green (which appears nearly white in photos) and coral; the trailing E7A has stainless-steel carbody sides that were an experiment aimed at reducing paint costs. Tavern-observation 6601 trails the long streamliner.—Two photos, DAVID W. SALTER. **ABOVE:** E4 3008 still wears the original colors in this view, circa 1947, but trucks and running gear had been painted black.—DICK SHARPLESS, COLLECTION OF DAVID W. SALTER.

ABOVE: In November and December 1955, Pullman-Standard delivered nine chair-lounge cars with 52 seats and a 10-seat lounge. Seven of the cars, Nos. 6235-6241, went to SAL; two others, the 861 and 862, went to RF&P. They were routinely assigned to the *Silver Meteor* and *Silver Star*. One of the cars typically operated as the New York-Venice coach on the *Meteor*.
ABOVE RIGHT: The interior of one of the coach-lounges shows the center lounge section, complete with plants. Heywood-Wakefield "Sleepy Hollow" reclining seats—possibly the most-comfortable reclining seat ever designed—were available to coach passengers. SAL cars had tropical murals or Florida scenes (such as shown) while RF&P cars had framed colonial scenes on the bulkheads.—BOTH PHOTOS, SMITHSONIAN INSTITUTION.

The *Silver Meteor*, December 1963

Baggage-dormitory	NYP-MIA
Combine	WWD-STP
10-6 sleeper	WAS-MIA
10-6 sleeper	NYP-MIA (3 days per week)
10-6 sleeper	NYP-MIA
5-2-2 sleeper	NYP-MIA
10-6 sleeper	NYP-MIA
5-d.br. Sun Lounge	NYP-MIA
11-double bedroom sleeper	NYP-STP
Diner	NYP-STP
10-6 sleeper	NYP-VEN
10-6 sleeper	NYP-STP
52-seat coach	NYP-STP
52-seat coach	NYP-VEN
52-seat coach	NYP-STP (last southbound 1/1/64; northbound 12/31/63)
Diner	NYP-MIA
52-seat coach	NYP-MIA
52-seat coach	NYP-MIA
52-seat coach	NYP-MIA (12/17/63 to 1/2/64)
Tavern-observation	NYP-MIA

The *Silver Star*, December 1963

Baggage-dormitory	WAS-MIA
Baggage	WWD-STP
Tavern-observation	WAS-MIA
52-seat coach	NYP-MIA
52-seat coach	NYP-MIA
52-seat coach	NYP-MIA
52-seat coach	NYP-MIA (holiday period only)
52-seat coach	NYP-STP
Diner	NYP-STP
5-1-4-4 sleeper	NYP-STP
10-6 sleeper	NYP-STP
Diner	NYP-MIA
10-6 sleeper	NYP-MIA
6-bedroom buffet-lounge	NYP-MIA
11-double bedroom sleeper	NYP-MIA
10-6 sleeper	NYP-MIA
10-6 sleeper	WAS-MIA
5-1-4-4 sleeper	RVR-MIA

Recorded just a month earlier, Consist of Note 5-E for the *Silver Star* shows the fluctuation in consist size

between the fall and winter schedules. In this consist for the *Star*, the tavern-lounge-observations typically assigned were the round-end postwar cars that had been modified with an end-of-car diaphragm for mid-train operation.

IN 1963, NEW YORK-FLORIDA rail passenger operations underwent an unexpected and, for ACL and FEC in particular, drastic change. On Jan. 23, 1963, a strike by non-operating employees, honored by operating unions, paralyzed the Florida East Coast. Miami-bound ACL trains were unable to use the FEC and instead were diverted to Coast Line's Jacksonville-Orlando-Auburndale line (used by the Tampa section of the *West Coast Champion*). At Auburndale they entered the SAL for the remainder of the trip to Miami, terminating at the Seaboard station there.

Although passenger revenue from the detoured trains went to ACL, SAL was compensated with nearly a half million dollars in 1963 for the use of its property. Unknown to anyone at the time, the detour would continue permanently. But, even up to the Seaboard Coast Line merger in 1967, SAL operated the visiting streamliners as Extra movements.

Passenger revenues for 1964 held virtually on a par with those of 1963. Seaboard pushed hard to attract passengers heading for fun in a different direction—northbound to the New York World's Fair. Even in May and November, traditionally a lull period between the summer and winter rush, the flagship *Silver Meteor* fielded an impressive 20-car consist, as evidenced in Consist of Note 5-F and 5-G (page 90).

Seaboard's trains were generally perceived as big-time, high-speed services linking the Northeast to Florida. In contrast, their connecting trains were often quaint, backwater operations with the look and feel of a shortline railroad.

Seaboard's East and West Coast sections of the *Meteor* were usually separated and combined at Wildwood, a division point some 130 miles into central Florida from Jacksonville. From Wildwood the West Coast trains ran to Tampa Union Station where they split again, with one section continuing around

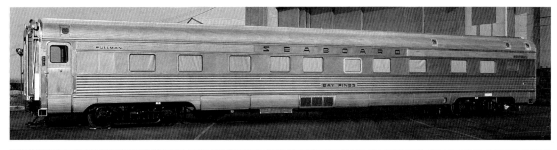

TOP LEFT: Budd built six sleepers with 5 double bedrooms, 1 compartment, 4 sections and 4 roomettes for Seaboard service in November 1955. They entered service covering a New York-Miami and a New York-St. Petersburg car line on the *Silver Star* in January 1956. Car names were *Bay Pines, Camden, Cedartown, Henderson, Pinehurst* and *Southern Pines.*—LAWRENCE S. WILLIAMS, INC. LEFT: Seaboard's *Tallahassee* and five sisters with 11 double bedrooms went into service on the *Silver Meteor* between New York and Miami and New York and St. Petersburg in January 1956.—PULLMAN TECHNOLOGY.

LEFT: *Boca Grande, Clearwater* and *Fort Lauderdale* offered 5 double bedrooms, 2 compartments and 2 drawing rooms to Seaboard patrons. Curiously, their rooms could not be opened en suite. The cars entered service in January 1956 on the *Silver Star* between New York and Miami but would spend most of their lives on the *Meteor.*—PULLMAN TECHNOLOGY. LOWER LEFT: Sometime in the 1960's, SAL added diaphragms to three of the postwar Budd-built tavern-observation cars, Nos. 6600, 6603 and 6604. The cars operated mid-train in the *Silver Star.* Taken in Miami, the photo dates from May 1968.—BOB PENISI, RAILROAD AVENUE ENTERPRISES.

Tampa Bay to St. Petersburg and other, smaller sections heading for the resort communities of Venice (via Bradenton and Sarasota) or Port Boca Grande. The Venice line was more popular and longer-lived, but the Port Boca Grande line with its yacht connection to the private golf and fishing resort of Useppa Island was more exotic.

The New York-Venice run was, for most of its life, strictly a through sleeping-car operation, with coaches and combines operated locally between Tampa and Venice. Typically a heavyweight 10-section, 1-drawing-room, 2-compartment car, the New York-Venice Pullman line had been handled on a variety of trains over the years on a year-round basis. At one point or another, the line had been incorporated into the *New York-Florida Limited, Orange Blossom Special, Sun Queen, Silver Meteor, Camellia* or the *Sunland.* By December 1947 it had been permanently shifted to the *Meteor.* By 1950 the 10-1-2 had been replaced by a streamlined 10-6 car, and in 1956 a through New

CONSIST OF NOTE 5-E
RF&P train 22, northbound *Silver Star*

Alexandria, Va.
Nov. 17, 1963

Car	Type
[RF&P 1013]	[Electro-Motive E8A]
[RF&P 1154]	[Electro-Motive E8B]
PRR*	X-29 express box car
PRR*	X-29 express box car
SAL 6054	Baggage-dorm
PRR 4060	52-seat coach
SAL 6244	52-seat coach
SAL 6208	56-seat coach
PRR 4061	52-seat coach
SAL 6218	52-seat coach
RF&P 862	Coach-lounge
SAL 6603	Tavern-obs (blunt-end, mid-train)
SAL 6103	Diner
SAL *Birmingham*	10-roomette, 6-d.br. sleeper
SAL *Avon Park*	11-double-bedroom sleeper
PRR *Imperial Point*	4-cmpt., 4-d.br., 2-drwg. rm. sleeper

*Number not recorded

RIGHT: It's March 9, 1955. There is probably still a snow covering throughout much of the Northeast, but here in St. Petersburg it's the soft evening hours of another day of relative warmth and sunshine—only light jackets and sweaters required. For many, the work (or school) day is over. The gentleman at right crossing the street is perhaps en route home to his family, toting a few items bought at the corner store. Across the street, folks gather on sidewalk benches to read newspaper stories about Eisenhower's new Federal Defense Highway System or whether Elvis Presley is a bad influence on American youth. For the policeman, the work day is still at hand with the task of monitoring traffic lanes to make way for an unlikely (except in St. Petersburg and a couple other locations) inhabitant of a palm-lined brick street: Seaboard E7A 3024 and its *Silver Star* connection train. In a few minutes, the last of the baggage will be loaded onto No. 122's combine and the diner (second car) readied for dinner patrons as the Pullman conductor makes a last-minute check of his diagram for the sleeper that trails the vestpocket consist. At 5:30 p.m., the 3024 will ease away from SAL's curbside depot, bringing to a close the buzz of station activity—until the next morning's *Silver Star* arrival and *Silver Meteor* departure.—JIM SCRIBBINS.

ABOVE: A tardy train 258, the *Meteor*'s Venice connection, resulted in this unusual maneuver at Valrico, Fla., on a dreary December morning in 1963. Normally, 258 went into Tampa Union Station to deliver its New York coach and sleeper to 158, the St. Pete section of the *Meteor*. So as not to hold up 158, the combining on this day was done at Valrico, junction with the Venice branch. Motor 2028 on 258 simply backed its cars onto the rear of 158.—DAVID W. SALTER.

York-Venice coach was added, eliminating the need for through coach passengers to make an across-the-platform transfer at Tampa to a local coach. The New York-Venice coach and sleeper lasted until the advent of Amtrak on May 1, 1971.

In the heavyweight era, the New York-Port Boca Grande car line was generally held down by either a 6-compartment 3-drawing-room car or a 10-1-2 which often alternated with each other on different days. This Pullman line was strictly a winter-only operation while across-the-platform coach connections at Tampa generally were available year round.

For the 1939 winter season, the West Coast *Orange Blossom Special* carried a New York-Port Boca Grande 10-1-2 or 6-3 which operated on alternate days. Coach connections were available across the

platform to local cars at Tampa for the same destination. This coach connection was offered on the *Blossom* in winter and the *New York-Florida Limited* in the off season. For the winter of 1941-42, the 6-3 and 10-1-2 were carried on the *Southern States Special*.

In the mid 1940's, the *Palmland* handled the sleeping-car lines in winter and offered the coach transfer year round. For the winter of 1946-47, coach transfers were available via the southbound *Advance Silver Meteor* and the northbound *Silver Meteor* while the *Palmland* carried the heavyweight sleeping-car lines.

The December 1948 timetable reveals that by then a winter-season 6-3 was being offered via the *Silver Star* while the *Palmland* offered a transfer at Tampa to a local train originating there and featuring a heavyweight parlor-diner and coach. This arrangement held

LEFT: In 1964-65, Seaboard acquired 20 SDP35 locomotives from EMD. Equipped with steam generators for train heating, these dual-service units were at home sprinting through the Piedmont with a passenger consist or grinding along with freight tonnage. SAL trains 9 and 10, the *Palmland*, became regular recipients of the utilitarian locomotives, a pair of which swing through the South Carolina countryside in June 1966 with No. 10. Note the C&O 10-6 serving as the Miami-New York sleeper. On occasion, the SDP's worked in tandem with E-units.—DAVID W. SALTER.

BELOW: With three local cars—a heavyweight baggage, combine and coach originating at Tampa—and a PRR 10-6 sleeper through from New York, Seaboard's Venice connection to the *Silver Meteor* putters across the Manatee River near Bradenton in March 1955. "Babyface" Baldwin locomotive No. 2700 powering the little *Meteor* was a rarity in railroading; only nine of these Baldwin model DR6-4-15's were built, three for Seaboard (Nos. 2700-2702) and the remainder for New York Central. Constructed in 1947-48, Seaboard's three units lasted until 1964.—JIM SCRIBBINS.

steady for a few years, but eventually the heavyweight sleepers were replaced by lightweights. By December 1955, the *Silver Star* was carrying a through winter-season 10-6, and the *Palmland* was still connecting with the Tampa-Port Boca Grande local to offer a transfer to coach passengers. Rail passenger service between Tampa and Boca Grande was finally discontinued after the winter season of 1958-59 on April 25, 1959. In this final season, the *Silver Star* handled a winter-season-only 4-4-2 to and from New York City while offering a coach transfer at Tampa.

Both of these branchline runs offered a unique journey to passengers who had spent the night aboard one of SAL's fast streamliners or standard trains. Once transferred to the locals, passengers enjoyed a leisurely journey into backwoods Florida over wooden trestles bridging tiny backwaters surrounded by scrub pines and palm trees. As if to confirm that subtropical ports-of-call were on the agenda, many of the stations on the branches were of Spanish architecture.

If the scenery was exotic, so was the motive power. Beginning in the early 1950's, both the Port Boca

Grande and the Venice lines hosted Baldwin passenger "Babyface" diesels 2700, 2701 and 2702. The 1500-h.p. oddities were displaced on the Venice run in the mid 1950's by something even stranger, an honest-to-goodness motor car, Seaboard Nos. 2028.

The quaint, shovel-nosed 1936 St. Louis Car Company product and its mate, the 2027 (later wrecked), had lived productive lives on the Seaboard, serving on runs between Savannah, Ga., and Montgomery, Ala., as well as in North Carolina and, briefly, in Florida handling the West Coast section of the *Silver Meteor* in 1939.

Like many of SAL's passengers, the 2028 was living in semi-retirement in balmier climes, paying its way by hauling the *Meteor*'s Tampa-Venice connection. The 600-h.p. beauty would make a reputation for itself among rail historians, continuing to provide reliable service in south Florida through the Seaboard Coast Line merger and right up through the day that Amtrak began on May 1, 1971.

Back on the main line things were changing as the decade of 1960's wore on. Despite the encouraging length of the flagship *Silver Meteor* in virtually any season, her alter ego, the *Silver Star,* was shrinking. Originally introduced as a winter-only train, the *Star* seemed to be reverting to that format unintentionally. In the off seasons of the mid-1960's, especially fall, the *Star* was down to a handful of cars. North of Washington, attached to a Pennsy corridor train, the *Star* was downright minuscule, as shown in Consist of Note 5-H (page 94). By contrast, the *Meteor* of the same day featured a healthy consist, as shown in Consist of Note 5-I. But, in the winter season, the *Star* still carried its weight, as shown in Consist of Note 5-J.

Revenues for 1965 climbed 1.6 percent over the previous year. The New York World's Fair, which continued into 1965, was certainly a contributory factor, and passenger revenues for the month of July were the highest since the Korean War year of 1953.

In 1965, too, a large group of passenger cars were purchased secondhand from Florida East Coast (see appendix). Their arrival in November of that year underscored Seaboard's continuing commitment to the passenger as the replacements were acquired to complement a roster already composed of a great deal of lightweight equipment. All told, Seaboard picked up 23 coaches, six diners, a diner-lounge, two tavern-lounge-observations, two baggage-dormitories, a baggage-dormitory-chair car and a baggage car.

Sadly, the 1965 purchase also marked FEC's de facto departure from the interstate passenger business thanks to the prolonged strike. For the small carrier which had contributed mightily to the success of

(Text continued on page 94)

TOP: Baldwin 2702 heads up the rarely photographed Tampa-Port Boca Grande train at Boca Grande on Oct. 5, 1952. Consist includes an RPO-baggage, deadhead coach, baggage, local coach, diner, local "American Flyer" coach and the New York-Port Boca Grande sleeper off the *Silver Star.*—G. W. PETTENGILL JR. VIA WARREN CALLOWAY. ABOVE: Seaboard motorcar 2028 at times also handled the Port Boca Grande connection. Shown on March 4, 1959, the train behind the 2028 stands at Tampa Union Station awaiting the through sleeper off the *Silver Star.*—JIM SCRIBBINS.

RIGHT: As the last passengers alight from the *Silver Meteor* at Miami on June 24, 1960, Seaboard Alco switcher 1433 ties onto the hind end of the train to pull it out to Hialeah Yard for servicing. Miami station was a stub-end affair whose platform tracks were bisected by a street (visible under the second car from the rear). On occasion, extra-long trains that would take a long time to load or unload were split in two and set into the station on two tracks so as not to tie up the street crossing.—JOHN DZIOBKO JR.

LEFT: The northbound *Silver Meteor* is making its grand entrance into Jacksonville on the afternoon of Aug. 5, 1965. Although it's the off-season, special summer-travel promotions have resulted in a healthy consist, which includes the famous Sun Lounge four cars back. The train is arriving from the south and is curving west onto the Jacksonville station leads at Beaver Street. Once clear of the interlocking, No. 58 will begin a backup move into Jacksonville Union Station. All SAL passenger trains passing through Jacksonville had to reverse direction when entering or departing JUS. BELOW: Evening is near as train 22, the northbound *Silver Star*, sets out from Miami on its overnight dash to the Northeast. It's two days after Christmas 1963 and the *Star*'s gleaming consist is undoubtedly swollen by holiday travelers. As was typical of the period, a tavern-observation car was second car out, adjacent to the baggage-dorm.
—DAVID W. SALTER.

(Text continued from page 91)

Florida passenger railroading and, indeed, the state itself, it was obvious—all bets on a comeback were off.

Seaboard passenger revenues in the 1960's held steady, but the cost of doing business rose constantly until it eventually eclipsed earnings. In part this was due to antiquated labor laws—and in an industry that was labor intensive, labor-related costs caught up fast. Time worked against the passenger carriers too. As the 1960's wore on, the railroads' streamlined passenger fleets—most nearing double digits in age—were one step closer to retirement. Given the revenue situation of the period, it was doubtful any road could seriously consider replacing those cars with private money.

Despite the circumstances, Seaboard was in no mood to tinker with its top streamliners. Although deficits had caused some great passenger railroads to do a 180-degree turnaround on their stance toward passenger business, the Florida roads still saw the glass as half full, not half empty. Part of this was due to one optimistic indicator. Unlike many other carriers, the passengers hadn't abandoned the Florida trains. Rather, aggressive marketing had ensured SAL trains a steady stream of the best customers—long-haul passengers. Another reason was the fact that the Florida roads were traditionally indulgent of their passenger trains, understanding their value as public relations tools. In essence, the attitude was, "As long as the passengers keep coming and as long as we can afford to—we'll run these trains."

A continued interest didn't prevent SAL from trying to eliminate unprofitable operations, however. An ominous cloud appeared in July 1965 when the U.S. Post Office began operating a new Zip Code mail-distribution system, which consisted of a number of regional distribution centers linked by trucks—not trains. Likewise, the Railway Express Agency was setting up a similar distribution center system with some of the new facilities located off of the railroad. Mail and express contracts had been the only thing keeping many unprofitable secondary trains from a belated date with discontinuance.

The railroad estimated the impact of the change in Florida alone to be $1.5 million in lost revenue annually. One round-trip operation, Nos. 11-12, between Wildwood and Tampa (the *Palmland*'s Tampa section), succumbed only four months after the Zip Code system went into effect. Fortunately, the effect on Seaboard's streamliner fleet would be minimal, even though the *Meteor* handled an RPO in Florida.

Even bigger changes were in the offing. Seaboard's attitude about the *Silver Star* and *Silver Meteor* remained "business as usual," but SAL itself was looking at former adversary ACL in a new light. Both roads were carefully planning a merger. Despite merger plans, SAL's overall passenger revenues continued to shine. Passenger earnings for 1966 increased $37,000 over 1965. Part of the credit went to the airlines. A strike against air carriers in July and August had helped fill the Silver Fleet.

But there was a down side to Seaboard's last full year of operations. Mail revenues dropped $930,000 over the previous year—less than anticipated but still enough to cast a long shadow of doubt. Thanks to the USPS, it appeared the Railway Post Office was going the way of the buffalo.

The RPO may have been an endangered species, but holiday specials on the Florida roads were not. Multiple sections in winter for the Florida trains had been the norm in the 1930's and 1940's. In the 1960's, passenger Extras at holiday times were just as common. Consider the Seaboard holiday special shown in Consist of Note 5-K. That Seaboard could fill the 16 or so Pullman lines regularly assigned to the *Silver Meteor* and *Star* as well as several other sleepers operated in holiday specials is mute testimony to the popularity of the Florida trains well into the jet age.

By the late 1960's, the *Silver Meteor* remained something special. With the exception of the *Broadway Limited*, the seasonal *Florida Special* and the *Congressional*, no other train on the Northeast Corridor regularly operated with observation cars. Shortly, none of those three would continue the tradition. The *Meteor* would. Always a good train, the *Silver Meteor* had become one of the finest in the country, partly by default as many of America's best trains were downgraded or discontinued as the decade wound down.

As popular as Seaboard trains were, a decidedly different future was just around the corner. Although the impending ACL-SAL merger raised many unan-

---

CONSIST OF NOTE 5-H
PRR train 115, southbound *Silver Star*
North of Washington, D.C.
Nov. 26, 1965

Car	Type
SAL 6249	52-seat coach
SAL 6240	52-seat coach
RF&P 856	52-seat coach
SAL 6223	52-seat coach
SAL *Columbia*	10-roomette, 6-d.br. sleeper
SAL *Hialeah*	11-double-bedroom sleeper

NOTE: Only SAL portion of combined PRR train is shown. At Washington, a coach, diner, baggage-dorm and mid-train tavern-observation—dropped from that day's northbound *Star*—were added for the run to Florida.

CONSIST OF NOTE 5-I
PRR train 114, northbound *Silver Meteor*
North of Washington, D.C.
Nov. 26, 1965

Car	Type
[PRR 4915]	[GG1 electric locomotive]
SAL 6054	Baggage-dorm
SAL *Boca Grande*	5-d.br., 2-cmpt., 2-drwg. rm. sleeper
RF&P *Lancaster*	10-roomette, 6-d.br. sleeper
PRR *Chester County*	10-roomette, 6-d.br. sleeper
PRR *Sumac Falls*	6-d.br. lounge (sub for Sun Lounge)
SAL 6113	Diner
SAL *St. Petersburg*	10-roomette, 6-d. bedroom sleeper
SAL *Lake Wales*	10-roomette, 6-d. bedroom sleeper
RF&P 861	52-seat coach-lounge
SAL 6235	52-seat coach-lounge
SAL 6104	Diner
RF&P 85	52-seat coach
PRR 4067	52-seat coach
SAL 6601	Tavern-lounge-observation

CONSISTS OF NOTE/5-J
RF&P train 21, northbound *Silver Star*
Alexandria, Va.
December 1965

Car	Type
SAL 6056	Baggage-dorm
SAL 6600	Tavern-lounge-obs (mid-train)
SAL 6217	52-seat coach
RF&P 853	52-seat coach
RF&P 862	52-seat coach-lounge
RF&P 855	52-seat coach
RF&P 856	52-seat coach
SAL 6109	Diner
SAL 6205	60-seat coach
PRR *Fairless Hills*	10-roomette, 6-d. bedroom sleeper
PRR *Club Creek*	12-duplex s.rm., 4-d.br. sleeper
SAL 6117	Diner
SAL *Miami*	10-roomette, 6-d. bedroom sleeper
SAL *Red Mountain*	6-double bedroom lounge
SAL *Venice*	11-double-bedroom sleeper
PRR *Greenwood*	10-roomette, 6-d. bedroom sleeper
SAL *Tampa*	10-roomette, 6-d. bedroom sleeper

swered questions, one thing was certain. Two contesting companies with outstanding and distinctive passenger services were about to become one. It was a time that called for a retrospective look at the Seaboard Air Line and what it had accomplished.

Since its inception in 1900, Seaboard had offered

CONSIST OF NOTE 5-K
Seaboard Holiday Special
On the PRR
Jan. 3, 1966

Car	Type
[PRR 4915]	[GG1 electric]
SAL 6245	52-seat coach
SAL 6500	Chair-buffet-observation
SAl 6213	56-seat coach
SAL 6208	56-seat coach-lounge
SAL 6207	60-seat coach
SAL 240	Diner (heavyweight)
PRR *Cascade Cliff*	10-roomette, 5-d. bedroom sleeper
PRR *Morrow Brook*	12-duplex s.rm., 5-d.br. sleeper
PRR *Imperial Path*	4-cmpt., 4-d.br., 2-drwg. rm. sleeper
PRR *Philadelphia Cty.*	13-double-bedroom sleeper
SAL 6108	Diner
PRR *Maple Brook*	12-duplex s.rm., 5-d.br. sleeper
PRR *Cascade Gardens*	10-roomette, 5-d. bedroom sleeper
PRR *Clinton*	10-roomette, 6-d. bedroom sleeper
PRR *May Brook*	12-duplex s.rm., 5-d.br. sleeper

through service from the Northeast to Florida on legendary runs like the all-Pullman *Seaboard Florida Limited* and the incomparable *Orange Blossom Special*. In the teeth of the Depression, Seaboard was its most impressive. In 1933, SAL had been the first Florida road to operate air-conditioned Pullmans. First, too, to install reclining seats (in 1936), SAL had also been the first to dieselize its passenger trains, in 1938. Finally—and for this it will always be remembered—Seaboard had been the first to offer streamlined service between New York and Florida. A better record as a leader in the industry would be hard to find.

Originally the underdog to Atlantic Coast Line in passenger operations, SAL pulled itself up by its own bootstraps to become not only a leader in innovation, but the leader in passenger earnings as well. A look at revenues tells the story. In 1946, with the railroads riding high on wartime earnings and planning for the future, ACL's yearly passenger income was $28.5 million; Seaboard's a little over $21 million. In 1966, the last full year of separate operations, ACL earned $14.4 million to SAL's $14.8 million. Clearly, SAL had done a better job of gaining, and retaining, customers.

Effective with the July 1, 1967, SCL merger, Seaboard Air Line passed into history. Happily, its tradition of fine passenger service would not.

6 POSTWAR COASTLINERS
Florida East Coast/
Atlantic Coast Line: 1945-1967

ABOVE: The *West Coast Champion* in all its postwar glory. Twin E7's clad in the original purple-and-silver scheme lead a long string of purple-letter-boarded rolling stock at Winter Park, Fla., circa 1952. Note the heavyweight RPO and, far back in the consist, an ex-C&O twin-unit diner. After 13 years of service, the train has proven itself a winner . . . and still champion.—R. R. WALLIN. RIGHT: What ACL lacked in editorial finesse with the questionable statement in which a key word had been omitted in this ad from a 1952 public timetable, the railroad made up for in aggressive promotion and advertising of its premier trains. In today's world of watchdog lawyers, Seaboard attorneys might have insisted that ACL reword the headline to read "The only lightweight streamliners between the East and Florida <u>that</u> speed over the only double-track route between the East and Florida."—AUTHOR'S COLLECTION.

AMERICA'S FAVORITE
Florida
AND THE
SUNNY SOUTH
WINTER VACATIONLAND

the only LIGHTWEIGHT STREAMLINERS
BETWEEN THE EAST AND FLORIDA SPEED OVER
"the only DOUBLE TRACK ROUTE BETWEEN THE EAST AND FLORIDA"

FLORIDA SPECIAL Streamlined Lightweight PULLMAN Train Between the East and Florida.

EAST COAST CHAMPION Streamlined Lightweight COACH Train Between the East and Florida.

WEST COAST CHAMPION Streamlined Lightweight PULLMAN-COACH Train Between the East and Central and West Coast Florida.

FIRST IN FLORIDA TRAVEL

ATLANTIC
COAST LINE
RAILROAD

S-M-O-O-T-H-E-R
NEW ROADBED — STREAMLINED FOR STREAMLINERS!

If major threats from the automobile and the airplane loomed over the horizon in 1946, they definitely were nothing new. Improved public highways had played a large role in permanently changing the travel habits of millions of Americans for decades. In the period between the first and second World Wars, railroads all over the country had suffered a steady decline of passenger-miles and revenues at the hands of the private auto. Innovation had been the key to regaining some of that business. First air-conditioning, then dieselization and streamlining had played a big part in getting passengers back on the train. With the advent of World War II, the influence of the auto was somewhat eroded by gas and tire rationing, but the railroads knew that, with the return of peace, the short reprieve from competition would be over.

Not surprisingly railroads turned again to the single most successful weapon in their arsenal—the streamliner. Nearly every major railroad in America was proceeding with or entertaining plans to streamline in the immediate postwar period. Among them were Atlantic Coast Line and its partners in New York-Florida service. In fact, ACL and partners had a bit of a jump on the competition. As a result of World War II, the roads had had an unfilled order on the books with the Budd Company since mid 1941. In the spring of 1946 and again in the spring of 1947, those cars arrived to freshen up ACL's war-weary consists. Even before these new coaches, diners, baggage-dormitories and observations were slated to arrive,

Coast Line was prodding its associates to add more cars, including streamlined sleepers, to the list.

In January 1946, ACL President Champion Davis suggested that the PRR, RF&P and FEC, along with ACL, consider purchasing a series of 86 new cars with which to re-equip the premier trains on the New York-Florida route—the *East* and *West Coast Champions* as well as the Washington section of the *Havana Special*. The idea was, obviously, to make the trains more attractive to the public and thereby attract more ridership. By recommending that only the premier trains be re-equipped, Davis was scaling back on the intentions previously expressed by some of the participating roads that the entire fleet be re-equipped. ACL was as cautious as ever in the way it spent its money.

Responses to Davis' proposal were, at once, indicative of the times and the individual railroads who comprised the alliance. Although all of the roads were in favor of re-equipping the trains and made few inquiries as to the costs and benefits, each had an individual concern. The Pennsylvania wanted its share to include only coaches and sleeping cars (i.e., revenue-producing cars) in the jointly owned pool. For the diminutive RF&P the problem was mileage equalization and how many cars the road would be required to provide. For the Florida East Coast, still in receivership, the concern was the competition of the Seaboard Air Line and court approval of FEC's pending equipment purchase.

In March 1946 at a conference in Philadelphia, the particulars of the re-equipping were ironed out.

For a time, and if both the northbound and southbound *East Coast Champions* were reasonably on time, Nos. 1 and 2 met at Fort Pierce, Fla., during their speedy journeys along the Florida East Coast. Photographer Scribbins was on hand for that meet between the two trains on March 11, 1955. As a gaggle of passengers crowd to board northbound No. 2, with tavern-observation *Hobe Sound* on the rear, brand-new FEC E9A No. 1031 leads No. 1 into town. —JIM SCRIBBINS.

UPPER RIGHT: New postwar cars arrived from Budd first. Here, 14-seat coach-baggage-dormitory No. 107 poses for the Budd Company photographer in April 1947.—BUDD COMPANY. LOWER RIGHT: ACL 54-seat coach 226 is pictured at Long Island's Sunnyside Yard in February 1949.—GEORGE E. VOTAVA. BELOW: Accommodations in the postwar Budd coaches were spartan.—BOMBARDIER.

RIGHT: RF&P also contributed coaches in the Budd postwar order. Number 801, another 54-seater, rests at Sunnyside Yard in February 1949.—GEORGE E. VOTAVA. LOWER RIGHT: FEC's streamlined diners were named for forts. *Fort San Marco*, a 48-seater bound for *Champion* assignment, is pictured at Budd's Red Lion plant near Philadelphia in April 1947. ABOVE RIGHT: Waiters set up tables in one of the postwar diners.—TWO PHOTOS, BOMBARDIER CORPORATION.

Despite the effort, within a year one third of the sleeping-car types and two out of three of the trains considered for re-equipping would be changed. What follows are the originally proposed car types and the way they would have been used:

Car types

21-roomette
10-roomette, 6-double-bedroom
4-compartment, 4-double-bedroom, 2-drawing-room
6-double-bedroom bar-lounge
2-double-bedroom, 2-compartment, 1-drawing-room bar-lounge

Proposed consists*

East Coast Champion (Pullman section)

2 - 21-roomette sleepers	NYP-MIA
4 - 10-6 sleepers	NYP-MIA
1 - 4-4-2 sleeper	NYP-MIA
1 - 6-double-bedroom bar-lounge	NYP-MIA
1 - 2-2-1 bar-lounge	NYP-MIA
1 - 21-roomette sleeper	WAS-MIA
1 - 10-6 sleeper	WAS-MIA
1 - 4-4-2 sleeper	WAS-MIA
2 - Diners	NYP-MIA

West Coast Champion

1 - 10-6 sleeper	NYP-STP
1 - 21-roomette sleeper	NYP-STP
1 - 6-double-bedroom bar-lounge	NYP-JAX
1 - 4-4-2 sleeper	NYP-TPA
1 - 10-6 sleeper	NYP-TPA
1 - 21-roomette sleeper	NYP-TPA
1 - 21-roomette sleeper	WAS-TPA
2 - Diners	NYP-TPA/STP
4 - Coaches	NYP-TPA/STP
1 - Coach	WAS-TPA/STP

Havana Special (Washington section)

1 - 4-4-2 sleeper	WAS-MIA
1 - 10-6 sleeper	WAS-MIA
1 - 21-roomette sleeper	WAS-MIA
1 - Diner	WAS-MIA
5 - Coaches	WAS-MIA

As a result of the Pullman litigation, the Clayton Act required railroads to issue specifications to and seeks bids from the major car manufacturers for their order. This was handled for all of the partners by ACL, the railroad with the most route-miles.

By January 1947, car types and selection of manufacturers had been finalized. The railroads had changed their order considerably.

Actual order

Mfr.	Road	Car type	Qty.	Delivery date
P-S	ACL	54-seat coach	20	11/49-1/50
P-S	PRR	54-seat coach	2	11/49-1/50
P-S	RF&P	54-seat coach	3	11/49-1/50
P-S	FEC	56-seat coach	5	11/49-1/50
P-S	ACL	36-seat diner	11	2/50 -5/50
P-S	FEC	36-seat diner	2	2/50-5/50
P-S	RF&P	36-seat diner	1	2/50-5/50
P-S	ACL	10-6 sleeper	25	9/49-10/49
P-S	FEC	10-6 sleeper	7	9/49-10/49
P-S	PRR	10-6 sleeper	6	9/49-10/49
P-S	RF&P	10-6 sleeper	4	9/49-10/49
P-S	ACL	21-roomette sleeper	5	9/49-10/49
P-S	FEC	21-roomette sleeper	2	9/49-10/49
P-S	PRR	21-roomette sleeper	2	9/49-10/49
P-S	RF&P	21-roomette sleeper	1	9/49-10/4
Mfr.	**Road**	**Car Type**	**Qty.**	**Delivery date**
ACF	ACL	6-d.br. bar-lounge	6	11/49-12/49
ACF	FEC	6-d.br. bar-lounge	2	11/49-12/49
ACF	RF&P	6-d.br. bar-lounge	1	11/49-12/49
ACF	ACL	14-2 sleeper	6	2/50-3/50
ACF	FEC	14-2 sleeper	1	2/50-3/50
ACF	PRR	14-2 sleeper	2	2/50-3/50
ACF	RF&P	14-2 sleeper	1	2/50-3/50
ACF	ACL	Baggage	2	2/50-3/50
ACF	FEC	Baggage	1	2/50-3/50

Coast Line and its partners experienced the same frustrating delays in delivery which affected the Seaboard. The cars above had all been ordered between March and June 1946, but delivery wouldn't come for another three and a half years. Still, they could hope. ACL's files were liberally sprinkled with memos estimating, then re-estimating the date their new fleet would arrive.

The winter season of 1946-47 saw Coast Line return to business-as-usual with a vengeance. Boasting the largest fleet of passenger diesels in the country, ACL could brag that every train between the Northeast and Florida was diesel-powered south of Rich-

A trio of E7's draw the northbound *East Coast Champion* at Jesup, Ga., in July 1949. Streamlined sleepers are still months away, and the train features a string of heavyweight sleepers behind the lightweight coaches.—HUGH COMER.

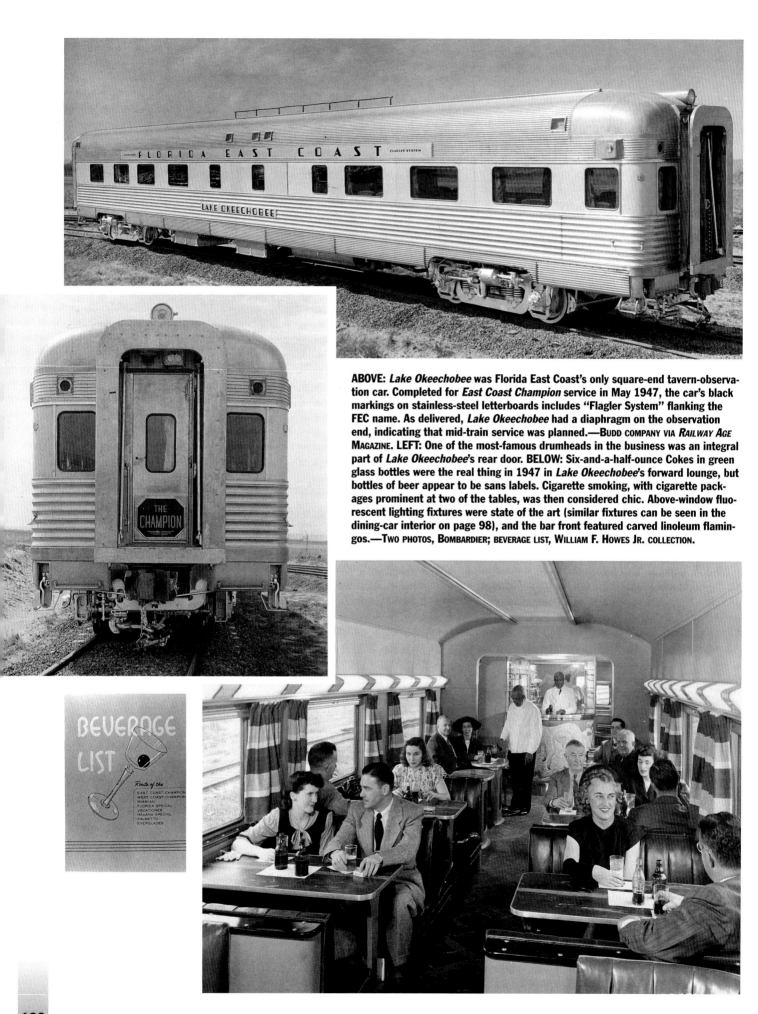

ABOVE: *Lake Okeechobee* was Florida East Coast's only square-end tavern-observation car. Completed for *East Coast Champion* service in May 1947, the car's black markings on stainless-steel letterboards includes "Flagler System" flanking the FEC name. As delivered, *Lake Okeechobee* had a diaphragm on the observation end, indicating that mid-train service was planned.—BUDD COMPANY VIA *RAILWAY AGE* MAGAZINE. LEFT: One of the most-famous drumheads in the business was an integral part of *Lake Okeechobee*'s rear door. BELOW: Six-and-a-half-ounce Cokes in green glass bottles were the real thing in 1947 in *Lake Okeechobee*'s forward lounge, but bottles of beer appear to be sans labels. Cigarette smoking, with cigarette packages prominent at two of the tables, was then considered chic. Above-window fluorescent lighting fixtures were state of the art (similar fixtures can be seen in the dining-car interior on page 98), and the bar front featured carved linoleum flamingos.—TWO PHOTOS, BOMBARDIER; BEVERAGE LIST, WILLIAM F. HOWES JR. COLLECTION.

mond (although occasionally an FEC Mountain would sneak into the picture south of Jacksonville). For the 1946-47 winter season, Coast Line fielded an all-Pullman heavyweight *Florida Special* (East Coast) and *Miamian*, both back after a five-year hiatus. The all-coach streamliner *Champion* (East Coast) ran side by side with a seasonal all-coach *Vacationer* serving the East Coast of Florida. To Tampa and St.Petersburg went the *Florida Special*'s West Coast section with a consist comprised of heavyweight Pullmans, diners and, within Florida, local coaches.

The *Champion* (West Coast) became an all-coach streamliner, the first time an all-streamlined *Champion* was offered to the West Coast—fullfillment of a dream dashed by World War II. To both coasts, the veteran *Havana Special* offered heavyweight sleepers and coaches. This train served the more exotic locations in Florida with a 10-section, 1-drawing room, 2-compartment car linking New York and Fort Meyers/Naples and a Jacksonville-Clewiston (on Lake Okeechobee) 8-section buffet-lounge. Also on the Northeast-to-Florida run were the *Everglades* and the *Florida Mail*, accommodation trains handling considerable head-end traffic as well as Washington-Florida coaches and, in the *Everglades*' case, heavyweight sleepers. All told, ACL could carry 2,700 passengers a day to Florida.

Although the railroad may have had to wait for improved rolling stock, it didn't hesitate to polish the skills of its passenger department people. Dining-car crews went back to "school" to brush up on courtesy and efficiency worn thin by the stresses of wartime service. Coast Line's diners had served four times as many meals in 1944 as they had in 1939. The new training program was part of an organized campaign to return spit and polish to one of the most-distinguished passenger fleets in the country.

In typical Coast Line fashion, schedules and consists didn't stay the same for long. Shortlived as a coaches-only streamliner, the *Champion* (West Coast) reverted to a coach-and-sleeper operation in the summer of 1947, staying that way for the rest of its career. The *Miamian*, reintroduced for the 1946-47 winter

season and traditionally a winter-only run, found itself a year-round operation starting with the summer of 1947. Coaches were added to the train in April 1948, but typically this operation reverted to all-Pullman status in the winter. For the winter season of 1948-49—its 60th season—the *Florida Special* made its last appearance as a heavyweight, running in two sections, a New York-Miami train and a Boston/ Washington section serving both coasts:

Florida Special (New York section)

12-1 sleeper	NYP-MIA
10-1-2 sleeper	NYP-MIA
6-3 sleeper	NYP-MIA
6-3 sleeper	NYP-MIA
10-1-2 sleeper	NYP-MIA
3-1 buffet-lounge	NYP-MIA
6-3 sleeper	NYP-MIA
12-3-2 sleeper	NYP-MIA
Diner	NYP-MIA
Diner	NYP-MIA
6-3 sleeper	NYP-MIA
7-2 sleeper	NYP-MIA
10-1-1 sleeper	NYP-MIA
10-1-1 sleeper	NYP-MIA
3-2 observation	NYP-MIA

Florida Special (Boston/Washington section)

6-3 sleeper	BOS-MIA
12-1 sleeper	BOS-TPA/SAR
12-1 sleeper	BOS-STP
12-1 sleeper	WAS-MIA
10-1-2 sleeper	WAS-MIA
10-1-2 sleeper	WAS-MIA
3-1 lounge	WAS-MIA
8-1-3 sleeper	WAS-MIA
10-2 sleeper	WAS-MIA
8-1-2 sleeper	WAS-TPA/SAR
10-1-2 sleeper	WAS-STP
Diner	WAS-MIA
Diner	JAX-TPA
Diner	JAX-STP

In December 1948, in keeping with the antitrust decision against Pullman, ACL purchased a variety of heavyweight sleepers (right) from the giant sleeping-car company, then leasing them back to Pullman for operation and maintenance. These cars would work with ACL-owned streamlined sleepers and with their heavyweight brethren still in Pullman ownership.

By December 1949, sufficient streamlined sleeping cars were on hand to introduce the *Florida Special* as a

Atlantic Coast Line tavern-lounge observation 256 and sisters 252-255 and 257 were, like FEC cousin *Lake Okeechobee*, square-end cars outfitted with diaphragms for mid-train service. The cars were used on the *Champion*s in both mid-train and rear-position assignments, but mid-train usage was longer lived. Clad in its purple letterboard, the 256 is at Washington, D.C., in May 1949. As with other cars of the era, this car series originally had (at the forward end only) full-width diaphragms. For maintenance reasons, they were later removed.—GEORGE E. VOTAVA.

ACL-heavyweights purchased from Pullman

10-1-2
Daggett
Gonzales
The Citadel
Fort Dodge
Chillicothe
Camp Cody
Camp Mills
Cape Cod
Cape Ferrelo
Cape Fortunas
Cape Lookout
Lake Elmo
Lake Louise
Lake Pelican
Lake Winnebago
Puerto Rico

8-1-2
Algonquin Park
Cameron Pass
Centcrest
Centolio
Charles E. Perkins
Rock Cliff
Rock Dell
Rose Isle
Rock Springs

8-section buffet-lounge
Oregon Club
Washington Club

10-2-1
Columbia College
Rollins College
Southern College
Swarthmore College
Sweet Briar College
Vassar College

8-5
Clover Bank
Clover Castle
Clover Creek

10-1-1
Fleetville
Island Home
La Boheme
La Fontaine
La Gioconda

8-single-bedroom lounge
Grosse Point
Palmer Woods

8-1-3
Anselin's Tower
Arsenal Tower
Brixworth Tower
High Tower
Silhouette Tower
West Tower

10-2
Quadrant Peak

6-6
Poplar Street
Poplar Terrace
Poplar Village
Poplar Vista

6-3
Glen Ayr

Rollins College, with 10 sections, 2 double bedrooms and 1 compartment, had been a car in long-term assignment to ACL before its purchase from Pullman in 1948. —O. H. BORSUM VIA FOSTER GUNNISON.

lightweight. To the casual observer, sprucing up the venerable *Special* seemed a natural extension of Coast Line's affection for its favorite train. What few knew was that the ACL and its partners had a tough time deciding what to do with the *Florida Special*. The problem was twofold: First, railroads were now required to purchase their own sleeping cars instead of relying solely on a cost-effective leased pool available from Pullman in the heavyweight era. Second, a four-month-per-year luxury operation required different equipment than a year-round coach-and-sleeper train.

Faced with those circumstances, ACL and partners had debated running an all-streamlined Pullman section of the *East Coast Champion* as well as an all-coach *East Coast Champion*. Instead, they compromised. An all-streamlined *Florida Special* would be operated but it would consist of streamlined cars with floorplans better suited to the railroads' year-round needs.

On Dec. 16, 1949, the *Florida Special* debuted as a streamliner for the winter season of 1949-50. Still all-Pullman and now all-room (i.e., no sections), the train featured accommodations which were quickly becoming the standards of the postwar era. All rooms offered toilet facilities, radio and piped-in music, a public-address system and individual climate controls. Although the *Special* was unique at the time as the only lightweight all-Pullman train to Florida, its consist did indeed reflect car types that could serve on more basic assignments during the eight months of the year the *Special* did not run. Hence, the *Special* carried no observation car—*de rigeur* for first-class trains of the day—and the train was top heavy with roomettes (150 of them), an accommodation decidedly unsuited to the luxury Florida tourist market, long the province of stateroom cars. Still, the re-equipped train was something fresh and new in an optimistic era desperate for new beginnings.

Here is how the new *Florida Special* looked:

Florida Special, 1949-50 season

10-6 sleeper	NYP-MIA
10-6 sleeper	NYP-MIA
10-6 sleeper	NYP-MIA
10-6 sleeper	NYP-MIA
10-6 sleeper	NYP-MIA
Diner	NYP-MIA
6-d. bedroom bar-lounge	NYP-MIA
6-d. bedroom bar-lounge	NYP-MIA
Diner	NYP-MIA
10-6 sleeper	NYP-MIA
21-roomette sleeper	NYP-MIA
14-2 sleeper	NYP-MIA
14-2 sleeper	NYP-MIA
10-6 sleeper	NYP-MIA
21-roomette sleeper	NYP-MIA
10-6 sleeper	NYP-JAX

The *Special* wasn't the only train to get streamlined sleepers that winter. The *West Coast Champion* was largely re-equipped as well, handling a range of new sleepers and coaches:

West Coast Champion, 1949-1950 season

(not in consist order)	
21-roomette sleeper	NYP-TPA
10-6 sleeper	NYP-TPA
14-2 sleeper	NYP-TPA
10-6 sleeper	NYP-SAR
10-6 sleeper	NYP-STP
10-6 sleeper	NYP-STP
6-d. bedroom bar-lounge	WAS-STP
10-6 sleeper	WAS-TPA
14-seat coach-baggage-dorm	NYP-TPA
54-seat coach	NYP-TPA
54-seat coach	NYP-STP
54-seat coach	NYP-STP
54-seat coach	NYP-SAR
46-seat coach	NYP-TPA
48-seat coach	JAX-TPA
14-seat coach-baggage-dorm	JAX-STP
Tavern-lounge	NYP-TPA
Diner	NYP-TPA
Diner	JAX-STP

Also, the *East Coast Champion* reverted to all-

Thirty-six *County*-series 10-6 sleepers arrived from Pullman-Standard in the fall of 1949. They would form the backbone of the *Florida Special* and *Champion* pool and would serve on secondary trains as well. Each new *Florida Special* consist in 1949 featured eight cars of this type.—PULLMAN TECHNOLOGY.

ABOVE: Back-to-back E6's shake the concrete overpass at Union Junction, Ga., on Independence Day 1948 as they accelerate out of Savannah with the southbound *Havana Special* having made its evening station stop. Coming in from the left is Seaboard's line through Savannah. ACL and SAL trains serving Savannah Union Station had to back into the stub-end facility.—DAVID W. SALTER.

BELOW: Steam was still in evidence in mainline passenger service on the Florida East Coast as late as March 1947. Here, 4-8-2 No. 422 has No. 79, the *Vacationer,* southbound at St. Augustine.—HUGH COMER. RIGHT: Florida East Coast was unquestionably in a prime position for delivering passengers to resort cities lining Florida's Atlantic coast. The ad, from a December 1946 timetable, also heralded dieselization of the Florida fleet.—AUTHOR'S COLLECTION.

coach status for the 1949-1950 winter, carrying 11 streamlined coaches (ten of which were the new Pullman-Standard 54-seaters), two diners, a tavern-lounge and a tavern-lounge observation. That season, too, the *Miamian* was an all-Pullman heavyweight and the *Vacationer* a mixture of heavyweight Pullmans and lightweight coaches. The *Havana Special* carried heavyweight coaches and sleepers to both coasts, while the *Everglades* was down to one heavyweight Washington-Jacksonville sleeper and a couple of coaches. The lowly *Florida Mail* was a one liner—a Washington-Florence (S.C.) coach with no through passenger service to Florida.

The lineup reflected what was the most-dramatic change to ACL's formidable fleet since the introduction of the *Champion*s a decade earlier. It was a time when Coast Line's $14 million investment in new equipment looked like the right move. The *Florida Special*, already popular before streamlining, began earning additional customers for Coast Line at the expense of Seaboard's *Orange Blossom Special*. And if the *Florida Special* was popular, the phenomenally successful *Champion*s paid their way even more dramatically as Coast Line's biggest money-earners. For the 12-month period ending May 31, 1949, the *East Coast Champion* posted a revenue-per-train-mile of $8.85 southbound and $8.99 northbound. Its West Coast counterpart earned $4.64 southbound and $5.86 northbound. Those numbers, especially the *East Coast Champ*'s figures, were extremely high. The future looked bright and, as such, the road launched a

plan to upgrade its existing heavyweight passenger fleet.

In November 1950, with the outshopping of coach 1084 at the road's Emerson Shops in Rocky Mount, N.C., Atlantic Coast Line embarked on an extensive modernization program which would span the decade and eventually encompass the rebuilding of 22 heavyweight head-end cars and 56 coaches. The railroad's facilities completely overhauled these cars, remodeling them to be the equals of streamlined equipment delivered by the major car builders. But one thing set them apart; the pioneering 1084 and brethren were attired in a new scheme, Coast Line's eye-popping colors of solid purple body, aluminum letterboard and yellow striping with black roof. The scheme was applied in the 1950's to most rebuilds and some standard heavyweights, as well as railroad-owned heavyweight sleeping cars. It was, arguably, one of the most-exotic car schemes ever applied, anywhere. The "new" cars could be routinely found in the consists of secondary runs like the *Everglades* and the *Havana Special*, but on occasion they also pinch hit in *Champion* service.

The heavyweight fleet wasn't the only thing changing. The *Vacationer* and *Miamian* were exchanging identities nearly every year in the early 1950's, so although Consist of Note 6-A is for the *Vacationer*, it also provides a good perspective of what the *Miamian* looked like. This consist shows the *Vacationer* in its guise as a lightweight coach/heavyweight sleeper operation to Miami, a role it would relinquish to the *Mi-*

amian the following winter season of 1951-52.

By the winter season of 1951-52, a pattern of operations had begun to emerge for Coast Line winter service which, with a few exceptions, would continue through the mid 1950's. The *Florida Special* was operated as an all-Pullman lightweight to Miami; the *East Coast Champion* continued to be offered as the all-coach lightweight counterpart to the *Special* over the East Coast of Florida route. The *Miamian* sported lightweight coaches and heavyweight sleepers from New York to Miami, and the *Vacationer*—once an all-coach companion to the *Champion*s—was now an all-Pullman operation with cars from Boston and New York destined for both coasts of Florida. See Consist of Note 6-B.

In summer, with the seasonal *Florida Special* and *Vacationer* dropped from the timecard, the *Miamian* continued to operate with roughly its same consist, as did the *West Coast Champion*. The *East Coast Champion* reverted to a coach-and-sleeper operation. In the winter season of 1953-54, the *Vacationer* was extended to operate as a through train to Boston via the New Haven Railroad. For many years, through sleeping cars had been handled via the New England carrier, but this marked a change from the norm. This time coaches, sleepers and diners moved as one consist through to Boston, although the train continued

CONSIST OF NOTE 6-A
FEC train 74, northbound *Vacationer*
Feb. 22, 1951
All cars MIA-NYP and lightweight except as noted

Car	Type	
[FEC 1007]	[E7A locomotive]	
[FEC 1012]	[E7A locomotive]	
FEC 501	Baggage (MIA-JAX)	
ACL 106	Coach-baggage-dorm	
FEC *Belleglade*	Coach	
FEC *Jacksonville*	Coach	
PRR 4053	Coach	
PRR 4027	Coach	
PRR 4056	Coach	
PRR 4029	Coach	
ACL *North Carolina*	Tavern-lounge	
FEC *Fort Dallas*	Diner	
Sun Dawn	2-1 lounge (heavyweight)	
SOU *Lake Childs*	10-1-2 sleeper (heavyweight)	
Glen Almond	6-3 sleeper (heavyweight)	
Oak View	12-1-4 sleeper (heavyweight)	
AT&SF *Glen Roberts*	6-3 sleeper (heavyweight)	
ACL *Poplar Vista*	6-6 sleeper (heavyweight)	
RF&P 807	Coach	

Other motive power

ACL 543	E7A locomotive	JAX-RVR
ACL 750	E6B locomotive	JAX-RVR
ACL 754	E6B locomotive	JAX-RVR
RF&P 618-		
James Madison	4-8-4 locomotive	RVR-WAS
PRR 4812	GG1 electric	WAS-NYP

The *East Coast Champion* (at left with E7A 1017) and the *Florida Special* make for a majestic pair at Miami station on the morning of March 11, 1955. First out will be the *Champ* at 10 a.m., and at 11:05 a.m. the brand-new E9's will lead the *Special* out of town and follow the wake of the *Champ* all the way north. Both trains were scheduled to arrive in New York exactly 24 hours later, at 10 and 11:05 a.m. respectively. —JIM SCRIBBINS.

to carry additional sleeping cars between Florida and New York City:

The *Vacationer*
Winter season 1953-54

54-seat coach	BOS-MIA
Coach	SPG-NHV
14-4 sleeper	BOS-MIA
6-3 sleeper	BOS-MIA
8-5 sleeper	BOS-MIA
6-3 sleeper	BOS-MIA
1-s.br, 1-drwg. room buffet-lounge	BOS-MIA
Diner	BOS-MIA
Diner	JAX-TPA
6-3 sleeper	BOS-SAR
6-4-4 sleeper	BOS-SAR
Diner	BOS-STP
8-1-3 sleeper	BOS-STP
6-3 sleeper	NYP-STP
6-3 sleeper	NYP-MIA
6-3 sleeper	NYP-MIA
6-3 sleeper	NYP-MIA
6-3 sleeper	NYP-MIA
8-5 sleeper	WAS-MIA
36-seat coach	JAX-NAP

CONSIST OF NOTE 6-B

The *Vacationer* (all Pullman)

Jan. 4, 1953
All cars heavyweight

Car	Type
Glen Huron	6-compartment, 3-double-bedroom sleeper
Glen Blair	6-compartment, 3-double-bedroom sleeper
NYC *Glen Pass*	6-compartment, 3-double-bedroom sleeper
Clover Field	8-section, 5-double-bedroom sleeper
Fir Springs	6-section, 4-roomette, 4-d.br. sleeper
ACL *Bradenton*	Diner (rebuilt)
Palm Valley	3-cmpt, 1-drwg. room buffet-lounge
Glen Alta	6-compartment, 3-double-bedroom sleeper
ACL *Silhouette Tower*	8-section, 1-drwg. room, 3-d.br. sleeper
ACL *Gonzales*	10-section, 1-drwg. room, 2-cmpt. sleeper
Glen Nevis	6-compartment, 3-double-bedroom sleeper
Lake Ontario	10-section, 1-drwg. room, 2-cmpt. sleeper
Oak House	12-roomette, 1-single-br., 4-d.br. sleeper
Glen Alice	6-compartment, 3-double-bedroom sleeper

The constant metamorphosis of the *Vacationer* and running mate *Miamian* was typical of the fine tuning Coast Line applied to its trains and schedules. It was a railroad which paid a lot of attention to its passenger trains.

In May 1954, *Modern Railroads* magazine devoted an entire issue to a profile of the Atlantic Coast Line, offering a glimpse behind the scenes at one of America's most successful passenger carriers in what would prove a pivotal decade. The article revealed a railroad as positive about the long-haul passenger business as it had been in 1939.

The optimism came as a bit of a surprise. Although the railroad had handled 2 million passengers and earned 12 percent of its operating revenue from them

in 1953, ACL was, according to the ICC's Fully Allocated accounting formula, spending $1.28 for every dollar it took in. But, unlike some railroads which used the Fully Allocated formula to justify a negative attitude toward passenger service, Coast Line recognized the formula for what it was: an accounting statistic, not the Ten Commandments. ACL justified its continued enthusiasm with an accounting statistic of its own: "avoidable costs." Simply put, the difference between the Fully Allocated formula and the Avoidable Costs formula was one of philosophy. The ICC method was actually a tool designed to be used for pricing a service, not evaluating profitability. Like any good tool, if used improperly it yielded poor results. The ICC formula assumed that by eliminating a

train you could eliminate all of the costs incurred in operating that train. But, taking track work as an example, unless you planned to eliminate *all* of your trains, lay off the maintenance people and tear up the track, that simply wasn't true. Some costs were simply unavoidable.

Avoidable costing took a different view. And, according to Coast Line President Champ Davis, on an avoidable-cost basis, ACL's long-haul passenger service of 1954 was still probably turning a profit. The enthusiasm went only so far, however. In contrast to the long-hauls, ACL was agressively eliminating local services which proved unprofitable. The railroad's philosophy was to move away from low-density branch-line service and concentrate on the long-haul passenger where there still might be some profit.

Any profit to be made was probably coming from the Northeast-Florida trains. In 1953, 75 percent of Coast Line's passenger revenues came from its Eastern long-hauls—revenues still coming in at the expense of Seaboard Air Line. In 1953, Coast Line controlled approximately 67 percent of the passenger business to Florida. That would change in the mid-to-late 1950's.

In the *Modern Railroads* article, ACL revealed it was experiencing one trend in common with Seaboard—more people were traveling to Florida in the summer. In 1940 ACL had earned 64 percent of its annual passenger revenue during the five months of

winter service; in 1950 only 54 percent of the revenues accrued during winter, and the trend was continuing. There were three basic reasons for the change: air-conditioning, new equipment and marketing. Of the three, air-conditioning may well have been the biggest contributor. As for new equipment, significant upgrades in coach travel in 1939 and 1949 lured the cost-conscious, and the cost-conscious traveled to Florida in summer. Finally, off-peak promotions ensured a continued interest in summer travel.

In May 1954, Coast Line launched what would prove its most successful marketing effort—Champion Vacations. All-expense-paid affordable summer trips were offered in conjunction with hotels in Mia-

TOP: In the early to mid-1950's, E7A 532 and two mates stand at Jacksonville with the *East Coast Champion* while another ACL locomotive set nearby awaits assignment. Shortly, the *Champ* departs (ABOVE), its long consist trailed by FEC tavern-observation car *Bay Biscayne.*—BARRIGER COLLECTION, ST. LOUIS MERCANTILE LIBRARY.

In December 1950, ACL acquired five twin-unit diners from Chesapeake & Ohio. ACL kitchen-dorm 126 and dining-room car *Winter Park* are at Tampa early in the 1950's. The non-fluted areas of the car sides were painted aluminum and letter and number boards were purple.—W. J. LENOIR VIA C. L. GOOLSBY.

mi Beach, Tampa, Sarasota, Bradenton, Clearwater and St. Petersburg. The immediate success of the venture encouraged the railroad to make Champion Vacation packages available yearround. With summer passenger loadings increasing, trains like the *East Coast Champion* could boast 13 cars even in the off season of fall, as evidenced in Consist of Note 6-C.

If Coast Line was still optimistic about the long-haul passenger business, some of its allies were playing it cautious. The first signs of disaffection came in the summer of 1955 when the Florida East Coast trustees insisted that the *Miamian* be scaled back to a winter-only run to save money. Likewise, before the winter of 1955-56, the New Haven opted out of through participation on the seasonal *Vacationer,* and that train was dropped from the timecard for good. The *East Coast Champion,* previously run as an all-coach companion to the *Florida Special* in winter and a coach/sleeper train in summer, picked up three 10-6 sleepers that winter to offset the loss of traffic from the *Vacationer.* The *Miamian* came back for the winter season of 1955-56 as a lightweight coach/ heavyweight sleeper affair. The *West Coast Champion* was enormous, of-

fering seven coaches, ten sleepers (including three heavyweights), diners and a tavern-lounge. The *Florida Special* consist offered more premium accommodations and fewer roomettes.

By 1954, the new 21-roomette cars purchased just five years earlier had vanished from the *Special.* In their place were leased 4-4-2's better suited to the demand for larger rooms. In the winter season of 1955-56, too, Seaboard was introducing more lightweight sleeping and coach-lounge cars on its Silver Fleet. Coast Line didn't counter this move, and there were probably several reasons for the decision. First, ACL was by nature still a conservative railroad. Second, passenger loadings seemed to encourage caution. The number of passengers transported in Coast Line assigned sleeping cars had dropped over 15 percent between 1953 and 1954. In 1955 it fell again —an additional 2 percent. Third, ACL felt that a Pullman room was a Pullman room. Whether that room was in a lightweight or a heavyweight was of little concern to the railroad.

It was of great concern to the customer. Over the years, passengers had even shown a marked preference for postwar lightweight accommodations versus prewar lightweight cars. Hence, Coast Line's reliance on heavyweights to cover peak period demand proved unpopular. The railroad remained unconvinced and grumbled that streamlining had consigned perfectly good heavyweight cars to pre-

RIGHT: ACL 2006 was part of a rolling-stock group built for the War Department by ACF in 1944 as hospital cars. The wrap-up of the war shortly after their construction rendered them surplus to the government, and many of them were sold to various roads. ACL purchased several in 1947 and rebuilt them into baggage-dormitories. They were regulars on the Florida streamliners. LOWER RIGHT: Coach 1082 was one of a series of heavyweights stripped down to the frame and remodeled by ACL's Emerson Shops. Finished in Coast Line's purple scheme, the cars ran in secondary trains and, on occasion, as back-up cars in *Champion* service.—BOTH PHOTOS, ACL VIA C. L. GOOLSBY.

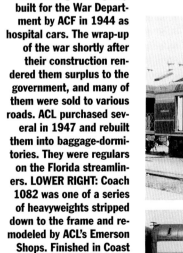

mature obsolescence. Having laid out a substantial investment just six years earlier, ACL decided to sit tight.

The decision may have hurt the railroad's chances at staying competitive. Whether by coincidence or not, from the mid 1950's through the early 1960's, Seaboard's passenger revenues remained stable while Coast Line's dropped.

CONSIST OF NOTE 6-C

FEC train 1, southbound *East Coast Champion*

Fort Lauderdale, Fla.
Oct. 20, 1954

Car	Type
[FEC 1013]	[E7A locomotive]
[FEC 1009]	[E7A locomotive]
PRR *Richelieu*	5-cmpt. buffet-lounge*
FEC 312	RPO (heavyweight)
FEC *New Smyrna Beach*	Coach
FEC *Bahamian*	10-6 sleeper
ACL *Clarendon County*	10-6 sleeper
ACL *Pass-A-Grille Beach*	6-d. bedroom buffet-lounge
FEC *Fort San Marco*	Diner
FEC *Chile*	10-6 sleeper
SOU 3786	Coach
FEC *Vero Beach*	Coach
FEC *Hypoluxo*	Coach
FEC *Lantana*	Coach
PRR 4049	Coach
FEC *Hobe Sound*	Tavern-observation

*Heavyweight, deadheading

Although ACL may have been reticent to invest in more new equipment, it had no such concerns about physical plant. Since 1943 a nearly continuous track improvement program had been underway. The result? Mile for mile, Atlantic Coast Line in the mid 1950's was one of the finest properties in the country. Effective Oct. 30, 1955, it set out to prove it. Operating speeds were increased to 100 mph in Automatic Train Control (ATC) territory for roller bearing-equipped trains (although speeds were later reduced to 90 mph to reduce wear).

Champ Davis' personal crusade to achieve those sustained 100-mph speeds on the Richmond-Jacksonville main line had been achieved through an outstanding program of maintenance and improvements. Line and grade revisions, heavier 132-pound rail, ballast and tie replacement (over 12 million of them in just ten years) had turned the Richmond-Jacksonville line into a racetrack, most of which was double track—in contrast to much of competitor Seaboard Air Line's route. Improved signaling went hand-in-hand with track improvements to allow the higher speeds. A modernized automatic block signaling system, ATC on most of the route and Centralized Traffic Control on specific single-track "choke points" allowed Coast Line's speedsters to take full advantage of its virtually sea-level main line. The railroad was so proud of the accomplishment that, instead of putting the usual artwork in its December 1955 timetable, it

Midwest-Florida trains provided important connections for some of ACL's New York-Florida runs. Here the northbound combined *Southland/Havana Special* steps out across the Manatee River at Bradenton, Fla., in March 1955. A single E6A is sufficient power for the heavyweight consist.—JIM SCRIBBINS VIA C. L. GOOLSBY.

The purple scheme was applied to Coast Line-owned heavyweight sleepers. Here, the 6-section, 6-double-bedroom Pullman *Poplar Terrace* is at Dallas, Texas, in December 1961. In the background, with the large Hertz sign, is the Texas School Book Depository, destined to become one of the most infamous buildings in America.—DE-GOYLER LIBRARY, SOUTHERN METHODIST UNIVERSITY.

Connecting trains fed passengers to the Florida fleet. Here at Wilmington, N.C., during the Dog Days of August 1957, Atlanta-Wilmington local train 54 behind E6A 517 arrives from Atlanta via Florence, S.C. Earlier in the morning, 54 had provided northbound connections to the New York-bound *Everglades* at Florence. —WILLIAM D. MIDDLETON.

published an unretouched photo of its main line.

The result of the upgrades was a wholesale shortening of schedules. Both the *East Coast Champion* and the *Florida Special* went onto 24-hour cardings New York to Miami. The *West Coast Champion* shortened its running time to St. Petersburg by 35 minutes. Likewise, the *Havana Special* and the *Miamian* benefitted from the improvements.

In the same year that Coast Line raised train speeds, it reached another milestone: complete dieselization. To haul its passenger fleet, Coast Line had been steadily purchasing EMD E-units, a thoroughbred well-suited to the railroad's level speedway. Between 1945 and 1948, thirty E7A&B units had arrived to bolster a tired fleet of prewar E3's and E6's. Again in the early 1950's, Coast Line had gone to EMD for its final E-units, this time seven E8A units which arrived in two orders in 1950 and 1953. Simply put, the E-units owned the Richmond-Jacksonville main.

Reliable diesel technology and skilled train handling in the cab, the tower and on the ground helped Coast Line's trains rack up a 95-98 percent on-time record, a distinct change from World War II when late northbound trains often had to be terminated at Washington, D.C., for fear of not reaching New York in time to be turned southbound (it happened on SAL, too). It was, in many respects, the zenith of ACL passenger operations, the culmination of its efforts and expenditures—new track, diesels and passenger cars—and a new postwar America hungry for travel.

Unfortunately, those travel-hungry Americans had for decades shown a marked preference for the private automobile. By the 1950's, better than 85 percent of all intercity travel was by auto. The railroads were counting on the new equipment and fast schedules to win and keep a portion of that market. It was not to be.

If there was such a thing as a defining moment in the struggle, it came on June 29, 1956. On that date, the Federal Aid Highway Act became law, and the nation turned its back on the passenger rail system, embarking on the construction of a brand-new 42,000-mile Federal Defense Highway System—the Interstate. Hundreds of billions of dollars of taxpayer monies would be spent for the system's construction, maintenance and operation, and well before it was finished, the railroads would know the game was up.

Some would go swiftly and others, like the Florida roads, would fight a seesaw battle, alternately encouraged, then discouraged by the numbers. Coast Line's yearly gross passenger revenues would skid from $28.5 million in 1946 to just $14.1 million in 1959. Nonetheless, throughout the 1950's there was still time to savor the American railroad passenger train at its best. And no one did it better than Coast Line. Proof positive could be had in the dining car. In the words of Champ Davis, "Good passenger service is the railroad's best . . . advertisement. With good dining-car service as a collateral, passenger service offers evidence of the character of those many unseen factors and services that enter into a railroad operation."

Coast Line wasn't about to disappoint. Within the confines of its sparkling diners, a fleet which included five high-capacity twin-unit cars purchased from the C&O in 1950, passengers could enjoy traditional Southern home cooking served as their train rocketed along track guaranteed to keep their complimentary coffee in the cup.

If you rode the *West Coast Champion* in the 1950's, you usually had a long walk to one of those twin-unit diners nestled mid-train. On the *East Coast Champion* there were generally two single-unit diners, a first-class dining car amidst the sleepers and a coach-class diner tucked in with the chair cars. The *Florida Special* of this era typically offered two 36-seat Pullman-Standard-built cars with distinctive angled tables. Later, the twin units would occasionally appear on the *Special*.

The china was, by now, Coast Line's Carolina pattern, a plain design with two medium gray stripes on an ivory body color. The silverware and hollowware were in what was known as the Zephyr pattern with ACL stamped in gothic-style letters.

The formality of the diner itself, arrayed in snowy white linen and gleaming tableware, was matched by the decorum of the passengers. America in the 1950's and early 1960's was still a nation which dressed for dinner. Jacket and tie for men was the norm even on those trains which catered to the tourist, but it was especially the case in the first-class diner. Patrons waiting in line to be seated (there were always lines during the winter season) were treated to enticing aromas, harbingers of better things to come—like North Carolina Country Ham with Eggs for breakfast or Southern Fried Chicken or Charcoal Broiled Sirloin for dinner.

Coast Line was visibly proud of its dining service, going so far as to bottle and sell its own salad dressing aboard the cars. The pride went beyond salad dressing, however, and lasted far longer than on most other

American roads. ACL took its dining operation seriously, refusing to downgrade service while introducing cost-saving meal options, like the American Plan.

Like all other roads, ACL was losing money on dining service. Yet, as late as 1962—when once-great passenger hauler Southern Pacific was introducing "Automat" cars with food vending machines—ACL hired one of the top restauranteurs in the country, Edwin Andraeus, as its general supervisor. A veteran of the Hamburg America Steamship company and some of the finest private clubs in America, Andraeus was given the job of taking a good dining service and making it better.

The history of Coast Line dining service was one of longstanding cooperation with partners FEC and RF&P. As far back as 1912, upon the Pullman Company's announcement of its intentions of quitting the dining car (but not meal service) business, the roads had entered into informal agreements for joint operation of dining-cars. At that point, ACL had purchased the cars and charged its partners a fee based on mileage for their operating expense. Later, FEC would purchase its own diners operating them in through service between New York, Washington and Miami or Key West. The cooperative arrangements between the roads would be based solely on a memorandum of understanding. This agreement, dating from February 1929, would govern the roads' dining operations through the streamlined era.

Typically, in the heavyweight era, FEC had about six diners in through winter service to equalize its mileage share. In addition, it provided diners for ser-

FEC locals provided connections to the Florida Fleet at Jacksonville. Here, E7A 1009 has a grip on head-end-heavy southbound local train 5 at St. Augustine, Fla., in December 1957. This was an all-day, all-stops train that took nearly 12 hours to make its way down from Jacksonville to Miami. It connected with the southbound *East Coast Champion* at Jacksonville and delivered connecting passengers to FEC stations at which the *Champ* sped through with nary a wisp of brakeshoe smoke.
—WILLIAM J. HUSA JR.

For travel fun without travel strain—Travel on a *Coast Line Train*

THERE IS NO MORE COMFORTABLE TRAIN RIDE THAN OVER THE RAILS OF ATLANTIC COAST LINE RAILROAD

A quick look at these illustrations will tell you why. And they also can help you visualize the travel comfort and fun you have as you speed to and from the World's Greatest Vacationland—regardless of weather—via the fastest train service between the East and Florida!

NEW YORK · MIAMI NOW ONLY 24 HOURS

ATLANTIC COAST LINE RAILROAD

RIGHT: ACL 54-seat coach 228 was one of a series of 25 similar cars delivered by Pullman-Standard in winter 1949-50 to Coast Line, RF&P and PRR. The cars formed the backbone of the postwar *Champion* fleet and, according to the railroad, offered the most-comfortable ride of any coaches in the fleet.

ABOVE: FEC received three 56-seat coaches from Pullman-Standard similar to the ACL order shown in the top photo. The FEC cars—the interior above is that of the *Lantana*—offered slightly different accommodations than their ACL, PRR and RF&P counterparts.
—PULLMAN TECHNOLOGY.

vice exclusively on its own line. In the streamlined era, FEC contributed one diner, the *Fort Pierce*, in the first set of cars for the *Champion* and, after World War II, the road would add another three Budd-built cars—*Fort Dallas*, *Fort Matanzas* and *Fort San Marco*—to the *Champion* pool and two P-S 36-seat cars—*Fort Drum* and *Fort Ribault*—to the *Florida Special* pool. RF&P would contribute its own Pullman-Standard diner, *Henrico*, to the *Florida Special* pool.

Although the equipment was contributed to equalize expenses, ACL was the operating railroad. Coast Line even handled the operation of FEC local dining service for a time. Throughout the streamlined era, crews working aboard ACL, RF&P or FEC diners in through New York-Florida service were provided by ACL. In the winter when more cars and service was needed, extra men came from roads like the Baltimore & Ohio and the Pennsylvania to fill out the ros-

ABOVE RIGHT: New 36-seat diners arrived from Pullman-Standard in the winter and spring of 1950. Two of this type were regularly assigned to each *Florida Special*. Here, ACL's *Moultrie* poses at Pullman-Standard in Chicago on March 14, 1950.—PULLMAN TECHNOLOGY.
RIGHT: The dining rooms of these cars were a departure from the norm, with angled tables and handy built-in settees (as part of the booth seating) between the windows to hold water pitchers and salt and pepper shakers. Bulkhead mirrors, with etched designs, enhanced an illusion of spaciousness. It was a time when the tradition of fine restaurant dining was routinely extended to rail travel.—ACL.

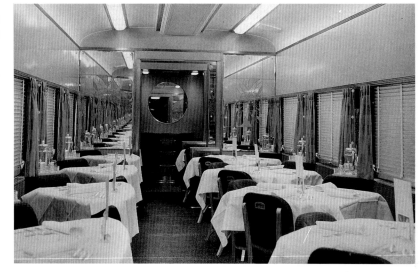

ters of stewards, cooks and waiters.

The standard crew consisted of four cooks, a steward and six waiters. The twin-unit diners featured a larger crew. As with some other roads like PRR, Coast Line established the practice of "swinging" crews between trains to save costly downtime. Even so, there were crew bases at New York, Washington, Jacksonville and Miami where provisions and tableware were stocked and replenished as well.

Despite its Deep South roots, the Coast Line larder was surprisingly middle-of-the-road. There were some regional specialties. Fresh Florida fruit abounded on the menu as did marmalade, a Florida staple. "Hush Puppies," a fried dough concoction that is still a Deep South tradition, appeared for a time. Seafood made a regular appearance with entree's like Crab Meat Norfolk and Florida Fried Shrimp. Lunches featured some items long out of favor today, such as Welsh Rarebit, a Coast Line specialty.

The dining-car experience is central to understanding what it was like to ride the Coast Line in those (if you will) salad days, but the streamliners themselves had unique personalities, too. The *Florida Special* was, by virtue of its all-Pullman status, a more formal operation. Sipping Manhattans and playing cards back in the bedroom-lounge were the folks who wintered in Palm Beach. Tourists and college kids traveled in coach on the *Champion*s, asked questions about the prices on the menu and, in general, behaved like tourists. Often, *Champion* clientele included school groups or other group-related moves.

Not surprisingly, a large percentage of these travelers were bound for Florida or returning home from there. The schedules of Coast Line's top trains catered to this market. With early afternoon departures from New York and morning departures from Florida, the fleet breezed through most of Virginia, North Carolina, South Carolina and Georgia in the dead of night.

Southward, after the night sprint through the coastal piedmont, the fleet descended on Jacksonville, where Jacksonville Terminal switch engines split up some of the trains. Both the *East Coast Champion* and *Florida Special* were handed over to FEC for the arrow-like run down the East Coast of Florida. FEC's double-track route was dotted with quaint wooden depots, such as at Hobe Sound, and Spanish-style beauties like the stations at Boca Raton and Hollywood. The FEC main bisected areas of tropical beauty which still graced the east coast of Florida in the 1950's as well as the urban sprawl that would displace it.

FEC's station at Miami was not, as would have been expected, an imposing big-city terminal with Roman columns and cavernous concourses, but a modest white, wooden-plank depot dating from 1912. This architectural shortfall posed a bit of a problem for the marketing people, and FEC publicity views taken of trains at Miami station seemed to imply that the skyscraper behind the trains (in reality the Dade County Courthouse) was the terminal. Nonetheless, the country-like depot was, at times, incredibly busy. Those who knew it best, loved the station for its history and hustle and bustle, but the love

LOWER LEFT: *Clover Castle* was one of several heavyweight Pullmans purchased from Pullman by ACL after World War II. It illustrates the exotic paint scheme applied to many of the road's flat-sided cars.—JOHN PLATT VIA PETER V. TILP. BELOW: Cousins to the FEC 14-2 sleepers illustrated on page 104 were the *River* series cars of ACL, PRR and RF&P. *Fairfax River*, complete with full-width diaphragms, ACL-inspired purple letterboards and black roof, gleams for its builder's portrait at the American Car & Foundry plant in Berwick, Pa. —ACF INDUSTRIES.

didn't extend to the general populace, which considered the depot an eyesore and pressed for its eradication. Nevertheless, FEC kept the station intact until September 1963, after the big strike had rendered it vacant of New York-bound streamliners.

At Jacksonville, the *West Coast Champion* was split into two sections, one for Tampa and the other for St. Petersburg. All sections of the *West Coast Champion* remained on home rails all the way to their terminals, tracing sometimes circuitous paths along portions of

ACL's fascinating network of steel covering western Florida. The Tampa section kept the New York diner and headed for the west coast via Winter Park and Orlando over a direct, well-maintained line featuring reasonably fast running times. At Lakeland, a winter-season-only 10-6 sleeper from New York was pulled from this train and matched with a local combine and coach for the run tracing two secondary ACL lines for some 150 miles to Fort Meyers and Naples near the northern boundary of the Everglades. In 1966, a

LEFT: Coast Line's *East Coast Champion* is pictured in its prime in this wonderful night scene at Richmond's Broad Street Station in August 1957. The A-B-A set of ACL E-units, led by veteran E6A 523, would race the train through the night over one of the best railroad properties in North America. During the small hours of the day at the ACL division point of Florence, S.C. (BELOW), the steeds would be serviced. This set of E-units was in charge of a 20-car *East Coast Champion*. Tight schedules and fast-running meant no-nonsense maintenance. ABOVE: Working RPO's were part of the *East Coast Champion*'s revenue base well into the 1960's. Tonight, this purple RPO is assigned to Wilmington-Atlanta train 55 and is being worked at Florence, where passengers from No. 55 will transfer to the Florida-bound *Everglades* out of New York.—ALL PHOTOS, WILLIAM D. MIDDLETON.

through New York-Naples coach was added.

Usually hauled by ACL F-units, the compact Naples train was a complete change from the 20-car *Champion* through passengers had ridden the night before. Creaking over wooden trestles, scaring snowy egrets into flight and offering glimpses of palm trees galore, the little branch run showed travelers a Florida worlds away from the bustle of the east coast.

Once in Tampa, the main section of the *West Coast Champion* was split again, with half terminating in

Tampa and several cars continuing on to Bradenton and Sarasota. The Bradenton-Sarasota train was required to make a two-mile back-up move out of Tampa Union Station to Uceta before proceeding down the 50-mile-long branch to Sarasota.

Owned in conjunction with the Seaboard Air Line, Tampa Union Station was an important terminal for ACL. The palm-fronded red brick depot was an eight-track stub-end facility. Its tropical flavor was accentuated by a widespread use of tile and its Span-

TOP: By the onset of the 1960's, FEC's vivid diesel scheme was beginning to show the effects of the hot Florida sun. Indeed, FEC's future in the rail-passenger market was but a couple of years away from virtual ruin by a massive strike that would alter all of the road's operations for years to come. But, on this fine morning of June 24, 1960, the *East Coast Champion* looks about as healthy as ever with a consist that stretches nearly to the vanishing point of this scene at Miami station. The wooden depot there (ABOVE) was usually overshadowed by the Dade County Court-house, but in its own right it was an attractive building, perhaps more suitable to a rural setting.
—BOTH PHOTOS, JOHN DZIOBKO JR.

ish-style waiting room. Outside were a metal-roofed patio and covered platforms. To the visitor, Tampa Union's most memorable features may have been the palms which graced the patio area or the distinctive wrought iron train gates past which thousands walked as part of the experience of a Florida vacation.

The St. Petersburg section of the *West Coast Champion* was the kid sister in everything from equipment to routing. Usually, this train got an add-on diner—or at times a cafe-lounge—at Jacksonville before heading for its namesake city on a meandering course using trackage quite unlike the Tampa line. Out of Jacksonville it headed cross state for Burnetts Lake on what was ostensibly a through line to Naples via Dunellon and Lakeland. But at Burnetts Lake, the train turned southeast onto another branch to reach the college town of Gainesville and then Ocala and Leesburg. At Croom, population 60, the train re-entered the Jacksonville-Naples line and headed south nine miles to Trilby where it turned west onto the line for Tarpon Springs, Clearwater and St. Petersburg.

The route itself offered a back country tour of Florida. With the exception of Gainesville and Ocala, most of the line linked small towns with quaint stations like the 1927 vintage white-clapboard affair at Trilby or Dunedin's trim stucco depot.

To reach the Clearwater depot, trains had to vie with automobile traffic on a section of street-running—a paradox to the 100-mph flight the night previous on ACL's double-track main down the Atlantic coastal plains. For much of the streamlined era, the road's St. Petersburg depot was a stucco, tile-roofed mission-style building, like many others in Florida. The street-level station with its "bell" tower, neatly trimmed hedges and palms was a fixture in the downtown area. The business community surrounded the station, hemming it in with local small-town charm, a reminder of just how tiny St. Petersburg seemed in the 1950's with a population less than 100,000. In 1963, ACL built a new station.

Aside from the inroads of the automobile in the 1950's, other notable events took place to influence ACL's Florida services. On Aug. 1, 1957, Champ Davis retired as CEO of the railroad after a 64-year career. By his hard work and determination, Davis had built the railroad into one of the finest properties in the country. Although freight revenues were the bread and butter of the company, Davis was enormously proud of Coast Line's passenger operations. Example: In December 1955, despite a harrowing schedule as top man on the railroad, Davis had time to bombard FEC management with a series of personal letters when he learned the railroad was tacking local Miami-Jacksonville coaches onto his beloved all-Pullman *Florida Special*. FEC curtailed the practice.

Davis had guided Coast Line in the expansion of streamliner service and had given those trains one of the finest physical plants in the country to operate over. In the tough times of the Depression, a world war and new competition, it was no mean feat. It can be said with little exaggeration that, as a bachelor, the hard-working Davis had been "married" to his railroad. If that were so, its streamliners had been his children. For the future, passenger operations would be dictated more by the bottom line than the heart.

That bottom line was getting tougher to meet. In a slump for much of the mid-1950's, Coast Line passenger earnings for early 1958 dropped off markedly, the result of a national recession and a Florida deep freeze which hurt traffic. Then, on Dec. 10, 1958, history was made with the introduction of the first regularly scheduled jet airliner service in the U.S. It's routing? New York to Miami via National Airlines.

Times were indeed changing for Florida-bound passenger trains. While ACL's Northeast-Florida service had held its own, services between the Midwest and Florida were being signficantly reduced. On Nov. 29, 1957, the Chicago-Miami *Dixieland*, which had been completely streamlined just three years earlier, was discontinued. Likewise, the *Southland* out of Detroit and Chicago ceased operation south of Jacksonville on Dec. 1. The *Southland*'s discontinuance meant that the Chicago-Miami streamliners *City of Miami* and *South Wind* would begin relaying their West Coast cars via the *West Coast Champion* from Jacksonville south. In addition, a Detroit-St. Petersburg 6-6-4 sleeper was now being handed over to the *West Coast Champ* by the *Dixie Flyer* at Jacksonville.

That *West Coast Champion* became a very large consist in the winter of 1957-58. With at least 19 regularly scheduled cars between Washington and Jacksonville, the train was too long to handle its winter-season New York-Naples sleepers. Hence, for that season only, the *Florida Special* did the job, carrying two New York-Naples sleepers, a 10-6 and a 6-double-bedroom lounge. In this way, the *Special* helped keep the *Champ*'s consist at a manageable size while increasing it own lounge capacity. At Jacksonville, the Naples sleepers were shifted to the Jacksonville-Tampa section of the *West Coast Champion*, giving that train a Pullman lounge.

Passenger revenues continued to decline in 1958 and 1959, but ACL didn't lose faith. Instead it continued to add amenities, introducing passenger service representatives on the *East* and *West Coast Champion*s in January 1958 to oversee the comfort of coach passengers. Likewise, American Plan meals were intro-

duced in February 1959, offering passengers a choice of several entrees at a fixed, low price through coupons handed out in advance. Finally, the road offered a "Travel Now, Pay Later" credit plan in conjunction with banks at 15 principal points on the railroad.

Although the marketing effort was first rate, the fleet had begun to look a little ragged as off-line cars filled out Coast Line consists. The *Florida Special* was the worst offender, having metamorphisized completely into what, from the exterior, looked like a multi-colored circus train with a hodge-podge of sleepers of varying pedigree. Fortunately, the train was still uniformly excellent on the inside.

On its re-equipping in 1949 and for the first few years of the 1950's, the *Special* had been a solid consist of ACL/FEC/RF&P/PRR sleepers purchased explicitly for Coast Line service. Slowly, that had changed as the 1950's wore on and the emphasis shifted to provide more premium room accommodations to meet demand. This required more use of off-line "extra" cars which had been idled for the winter by non-Florida-related carriers. The Consist of Note 6-D

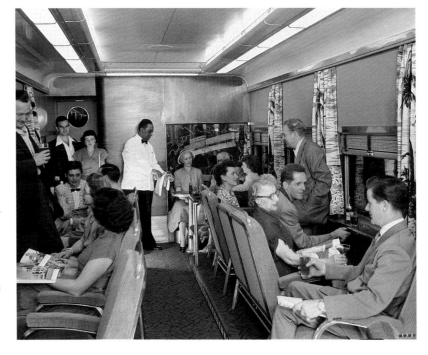

BOTTOM: RF&P contributed one 6-double-bedroom lounge to the *Florida Special/Champion* pool. Named *Colonial Beach*, the car is pictured wearing the paint scheme of purple letterboards and silver gray lettering it would carry until after ACL changed its car colors in 1959. It and the sister cars were delivered in 1950. BELOW: Lounge section of the ACL/RF&P/FEC sleeper lounges featured a raised-floor seating area and seats that faced outward.—BOTH PHOTOS, ACF INDUSTRIES.

CONSIST OF NOTE 6-D
Florida Special
En route on the PRR
January 1959
All cars lightweight

Car	Type
[PRR 4903]	[GG1 electric locomotive]
FEC *St. Johns River*	Baggage-dorm
AT&SF *Hualpai*	4--4-2 sleeper
UP *Verdugo*	4-4-2 sleeper
UP *Palos Verdes*	4-4-2 sleeper
PRR *Imperial Meadows*	4-4-2 sleeper
ACL *Virginia Beach*	6-double-bedroom lounge
ACL *Plant City*	36-seat diner
PRR *Sturgeon Rapids*	10-6 sleeper
FEC *Havana*	10-6 sleeper
C&O *City of Alderson*	10-6 sleeper
PRR *Fairless Hills*	10-6 sleeper
RF&P *Henrico*	36-seat diner
FEC *Bahamian*	10-6 sleeper
FEC *Brazil*	10-6 sleeper
ACL *Putnam County*	10-6 sleeper
GN *Big Horn Pass*	6-rmtte, 5-d.br., 2-cmpt. sleeper
UP *Pacific Forest*	10-6 sleeper

ABOVE: Atlantic Coast Line diner *Greenville* (P-S, 1950) was reconfigured as a diner-lounge in the 1960's, with 24 table seats and eight lounge seats. As was the case when it was a 36-seat diner, half the tables seated two patrons and the other half four. To make eight lounge seats, ACL simply removed two tables; the built-in wall-side booths became the lounge seats.—ACL. BELOW: An *East Coast Champion* menu from March 1960 featured American Plan dinners for the cost-conscious traveler.—WILLIAM F. HOWES JR. COLLECTION.

from January 1959 (above right), the last season the *Special* ran as an all-Pullman operation, illustrates the point. The consist contains cars built for the 1938 Santa Fe *Chief*, UP's 1941 *City of Los Angeles*, the 1950 GN *Empire Builder*, Pennsylvania Railroad's postwar "Blue Ribbon" fleet and numerous other car orders.

Even on Coast Line's own fleet, new colors were appearing. Perhaps wary of the escalating costs of maintaining its trademark scheme of purple and silver gray, ACL changed its locomotive scheme to basic black with silver lettering and yellow stripes. Stainless-steel passenger cars lost their distinctive purple letterboards in favor of the all-stainless-steel look, with black roofs and lettering. For passenger cars, the change officially became effective on April 20, 1959, and would extend to PRR and RF&P cars in the Florida pool as well (FEC cars had always fit the mold).

More drastic changes were in the works come win-

ter. Starting with the 1959-1960 winter season, the *Florida Special* became a coach/sleeper operation. Although the train had enjoyed an enviable record as an all-Pullman operation dating from 1888—and had been considered by many to be an equal to the great *20th Century Limited*—it could *not* be said that the addition of coaches broke an inviolate tradition of first-class operation. Several times during its career the *Special* had, either by design or happenstance, carried chair cars. What was different this time was that the train was virtually swapping identities with the *Miamian*. For the 1959-1960 season, the *Florida Special* went to a morning departure schedule from New York. The seasonal *Miamian*, previously Coast Line's morning-departure coach-and-sleeper operation, regained its former all-Pullman status and moved to an afternoon departure. Most likely, Coast Line wanted to bolster its morning departure slot with a famous, well-patronized train, thereby putting it into a better competitive position against Seaboard's morning Florida departure, the *Silver Star*. Since this was essentially the only Coast Line train departing New York on a morning carding (the only other was the *Everglades*, by this time a virtual milk run), it became necessary to offer coach service. This "new" *Florida Special* was still a wild mixture of equipment, as Consist of Note 6-E on the following page shows.

Never short of marketing ideas and drawing on a long tradition of on-board promotions, Coast Line introduced fashion shows on the *Florida Special* in 1959. It was the precursor of a renewed marketing campaign which would center on the *Special's* 75th anniversary a few years hence.

But it was more than just fashion shows. Coast Line was putting the passenger first in many different ways. The decade of the 1960's dawned with the railroad taking still more concrete steps to lure and keep

---

EAST COAST CHAMPION

Car in Charge of _____

PATRONS are respectfully requested to write their orders on meal checks, and pay only on presentation of such checks. Waiters are forbidden to accept verbal orders. Please notify Steward in charge of car if the service is not entirely to your satisfaction.

American Plan Dinners
No Substitutions
2.25
Choice of Soups or Juices

BAKED SUGAR CURED HAM, RAISIN SAUCE
SLICED TURKEY WITH ASPARAGUS SPEARS, AU GRATIN
CRAB MEAT NORFOLK OR FILLET OF OCEAN PERCH

Snowflake Potatoes   Brussels Sprouts in Butter
Rolls   Assorted Breads
Choice of Beverage   Bread and Butter Pudding

Plate portion of salad served with these meals, 30 cents extra

For Children • Under 12 years of age, choice of American Plan Dinners with reduced portions. 1.10

Table d'Hote Dinner
Please Write On Check "Table D'Hote Dinner" and Each Item Desired
Choice Of

Cream of Celery Soup
Mixed Fruit Cocktail   Crab Meat Cocktail .30 Extra
Consomme, Julienne

Florida Orange Juice
Celery and Olives
Chilled Tomato Juice

The Amount Shown After Each Entree Denotes Price Of Meal

★ TENDER BEEF POT ROAST, BROWN GRAVY, SPICED APPLE 3.00
★ SIRLOIN STEAK, BROILED OVER CHARCOAL 5.25
FRENCH FRIED ONION RINGS

Snowflake Potatoes   Selection of Two
Brussels Sprouts in Butter   French Fried Potatoes
Condied Carolina Sweets
Succotash

Spring Vegetable Salad, "Coast Line" Dressing
Dinner Rolls   Assorted Breads
Choice of Beverage and Dessert

★ Guests holding American Plan Dinner Coupons will be allowed 2.25 on Table d'Hote selection

An extra charge of 50 cents per person will be made for meals served on this car. This service is subject to delay when dining car is busy.

A La Carte

Soups and Appetizers

Cream of Celery Soup .40   Spanish Bean Soup .40   Consomme, Julienne .40
Celery and Olives .40   Olives .40   Iced Florida Celery .40
Fruit or Vegetable Juice .25   Florida Orange Juice .25   Mixed Fruit Cocktail .65
Crab Meat Cocktail .85

Suggestions

Cold Salmon, Tartar Sauce, Potato Salad, Sliced Tomatoes 1.85
Welsh Rarebit, Chef's Salad, Dry Toast, Beverage 1.75
Sardines in Oil, Potato Salad, Sliced Tomatoes 1.60
Vegetable Plate with Poached Egg 1.45

Sliced Tomatoes .55   Turkey Salad 1.65   Lettuce and Tomato Salad .70
Tomato Stuffed with Turkey Salad 1.60   Tuna Fish Salad 1.50   Hearts of Lettuce .60

Bread

Assorted Bread .25   Toast or Rolls .25   Ry-Krisp .10
Milk Toast .65   Cream Toast .85

Desserts

Blueberry Pie .35   Baked Apple .50   Ice Cream, Wafers .35
Florida Grapefruit .30   Stewed Prunes .40
Swiss Gruyere Cheese .45   Blue Cheese .45   Camembert Cheese .45

Beverages

Coffee, Postum, Cocoa, Sanka, Tea .35   Milk, Buttermilk .35

You Will Like Our New Specialty
Southern Fried Chicken
Served in a Basket
with
French Fried Potatoes
Mixed Salad
Rolls   Beverage
2.25

The State of Pennsylvania assesses a sales and use tax of 4% on all meals, food items, cigars, playing cards and other articles, which must be collected from the buyer.
The State of North Carolina assesses a sales tax of 3% on all meals and food items, which must be collected from buyer.
The States of Florida, Georgia and South Carolina assess a tax of 3% on all sales, which must be collected from the buyer.

SUGGESTIONS FOR THE BETTERMENT OF THE SERVICE ARE INVITED
J. R. Heddleston, Supt. Dining Cars, Atlantic Coast Line R. R. Co., Washington, D. C.

Back-to-back E7A's hurtle north with a 16-car *East Coast Champion* in August 1957.—DAVID W. SALTER.

new customers. In Lakeland, Fla., a new station was opened on Sept. 1, 1960. Plans were under way for new facilities at Fort Meyers, Savannah and St. Petersburg to name a few. Passenger revenues were up 4.29 percent over 1959.

The railroad was also in the process of establishing a central reservation bureau in its Jacksonville offices. Going into operation in March 1961, the office would be one of the most advanced reservation systems in the country, offering passengers faster service and saving the railroad money by helping allocate sleeper and coach space more accurately.

By far, though, the biggest news of 1960 was the proposed merger of Atlantic Coast Line with long-time rival Seaboard. Both lines, as well as an outside consulting firm that had studied the issue, agreed that the merger of the largely redundant properties would

---

CONSIST OF NOTE 6-E

FEC train 88, *Florida Special*

Miami, Fla.
Feb. 22, 1960

Car	Type
[FEC 1022]	[E7A locomotive]
[FEC 1053]	[E7B locomotive]
[FEC 1003]	[E6A locomotive]
ACL 586	Baggage
Glen Blair	6-3 sleeper (heavyweight)
PRR *Imperial Range*	4-4-2 sleeper
UP *North Beach*	4-4-2 sleeper
FEC *Brazil*	10-6 sleeper
ACL *Myrtle Beach*	6-double-bedroom lounge
RF&P *King and Queen*	10-6 sleeper
NKP *City of Erie*	10-6 sleeper
C&O *Yorktowne*	10-6 sleeper
ACL *Port Tampa*	Diner
ACL 125	Kitchen-dorm
C&O *City of Grand Rapids*	10-6 sleeper
FEC *Argentina*	10-6 sleeper
ACL 246	Coach
FEC *St. Augustine*	Coach
FEC *Salerno*	Coach
FEC *Titusville*	Coach
ACL 203	Coach
ACL 256	Tavern-observation (sq. end)

CONSIST OF NOTE 6-F

Miamian

En route on the PRR
December 1960

Car	Type
[PRR No. unknown]	[GG1 electric locomotive]
FEC *Homestead*	54-seat coach
FEC *Boca Raton*	60-seat coach
RF&P 803	54-seat coach
RF&P 806	54-seat coach
ACL *Florida*	Lounge (rebuilt heavyweight)
PRR 4470	Diner (rebuilt heavyweight)
PRR *Illinois Rapids*	10-roomette, 6-d.br. sleeper
GN *Hanging Glacier*	16-dplx rmtte, 4-d.br. sleeper
GN *Sheyenne River*	4-sec.,1-cmpt., 7-dplx. rmtte, 3-d.br. sleeper
NYC *Suspension Bridge*	4-4-2 sleeper
NYC *Elkhart County*	13-double-bedroom sleeper

ABOVE: Beginning in late 1957, the *West Coast Champion* began handling through West Coast cars off the daily *Dixie Flyer* and the alternating-days *City of Miami* and *South Wind* south of Jacksonville. In this idyllic scene of northbound 92, the Tampa section of the *West Coast Champ* crossing the Palm River near Tampa, we can see that it is a *City of Miami* day. Despite that train's name, it fielded a through sleeper and coaches to several West Coast points, and its handsome brown-and-orange cars stood out even more than ACL's purple equipment. FP7 850 leads the colorful train. ABOVE RIGHT: ACL train 291, the *Champion* connection for Naples, scampers along north of Bartow, Fla., with its through coach, sleeper and local combine.—BOTH PHOTOS, DAVID W. SALTER.

yield a leaner company, better able to meet the competition. Estimates predicted the new combined carrier could save as much as $38 million every year. With the unanimous support of board members and stockholders, a merger plan was submitted to the Interstate Commerce Commission on July 22, 1960. Due to litigation, the merger would be delayed for several years.

For the winter season of 1960-61, the *Miamian* returned, again with a changed look. A coach/sleeper operation once more, it too carried a bevy of off-line cars, as shown on page 119 in Consist of Note 6-F.

As evidenced by *Florida Special* and *Miamian* consists of the period, ACL continued to use foreign-road cars to meet the demands for larger rooms. Leasing cars from Pullman while home-road cars stood idle due to inappropriate floor plans was counterproduc-

tive, so ACL sent its six ACF-built *River*-series cars (14 roomettes, 2 drawing rooms) to Pullman-Standard for rebuild into 7-double-bedroom 2-drawing-room cars. By the summer of 1961, three of the cars, renamed *Surf Bird*, *Blue Bird* and *Humming Bird*, were holding down a New York-Tampa/Sarasota car line in the *West Coast Champion*. The other three cars—*Honey Bird*, *Jay Bird* and *Rice Bird*—would all be back by autumn assigned to a New York-St. Petersburg car line on the same train.

More cars were rebuilt in 1962 with the same goal in mind. In July, sleeper *Magnolia Gardens* was outshopped by Pullman. Originally the 21-roomette car *Parris Island*, the new incarnation featured 11 double bedrooms. Alas, it was the only rebuild of its type on the railroad, and the rest of the 21-roomette cars

would remain in their original configurations and largely relegated to white-elephant status.

Then in mid 1962, six prewar 4-double-bedroom, 4-compartment, 2-drawing-room cars in the *Bridge* series, veterans of New York Central's *20th Century Limited,* were purchased. The cars were completely rebuilt on the interior. The result was a sleeper with a unique floorplan: 4 compartments and 4 drawing rooms, with all bathrooms enclosed ("annexed"). The smooth-sided Pullmans were finished in a dull aluminum with black roofs, underbody and lettering. Destined for a *Florida Special* assignment, the rebuilt room cars arrived on the property in October 1962.

December would mark the beginning of the 75th anniversary for the *Florida Special.* Coast Line planned a show-stopping anniversary season train. The first order of business was to bring back some semblance of consistency to the liverics of regularly assigned cars. An edict came down from top management calling for all cars assigned to the *Special* for the anniversary season to be finished in standard ACL passenger "colors"— stainless steel with black roof and lettering. The practice even spilled over to affect six ACL-assigned PRR *Imperial*-series 4-4-2's (*Imperial Park, Pass, Plateau, Point, Range* and *Terrace*) which were painted in silver from October 1962 through May 1963 just for the occasion.

Original intentions were for these cars to hold down regular line assignments in the *Special*, but at the last minute they were replaced by cars in the *Bird* series. As such, the *Imperials* were often found on the *East* and *West Coast Champions* as well as being available as extra cars for the *Florida Special.* In either case, they still matched.

The Pullman Company assigned the following sleeping cars to the *Florida Special* for the 75th anniversary season:

Sleeping cars in assignment to the *Florida Special* 12/14/62-4/21/63

Owner	Car name	Type
ACL	*Bryan County*	10-6
ACL	*Halifax County*	10-6
ACL	*Volusia County*	10-6
ACL	*Blue Bird*	7-2
ACL	*Honey Bird*	7-2
ACL	*Humming Bird*	7-2
ACL	*Jay Bird*	7-2
ACL	*Rice Bird*	7-2
ACL	*Surf Bird*	7-2
ACL	*Cape Fear River*	4-4
ACL	*Kissimmee River*	4-4
ACL	*Manatee River*	4-4
ACL	*Berkeley County*	10-6
ACL	*Colleton County*	10-6
RF&P	*Hanover County*	10-6
FEC	*Havana*	10-6
PRR	*Hudson County*	10-6
ACL	*Osceola County*	10-6
FEC	*Magnolia*	6-d.-bedroom lounge
FEC	*Oleander*	6-d.-bedroom lounge
ACL	*Ponte Vedra Beach*	6-d.-bedroom lounge
ACL	*Ortega River*	4-4
ACL	*Savannah River*	4-4
ACL	*Suwanee River*	4-4
ACL	*Polk County*	10-6
ACL	*Prince George County*	10-6
ACL	*Seminole County*	10-6

A consist for one of the *Florida Special*s of the season is shown in Consist of Note 6-G.

Coast Line planned a once-in-a-lifetime train to commemorate the original *Florida Special.* After all, just surviving for 75 years in the face of government-sponsored competition like a national highway system and the jet airplane was something to celebrate. For

E6A 508 leading No. 92, the *West Coast Champion* (Tampa section) had been moving *Champions* for nearly a quarter century when photographer Salter recorded the train backing into Jacksonville Union Station in September 1965. Note that it is a *City of Miami* day; the brown-and-orange cars— a sleeper toward the head end and a coach at the rear—painted for the famous Illinois Central train will be pulled from the consist here at Jacksonville for transfer into the the main section of the *City,* coming up the Seaboard from its namesake. ACL train 192, the St. Petersburg section of the *West Coast Champ,* due into Jacksonville only a few minutes after No. 92, also carried through cars for the *City of Miami.*—DAVID W. SALTER.

bingo, horse-racing games, group sing-a-longs and fashion shows brought hyperactivity to the recreation car. Even radio/telephone service was available. If sleeping-car passengers wanted some peace and quiet, there was always the Pullman lounge.

The anniversary-season marketing efforts paid off. Such luminaries as Art Buchwald and NBC's *Today* Show featured the anniversary train in their coverage. Standing-room-only crowds were common in the recreation car, and the reserved dining-car service for Pullman passengers proved very successful. The ultimate tribute came from the passengers themselves who flocked to the train and weren't shy about telling ACL how much they liked the experience. As one Coast Line executive put it, "We have had more compliments on this train than any other we have ever operated." That was pretty heady stuff in an era of overall industry decline. The *Special's* premier companion trains enjoyed continued patronage, too, as the winter season 1962-63 consists attest:

East Coast Champion consist
effective Dec. 14, 1962

Baggage-dorm	NYP-MIA
10-6 sleeper	WAS-MIA
54-seat coach	WAS-MIA
54-seat coach	NYP-JAX
Diner	NYP-JAX or MIA
54-seat coach	NYP-MIA*
54-seat coach	NYP-MIA*
54-seat coach	NYP-MIA
52-seat coach	NYP-MIA
Tavern-lounge	NYP-MIA
54-seat coach	NYP-MIA
54-seat coach	NYP-MIA
6-d.-bedroom lounge	NYP-MIA
4-4-2 sleeper	NYP-MIA
Diner	NYP-MIA
4-4-2 sleeper	NYP-MIA
10-6 sleeper	NYP-MIA
10-6 sleeper	NYP-MIA
10-6 sleeper	NYP-MIA**
10-6 sleeper	NYP-JAX

*Operated only on specific dates
**Did not operate 12/23-25, 1/6-1/31

West Coast Champion consist
effective Dec. 14, 1962

10-6 sleeper	WAS-STP
10-6 sleeper	WAS-SRA
10-6 sleeper	WAS-JAX
Tavern-lounge	WAS-TPA
46-seat coach	WAS-TPA
54-seat coach	NYP-STP
54-seat coach	NYP-STP
Diner	NYP-STP
54-seat coach	NYP-TPA
54-seat coach	NYP-SRA
10-6 sleeper	NYP-TPA
10-6 sleeper	NYP-TPA
Diner	NYP-TPA
4-4-2 sleeper	NYP-STP
10-6 sleeper	NYP-STP
6-d.-bedroom lounge	NYP-STP
10-6 sleeper	NYP-NAP
Local coach	LAK-NAP
4-4-2 sleeper	NYP-SRA
Southbound only	
10-6 sleeper	NYP-AUG
10-5 sleeper	NYP-WIL
10-5 sleeper	WAS-WIL

Dining was a particularly elegant affair aboard the *Florida Special*. In this posed scene from the 1960's, ACL's *Florida Special* hostess checks with dining patrons to ensure that their steaks have been cooked to order. Perhaps to keep the riff-raff from peering in at them during station stops, the party has lowered the window shade in this Budd diner.—ACL.

the anniversary season, the "new" train reverted to a 24-hour New York-Miami carding. An extra fare of $5/Pullman and $2.50/coach was levied, but passengers got their money's worth with reserved-seat dining, complimentary champagne and train hostesses. New recreation cars returned, and with them the memories of the prewar cars which had made the train famous. The "new" cars were actually the all-dining-room halves of twin-unit diners *Port Tampa*, *Winter Haven* and *Winter Park*, separated from their kitchen-car mates. Recreation-car activities mimicked group activities offered on the *Special's* recreation cars of the 1920's and 1930's.

Perhaps in imitation of the frenetic pace of onboard amusement forced on ocean-liner passengers by merciless ship's pursers, the *Special's* recreation cars of the bygone era had offered everything from dancing to bingo. In one memorable season, 1932-33, and in the face of all logic, the train had even offered a small "swimming pool" in a club car that had also been outfitted with gym equipment for those passengers intent on exercise.

No such contraptions were available on the 1962 *Florida Special,* but there was no shortage of entertainment as movies,

CONSIST OF NOTE 6-G

PRR train 107, southbound *Florida Special*

Newark, N.J.
Dec. 17, 1962

Car	Type
[PRR 4881]	[GG1 electric locomotive]
ACL 106	Baggage-dorm
FEC *Homestead*	54-seat coach
FEC *Salerno*	56-seat coach
ACL *Tarboro*	36-seat diner
ACL 231	54-seat coach
ACl 210	56-seat coach
ACL *Port Tampa*	Recreation car
ACL *Honey Bird*	7-2 sleeper
ACL *Rice Bird*	7-2 sleeper
ACL *Cape Fear River*	4-4 sleeper
FEC *Havana*	10-6 sleeper
ACL *Orlando*	48-seat diner
ACL *Berkeley County*	10-6 sleeper
ACL *Virginia Beach*	6-d-bedroom lounge
ACL *Kissimmee River*	4-4 sleeper*

*Carrying 75th Anniversary drumhead

Picked up from *City of Miami* on alternate days

(Tampa section)
10-6 sleeper	CHI-SRA
54-seat coach	CHI-SRA

(St. Pete section)
10-6 sleeper	CHI-STP
52-seat coach	CHI-STP

Picked up from the *South Wind* on alternate days

(Tampa section)
5-4-4 sleeper	CHI-SRA
52-seat coach	CHI-SRA

(St. Pete section)
5-1-4-4 sleeper	CHI-STP
52-seat coach	CHI-STP

One famous name that wouldn't return that winter or evermore was the *Miamian*. Changing times and Coast Line's reshuffling of priorities to focus on the *Florida Special* left no room at the table for a second winter-season train to Florida. Overshadowed by the enthusiasm for the anniversary of the *Florida Special*, the *Miamian* quietly faded from the scene.

Things appeared to be on the upswing for Coast Line's passenger operations as the 1960's marched on, but a watershed event cast doubts about the future. On Jan. 23, 1963, the Florida East Coast was struck by unions after it had refused to go along with 192 other Class 1 railroads in accepting a negotiated salary increase to members of 11 non-operating unions. Because operating employees honored the picket lines, the Florida East Coast railway came to a virtual halt. What started out as a simple work stoppage over 10

ABOVE: Having traded their regal purple and silver for somber black with yellow stripes, triple ACL E-units thunder onto the St. Lucie Canal bridge near Indiantown, Fla., with the northbound *Florida Special* on Dec. 25, 1963. The FEC strike had taken hold, and No. 87 was detouring—permanently—on the Seaboard.—DAVID W. SALTER.

cents an hour eventually turned into one of the longest and most-bitter labor disputes in modern American history.

The railroad's and the unions' inability to settle the issue spawned an amazing amount of violence. Over 200 bombings and dynamiting of trains resulted. Five trains were wrecked by vandals. The FEC was obviously no place to be operating streamliners loaded with people. After an FEC freight was dynamited near where then-President Lyndon Johnson was speaking, the FBI was called in, eventually arresting four FEC employees. But the damage had already been done, in more ways than one.

Immediately after commencement of the work stoppage, arrangments were made to reroute Miami-bound Coast Line trains via ACL's Tampa line to Auburndale, Fla., then on the Seaboard to Miami. Service to selected FEC points such as Daytona Beach, Melbourne, Vero Beach and Fort Pierce was maintained through special buses connecting with trains at ACL's Sanford station. Northeast-Florida schedules were lengthened on account of the greater mileage of the inland route.

Coast Line received all of the operating revenue from the makeshift Miami service, not having to share it with SAL, but it did have to reimburse SAL

RIGHT: *Manatee River* was formerly New York Central's 4-4-2 *Suspension Bridge*. In October 1962, the car was sold to ACL and remodeled with 4 drawing rooms and 4 compartments to provide premium room accommodations on the *Florida Special*. LOWER RIGHT: *Blue Bird*, formerly the 14-2 sleeper *Cape Fear River*, was remodeled in the summer of 1961 with 7 double bedrooms and 2 drawing rooms. It was assigned to the *Florida Special* for its 75th anniversary season.—BOTH PHOTOS, PETER V. TILP.

for the use of its property, including Seaboard's Miami station which became the new terminus for ACL East Coast trains.

Aside from the human consequences of the strike, perhaps the saddest thing was FEC's *de facto*—and sudden—departure from big-time passenger railroading. For although the intrastate carrier would be forced to offer local Jacksonville-Miami service, it would never again host Floridaliners from the Midwest or Northeast. FEC would eventually re-emerge from its isolation a wholly new entity, bereft of costly passenger operations and union ties. In the process, the road discarded 75 years of passenger history which had included the establishment of some of the greatest passenger trains in American history.

Despite the strike, Coast Line's attitude about passenger service remained upbeat. It appeared the slump was over. Passenger revenues for 1962 were higher than those of 1961, and 1963 topped 1962. Appraising his trains' performance in 1962, Ray Paschall, ACL's manager of passenger sales and service said, "Business has been very good. We did not have an out-of-pocket loss." He was echoed by ACL Assistant Vice President D. T. Martin who remarked, " We know there is money to be made in the passenger business, and we are going to do our utmost to make it." Their optimism was buoyed by a general national upturn in passenger revenues. For most railroads, however, the upswing had resulted only in lower overall losses rather than Coast Line's break-even situation. This accounted for the difference in attitude between the Florida roads and others across the country regarding passenger operations. ACL and SAL were still enthusiastic because they could afford to be.

Even so, ACL was taking measures to tighten its belt. One economizing practice becoming more common was the combining of the *Champion*s between New York and Jacksonville during the off season, thus saving crew costs (the biggest expense of passenger-train operation) and equipment wear. Unlike the competing *Silver Meteor,* which had long carried cars for both coasts and operated as one consist all the way

between New York and Wildwood, Fla., the *Champion*s had always operated as separate East and West Coast trains. But as traffic shrunk, it became impractical to operate two separate trains. Here is an example of what the combined trains looked like:

Consolidated *Champion*s effective April 26, 1965

7-2 sleeper	NYP-MIA
6-d.br. lounge	NYP-MIA
Diner	NYP-MIA
54-seat coach	NYP-MIA
54-seat coach	NYP-MIA
Tavern-lounge	NYP-MIA
54-seat coach	NYP-STP
54-seat coach	NYP-SRA
Diner	NYP-TPA
10-6 sleeper	WAS-TPA
10-6 sleeper	NYP-SRA
10-6 sleeper	NYP-STP
10-6 sleeper	NYP-JAX
52-seat coach	NYP-MGY
10-6 sleeper	NYP-AUG
Tavern-lounge	JAX-TPA
Cafe-lounge	FLO-AUG
Cafe-lounge	JAX-STP

Separately operated, regular consists for the off season of autumn had indeed shrunk considerably as the Consist of Note 6-H for the *East Coast Champion* from a year and a half earlier shows.

Things stayed much the same through 1964. Exceptions: The *West Coast Champion* began handling a New York-Montgomery (Ala.) streamlined coach that December, and the *Havana Special* was renamed *Gulf Coast Special.* The latter change was, perhaps, motivated by the fact that Cuba hadn't been an achievable destination via ACL and connecting steamships

CONSIST OF NOTE 6-H PRR train 105, southbound *East Coast Champion*
Newark, N.J.
Nov. 6, 1963

Car	Type
[PRR No. unknown]	[GG1 electric locomotive]
ACL 105	Baggage-dorm
ACL 203	60-seat coach
ACL 217	54-seat coach
ACL 249	54-seat coach
ACL 227	54-seat coach
ACL 255	Tavern-lounge
ACL *Newark*	Diner
ACL *Beaufort County*	10-6 sleeper
ACL *Jay Bird*	7-2 sleeper
PRR *Bucks County*	10-6 sleeper
FEC *Bahamian*	10-6 sleeper

ABOVE: In 1962-63, the *Florida Special* achieved its diamond anniversary. Arriving at the FEC Miami station, the 75th anniversary *Florida Special* is bustin' the banner held by Joan Cooke (at left), typifying swimming attire from 1888, and Michal Flotkin in more-revealing modern-day swimwear. She is assisted by Roger Baretto, district passenger agent for FEC. E9 1034 wears the newer simplified scheme of solid light blue. In the cab is Miami Mayor Robert King High.—BROTHERHOOD OF LOCOMOTIVE ENGINEERS. ABOVE RIGHT: Florida East Coast's last full-fledged public timetable, dated Dec. 12, 1962, featured this ad for the *Florida Special*'s 75th anniversary.—AUTHOR'S COLLECTION. RIGHT: The *Florida Special* hostess leads passengers in a full range of activities, including sing-a-longs in recreation car *Winter Haven*.—ACL. LOWER RIGHT: In time for the *Special*'s anniversary season, dining-room cars *Port Tampa*, *Winter Park* and *Winter Haven* were separated from their kitchen car mates and designated as recreation cars.—PETER V. TILP.

for some time. Fidel Castro, the Bay of Pigs debacle and the Cuban missile crisis had seen to that.

Still, it was sad to lose the name, for the *Havana Special* had in fact been the patriarch of Coast Line's New York-Florida service. Its forunner, the *New York & West Indian Limited*—nicknamed the "Havana Mail"—had been ACL's first train between New York and Florida, predating the *Florida Special* by ten years.

But something that *didn't* happen that year hurt worst of all. Despite a strong marketing effort to encourage people to travel to the 1964 New York World's Fair (which resulted in 11,000 customers taking advantage of all-expense-paid Coast Line vacation packages to New York), overall passenger revenues for the year dropped. It was a blow to ACL's optimism.

Even so, the railroad's tireless effort to attract passengers continued. A review of Coast Line's earnings and timetables reveals that the carrier was still losing ground not only to the auto and airliner, but to the Seaboard Air Line. For 1965, in an effort to attract more budget-minded travelers, the road introduced the "Budget Room Coach."

Between June and September, a New York-Miami Budget Room Coach—car line BC-9—was included in the consist of the *East Coast Champion*. Four 21-roomette cars were assigned: RF&P's *Byrd Island* and ACL's *Edisto Island*, *Roanoke Island* and *Sullivans Island*. It was a good deal for all parties. For some time, Coast Line had been struggling to find a use for the all-roomette cars, which had been deemed unsuitable for the Florida market. Some had been farmed out to other roads. In the mid-1950's, for example, the *Roanoke Island*, *Parris Island* and *St. Simons Island* had operated on the Rock Island in Minneapolis-Kansas City service.

Now Coast Line was creating a market to fill the cars right at home. The cars' full-sized roomettes were sold for just a $15 supplement above coach fare. Perhaps at Pullman's request and to avoid selling two identical accommodations at entirely differ-

This rare photo shows B&O dome sleeper *Sunlight Dome* on the rear of the southbound *Florida Special* at Wilson, N.C., on an evening in 1965. Note the ACL herald applied near the vestibule door, an unusual if not unique use of ACL's herald on streamlined rolling stock. The drumhead hung on the rear safety railing reads ATLANTIC COAST LINE FLORIDA SPECIAL.—TOM KING.

ent prices, the *East Coast Champion* offered no standard roomettes in its consist that summer.

That winter other "new" cars appeared. For the 1965-66 winter season, ACL and partners took advantage of B&O's recent idling of its 5-roomette 3-compartment 1-single bedroom Strata Dome sleepers, a unique Budd-built threesome which had been fixtures on the Chicago-Washington *Capitol Limited*. Leasing the cars, ACL operated them on the rear of the *Florida Special*. Two of the cars were assigned by Pullman to the train, but it is probable that all three—*Moonlight Dome*, *Starlight Dome* and *Sunlight Dome*—had been made available to ACL. Even though these domes were designed to operate within the restricted clearances of Northeastern railroad right-of-way, they only operated between Richmond and Miami when in *Florida Special* service, in part because of the extra-tight clearances of the Capitol Hill Tunnel leading to Washington Union Station from the south, but also because by dropping the dome at Richmond northbound, it could turn back south on that same day's southbound *Florida Special*. That, coupled with same-day turnaround at Miami, meant that only two cars were necessary to protect schedules (three sets of *Florida Specials* were needed to protect its New York-Miami schedule). Innovations extended beyond new equipment. The 1965-66 season also saw the intro-

duction of the popular Candlelight Dinners.

During winter, the *Special*'s companions—the *Champion*s—were still heavily patronized as Consists of Note 6-I and 6-J betray. Interestingly, Consist of Note 6-I shows the *Port Tampa*, formerly a recreation car for the *Florida Special*, reunited with its kitchen car mate for twin-unit diner service.

The *Champion*s weren't the only big winter consists on the ACL. On certain heavy travel days bracketing the holidays, both Coast Line and Seaboard operated "Holiday Specials" filled with cars idled on off-line roads. The trains were fixtures for many years in Florida service. Consist of Note 6-K (page 128) illustrates one of them.

By 1966, the *Florida Special* was beginning to pick up off-line cars again as the railroad strived to offer the most modern interior accommodations. Consist

CONSIST OF NOTE 6-I
PRR train 105, southbound
East Coast Champion

New York City
December 1965

Car	Type
ACL 103	Baggage-dorm
ACL 1085	54-seat coach (hvywt. rebuild)
ACL 225	54-seat coach
RF&P 811	54-seat coach
ACL 218	54-seat coach
ACL 244	54-seat coach
ACL 256	Tavern-lounge
ACL *Baltimore*	Diner
ACL *Wrightsville Beach*	6-double-bedroom lounge
ACL *Beaufort County*	10-6 sleeper
ACL *Savannah River*	4-4 sleeper
ACL *Kissimmee River*	4-4 sleeper
ACL *Atlanta*	Diner
SP 9106	4-4-2 sleeper
PRR *Imperial Plateau*	4-4-2 sleeper
PRR *Delaware County*	10-6 sleeper
ACL *Harnett County*	10-6 sleeper
RF&P *King George*	10-6 sleeper

CONSIST OF NOTE 6-J
PRR train 101, southbound *West Coast Champion*

New York City
December 1965

Car	Type
ACL 106	Baggage-dorm
RF&P 802	54-seat coach
ACL 239	54-seat coach
ACL *Naples*	Diner
RF&P 801	54-seat coach
ACL 1112	54-seat coach (hvywt. rebuild)
ACL 207	52-seat coach
ACL 222	46-seat coach
FEC *Argentina*	10-6 sleeper
ACL 253	Tavern-lounge
ACL 125	Kitchen-dorm
ACL *Port Tampa*	Dining-room car
ACL *Hillsborough County*	10-6 sleeper
C&O *City of Charlottesville*	10-6 sleeper
ACL *Sea Island Beach*	6-double-bedroom lounge
C&O *City of Marion*	10-6 sleeper
RF&P 810	54-seat coach
ACL *Duval County*	10-6 sleeper
ACL *EdgecombeCounty*	10-6 sleeper

Although Florida is synonymous with surf, sand and sun, the state is also a haven for sportsmen, and ACL did not forget them in this bucolic publicity photo dating from about 1963. Undoubtedly, the ACL photographer has staged the fishermen in this scene, but a slight speed blur on the nose of the E8 leading this all-stainless *Florida Special* is a certain indication that the train was not stopped. The location is unknown, but the scene may have been taken on the *Special*'s new Seaboard routing through central Florida, where lakes like this abound.—ACL.

of Note 6-L, taken north of Richmond, shows the train minus the 5-1-3 dome sleepers which operated on the rear. The interesting thing about this consist is the presence of the *Fort Meyers* as a recreation car. Normally a twin-unit diner, the *Fort Meyers* appears to have been separated so that the dining-room car pro-

vided another recreation car in the *Florida Special* pool, perhaps to replace the *Port Tampa* which ACL was using once again as part of a twin-unit diner.

The Budget Room Coaches returned again to the *East Coast Champion* for the summer of 1966. This year Pullman assigned six 21-roomette cars to cover line BC-9: RF&P *Byrd Island*, ACL *Edisto Island*, ACL *Roanoke Island*, ACL *Sullivans Island*, PRR *Vincennes Inn* and PRR *Zanesville Inn*.

This summer, like the last, no 10-6 sleepers or other first-class roomettes ran in the *East Coast Cham-*

CONSIST OF NOTE 6-K
ACL Holiday Special

On the PRR
Jan. 3, 1966

Car	Type
[PRR 4922]	[GG1 electric]
SP 9106	4-4-2 sleeper
PRR *Imperial Path*	4-4-2 sleeper
PRR *Imperial Range*	4-4-2 sleeper
PRR *Sassafras Falls*	6-double-bedroom lounge
PRR *Cascade Ledge*	10-5 sleeper
PRR *Lake County*	13-double-bedroom sleeper
PRR *Jefferson County*	13-double-bedroom sleeper
PRR *Maple Brook*	12-5 sleeper
PRR *Meadow Brook*	12-5 sleeper
PRR 4480	Class D78f diner (hvywt. rebuild)
ACL *Fitzgerald*	Diner
PRR *Middle Brook*	12-5 sleeper
PRR *Maple Brook*	12-5 sleeper
PRR *Imperial Lawn*	4-4-2 sleeper
ACL *Virginia*	Lounge
ACL 1084	54-seat coach (hvywt. rebuild)
ACL 1087	54-seat coach (hvywt. rebuild)
ACL 1088	54-seat coach (hvywt. rebuild)
ACL 1111	54-seat coach (hvywt. rebuild)

CONSIST OF NOTE 6-L
PRR train 107, southbound *Florida Special*

Pennsylvania Station, N.Y.
March 26, 1966

Car	Type
[PRR 4923]	[GG1 electric locomotive]
ACL 100	Baggage-dorm
RF&P 801	54-seat coach
ACl 240	54-seat coach
ACL 237	54-seat coach
ACL *Fort Meyers*	Recreation car
ACL *Sumter County*	10-6 sleeper
ACL *Ponte Vedra Beach*	6-double-bedroom lounge
ACL *Tampa*	Diner
SOU *Royal Court*	11-double-bedroom sleeper
ACL *Jay Bird*	7-2 sleeper
ACL *Surf Bird*	7-2 sleeper
PRR *Imperial Trees*	4-4-2 sleeper

pion. Rather, PRR 12-duplex-room, 4-double-bed-room *Creek* sleepers were assigned; see Consist of Note 6-M (page 130). The Budget Room Coach service would end temporarily in September 1966, only to be revived again that December with the commencement of winter schedules. The regular use of the 21-roomette cars on this car line ended for good in September 1966. Beginning in December, Budget Room Coach service (the first such effort in the winter season) featured leased Baltimore & Ohio 16-duplex-roomette, 4-double-bedroom cars. The cars operated on a year-round basis through the Seaboard Coast Line era and into Amtrak. Consist of Note 6-N (page 131) illustrates the operation during this period.

That December, too, the *Florida Special* would get a round-end 5-double-bedroom lounge-observation in the form of former L&N cars *Royal Canal* and *Royal Street*. The B&O domes used the previous season were now on lease to Canadian National through March 1968. The distinctive L&N observations would work on the *Special* for the 1966-67 and the 1967-68 seasons, operating Richmond-Miami.

Also in 1966, ACL commenced studies in cooperation with the U.S. Department of Commerce and the Department of Transportation to determine the feasibility of transporting passengers and their autos on the same train between Washington and Jacksonville. The practice of shipping passengers' autos to their destinations was nothing new to the Florida roads. Both Seaboard and ACL had had successful programs in place doing just that for decades. In the winter of 1939-40 for instance, Coast Line had shipped almost 9,000 autos in one season. What was different about this new effort was that passengers were to stay with their autos, using them as their primary lodging—a concept similar to that of a ferryboat operation.

Early tests included shipping autos in PRR Class B70A theatrical scenery cars, which featured large doors on the car ends. ACL brass riding in the autos

ABOVE: It's New Year's Eve day 1959 and the photographer was at trackside on the Florida East Coast at Vero Beach to witness the *Miamian*'s passage through town. Heavyweight sleepers dominate the forward half of the train.—PETER McLACHLAN.

LEFT AND LOWER LEFT: Holiday specials were commonplace on both Seaboard and ACL. This southbound passenger Extra screaming along the Seaboard Air Line between Avon Park and Sebring, Fla., just before Christmas 1963 has a little bit of everything in its consist—heavyweight, purple-painted ACL rolling stock, ubiquitous Pennsy sleepers and, trailing the whole consist, a rebuilt RF&P heavyweight coach. The heavyweight coach in Illinois Central orange and brown near the center of the train is probably a modernized ACL car painted in IC colors for the *Seminole* pool.—BOTH PHOTOS, DAVID SALTER.

RIGHT: Diner *Boston* was delivered in December 1940 as part of the pre-war expansion of *Champion* service. It is pictured in 1966 with several modifications, most notable of which are the oval kitchen windows.—C. L. GOOLSBY.

RIGHT: ACL diner *Orlando* operated on the 75th anniversary *Florida Special*. It had an interesting past. Originally it was delivered as diner-lounge *St. Petersburg* in 1947. In 1950 it was renamed *Orlando*. Sometime in the early to mid-1950's the car became a 48-seat diner.—GEORGE E. VOTAVA.

were subjected to a high-speed adventure on the tail end of a *Champion* to test feasibility. According to participants, the B70A's did all right for themselves. A similar test using auto-rack cars didn't turn out nearly as well.

Ultimately, the idea was to transport passengers in specially designed, air-conditioned double-deck auto carriers (four cars to each level) equipped with windows. Passengers would be free to walk about the train and have access to special-service cars, one at each end of the 12-car train, which would provide dining and lounge space. Additional rest rooms were to be provided at other locations in the auto carriers. Of course, the key assumption was that people wouldn't mind sleeping or staying in their automobiles in a claustrophobic car carrier for large portions of the 12-hour trip.

Nevertheless, the think-tankers were on to something, despite the fact that the assumptions about passenger tolerance for this kind of thing would have to be re examined. The concept was the forerunner to the *Auto-Train,* which would debut just three years later under the direction of a private company.

Coast Line's passenger roster continued to soldier on in 1967, the final half year of operation. Consist of Notes 6-N and 6-O from April, just before the end of the winter season, show a sampling of the ACL's fleet shortly before merger with Seaboard.

For the last summer season in 1967, the *East* and *West Coast Champion*s were combined between New York and Jacksonville. Each train contributed a small group of cars to the entire consist with the *East Coast Champ* offering a New York-Miami Budget Room Coach and a 7-double bedroom, 2-drawing-room car as well as a New York-Augusta 10-6 via a connection. Once again, you couldn't get to Miami in a roomette on the *Champion.* The *West Coast Champion* portion in the final ACL period offered a New York-St. Petersburg 10-6, a New York-Sarasota 10-6 and a New York-Tampa 6-double-bedroom lounge.

The combined train offered dining cars between New York, Miami and Tampa. A cafe-lounge was

CONSIST OF NOTE 6-M
RF&P train 1, *East Coast Champion*

Alexandria, Va.
June 21, 1966

Car	Type
[ACL 520]	[E6A locomotive]
[ACL 545]	[E8A locomotive]
[ACL 764]	[E7B locomotive]
[ACL 510]	[E6A locomotive]
ACL 3	RPO
PRR ??	X-29 express box car
ACL 103	Baggage-dorm
ACL *Roanoke Island*	21-roomette BRC
PRR *Vincennes Inn*	21-roomette BRC
PRR *Chimney Creek*	12-4 sleeper
ACL *Ponte Vedra Beach*	6-double-bedroom lounge
ACL *Washington*	Diner
ACL 227	54-seat coach
ACL 228	54-seat coach
ACL 251	Tavern-lounge
ACL 232	54-seat coach
ACL 219	54-seat coach
ACL *Talladega*	Diner
ACL 218	54-seat coach
ACL 201	60-seat coach
ACL 204	60-seat coach
ACL 275	36-seat coach-lounge
PRR 1568	60-seat coach
PRR 1829	Coach
ACL 215	56-seat coach

LEFT: The still of a Florida afternoon is interrupted briefly as the *West Coast Champion's* St. Pete section hurries north out of Lady Lake in 1965. Train 192 has a date with the Tampa section at Jacksonville.—DAVID W. SALTER.
BELOW: An interior view of ACL's square-end tavern-observation car 254 shows its appearance early in the 1960's.—ACL.

CONSIST OF NOTE 6-N
PRR train 104, northbound
East Coast Champion
April 2, 1967

Car	Type
[PRR 4894]	[GG1 electric locomotive]
ACL 106	Baggage-dorm
ACL 249	54-seat coach
ACL 203	60-seat coach
ACL 1077	54-seat coach (hvywt. rebuild)
RF&P 841	70-seat coach
ACL 260	52-seat coach
RF&P 804	54-seat coach
ACL 212	56-seat coach
ACL 275	36-seat coach-lounge*
ACL *Newark*	Diner
RF&P *Colonial Beach*	6-double-bedroom lounge
PRR *Imperial Trees*	4-4-2 sleeper
PRR *Joseph Horne*	12-4 sleeper
PRR *College Creek*	12-4 sleeper
ACL *Fitzgerald*	Diner
PRR *Mackinaw Rapids*	10-6 sleeper
PRR *Hanover County*	10-6 sleeper
PRR *Samuel M. Kier*	10-6 sleeper
ACL *Suwanee River*	4-4 sleeper
B&O *Bob-O-Link*	16-4 Budget Room Coach

*Subbing for tavern-lounge

available between Jacksonville and St. Pete, and a single tavern-lounge ran New York to Miami. Coaches operated between New York, Washington and Miami as well as to Sarasota, Naples and St. Petersburg on the West Coast. Also included was the New York-Montgomery coach which had proven quite popular.

What had once been a 24-hour service between New York and Miami now took 26½ hours; likewise, the trip into St. Petersburg now took 25½ hours. At Jacksonville, the *West Coast Champion* was still picking up cars from the *City of Miami* and *South Wind*. Among the minor players in Coast Line's Florida fleet which survived to this final season was the *Gulf Coast Special*, which operated reclining-seat coaches

BELOW: The southbound *Champion* is strung out around one of the curves at the junction point of Waycross, Ga., on a spring morning in 1966. Visible are the baggage-dorm, a 7-2 *Bird*-series sleeper, three *County*-series 10-6's (one ex-C&O) and a 6-double-bedroom lounge.—TOM KING.

LEFT: The FEC strike sent ACL streamliners away from coastal waters for much of their trip through Florida. Trains that normally headed south from Jacksonville over FEC rails now remained on ACL's Tampa line as far as Auburndale, Fla., where ACL crossed Seaboard's main to Miami. Here at Auburndale on April 15, 1964, the *East Coast Champion* negotiates the connection, leaving the Tampa line to enter Seaboard rails.—DAVID W. SALTER. BELOW: Looking a bit out of place at the Seaboard Air Line station in Miami, the *Florida Special* awaits its evening departure in the fall of 1965. Thanks to the FEC strike, this would be the train's permanent home in Miami.—JOHN DZIOBKO JR.

ABOVE: Atlantic Coast Line coach 271 featured 36 seats and an 8-seat lounge. It and several other cars were purchased from the C&O. This one was built for C&O's planned-but-never-run *Chessie* streamliner between Cincinnati and Washington/Newport News. The clue is the long, flat letterboard which on C&O was painted yellow.—R. W. YOUNG VIA C. L. GOOLSBY. BELOW: RF&P's 21-roomette sleeper *Byrd Island* kept its purple letterboard for its entire career. The car was used in Budget Room Coach service on the *East Coast Champion* in 1965 and 1966.—O. H. BORSUM VIA FOSTER GUNNISON.

between New York and Jacksonville, a lone 10-6 and an overnight coach between Jacksonville and Tampa. This train departed New York in the late evening, arriving in Jacksonville the following night after nearly a 22¾-hour journey. Also in the timecard was the *Everglades*, offering a Washington-Jacksonville reclining-seat coach which put the traveler into Jacksonville at the not-so-convenient hour of 4:30 a.m. Obviously, through traffic on this *de facto* local train was minimal.

Time was running out for the ACL. A look back revealed a great passenger railroad whose hopes and expectations for the future had been dashed by a general national downturn in rail passenger travel. In the twenty years between the end of World War II and the SCL merger, ACL's passenger revenues would be cut in half despite a huge investment in new equipment. To its credit, the railroad never gave up. New stations, rebuilt cars, package tours and a world-class marketing effort were the railroad's response to a challenge which many other carriers had reacted to with service cuts and massive discontinuances. By the mid 1960's, only a handful of American trains could rival Coast Line's revitalized, extra-fare *Florida Special* for its amenities. And no other railroad in the country was planning a whole new service—an auto train.

Happily, all of these efforts would not be in vain. For, come July 1, 1967, Coast Line's best would continue under a new banner—Seaboard Coast Line—as the merger with SAL, on the drawing board since at least 1960, would become reality.

ABOVE: In an August 1965 scene that is at once pretty and sad, FEC E9 1034—which only a couple years earlier had led the 75th anniversary *Florida Special* into Miami (page 126)—trundles across the St. Johns River in Jacksonville with the vestigal remains of FEC's once-grand fleet of Floridaliners.—DAVID W. SALTER.

LEFT: ACL's modernized coaches in the 1960's featured attentive passenger representatives and murals of Florida scenes.—ACL. LOWER LEFT: Former 21-roomette car *Parris Island* was remodeled in July 1962 to become *Magnolia Gardens*, Atlantic Coast Line's only 11-double-bedroom car. This rare photo shows the car shortly after rebuilding.—R. W. YOUNG VIA C. L. GOOLSBY.

CONSIST OF NOTE 6-O
PRR train 100, northbound
West Coast Champion
April 2, 1967

Car	Type
[PRR 4868]	[GG1 electric locomotive]
ACL *Marion County*	10-6 sleeper
ACL *Virginia Beach*	6-double-bedroom lounge
SOU *Holston River*	10-6 sleeper
RF&P *Stratford County*	10-6 sleeper
ACL *Polk County*	10-6 sleeper
ACL *Talladega*	Diner
SP 9034	10-6 sleeper
ACL *Duval County*	10-6 sleeper
PRR *Benjamin Bakewell*	12-4 sleeper
SOU *Cashier's Valley*	14-4 sleeper
ACL *St. Petersburg*	Dining-room car (twin unit)
ACL 127	Kitchen-dorm
ACL 1076	54-seat coach (hvywt. rebuild)
ACL 254	Tavern-lounge
ACL 211	56-seat coach
RF&P 801	54-seat coach
ACL 220	54-seat coach
RF&P *Caroline County*	10-6 sleeper

7

A SUCCESSFUL MARRIAGE
Seaboard Coast Line: 1967-1971

In its first half year of operations, the new Seaboard Coast Line made few changes to the principal passenger trains of the former SAL and ACL. It was a typical response for a company ironing out the complexities of a recent merger. Summer schedules for 1967 featured the former Silver Fleet and the *Champion*s operating to their normal destinations with consists similar to those offered in previous summers.

Several name changes were applied to sleeping and dining cars in the fleet of the new railroad to avoid confusion between ACL and SAL cars. For example, the former Seaboard Sun Lounge sleepers *Hollywood Beach, Miami Beach* and *Palm Beach* became *Sun Ray, Sun View* and *Sun Beam*.

Likewise, their prior names were applied to three former-SAL six-double-bedroom lounges to bring the SAL cars into conformity with former-ACL *Beach*-series six-double-bedroom lounges. Thus, *Kennesaw Mountain, Red Mountain* and *Stone Mountain* became *Hollywood Beach, Palm Beach* and *Miami Beach*. ACL's former diner and recreation car fleet, which had always carried names, lost them and were renumbered in the 5900 series along with all former-SAL diners.

But, as time went on, the changes would become more substantial. The inexorable abandonment of the rails by the United States Post Office continued to spell doom for a bevy of lightly patronized secondary runs across the country. SCL was no exception. Mail revenues on the SCL decreased 21 percent in just one year. In late December 1967, SCL would axe trains 77 and 78, the former-ACL *Palmetto* between Richmond and Florence, S.C.; RF&P would also discontinue its portion of the train. With an average of only 52 passengers per day, the *Palmetto* had been almost completely dependent of mail revenues.

Fall schedules saw the by-now-routine combining of the *East* and *West Coast Champion*s, but winter brought the first signs of the inevitable consolidations which would result from SCL's elimination of near-duplicate services. When the winter-season timetable went into effect on Dec. 15, 1967, the *East Coast Champion* no longer existed. Now simply called the *Champion*, it served Gulf Coast points only. Consist of Note 7-A (following page) shows how it looked a few days before Christmas 1967. The presence of the leased B&O 16-4 in the this train shows that Budget Room Coach service was now available to West Coast points. No other drastic changes had taken place, but, equipmentwise, things were as interesting as ever. Consider the line-up for the *Silver Meteor* shown in Consist of Note 7-B. Note the presence of C&O's *City of Logan* and PRR's Tuscan *Mahoning Rapids*. By contrast, the *Silver Star* was a bit more normal-looking, as Consist of Note 7-C shows, although B&O's *Wren* in the lineup was covering a Budget Room Coach line between New York and Miami.

The winter flagship *Florida Special* was still drawing a crowd, too, and it offered first-class riders a smorgasbord of off-line cars. In the 1967-68 season, the *Special* again featured L&N "Lookout Lounges," five-double-bedroom observation cars *Royal Street* and *Royal Canal*, as well as PRR's six-double-bedroom lounges *Catalpa Falls* and *Larch Falls*. Come February

FACING PAGE: Waves are exchanged as Seaboard Coast Line's *Silver Meteor*s pass in central Florida.—KARL ZIMMERMANN. **TOP:** E6A 503 was well into its third decade of service when it became a locomotive of SCL. On the evening of March 22, 1968, it leads the famed *Florida Special* at Jacksonville Union Station. SCL's headquarters building rises in the distance to the right of the train.—DAVID W. SALTER. **ABOVE:** In the late 1960's and beyond, few trains in the U.S. still carried round-end observation cars. SCL's *Silver Meteor* was an exception. Tavern-obs 5842 is pictured at Sunnyside Yard in September 1970.—D. T. HAYWARD VIA TOM MARTORANO.

RIGHT: SCL's ex-B&O *Cardinal* (16 duplex roomettes, 4 double bedrooms) and sister cars *Bobolink, Gull, Oriole, Robin, Swan, Thrush* and *Wren* were regulars on the *Silver Meteor* and *Champion*. —D. T. HAYWARD VIA TOM MARTORANO. LOWER RIGHT: Former C&O 11-double-bedroom sleeper *Homestead* kept its name and its C&O paint scheme when SCL purchased it in 1970. The car originally catered to resort traffic on such C&O trains as the *F.F.V.*, which fielded a through sleeper between New York and Hot Springs, W. Va.—PETER V. TILP. BOTTOM RIGHT: Former SAL Sun Lounge *Palm Beach* was renamed *Sun Beam*. —D. T. HAYWARD VIA TOM MATORANO.

BELOW: One of the *Champion*'s more-unremarked through-car operations was that of a New York-Montgomery (Ala.) coach, which came off the *Champ* at Waycross, Ga. From there, a Waycross-Montgomery local handled the car west to the Alabama state capital. SCL train 189 has just pulled into Montgomery station in August 1968; the through coach (ex-Nickel Plate) is at the end of the train and still wears ACL markings.—MIKE SCHAFER

1968, Pennsy's classic *View*-series sleeper-observations, *Mountain View* and *Tower View*, off the *Broadway Limited*, would appear too, offering Florida travelers top-of-the-line master room accommodations, complete with a shower. Consist of Note 7-D from the late winter of 1968 illustrates the arrangement.

In contrast to sleeper-laden consists like the *Florida Special* and *Champion*, SCL's secondary trains on the New York-Florida route featured mostly head-end cars; Consist of Note 7-E shows one example.

On Feb. 1, 1968, SCL's principal northern partner, the Pennsylvania Railroad, ceased to exist. On that date, the long-awaited merger between Pennsy and New York Central—destined to become one of the biggest business blunders in American history—became official. For SCL, things wouldn't change much at first. Penn Central would be as overbearing with its Southern partner on passenger matters as PRR had

been. Penn Central's mismanagement of its own affairs, however, would lead to increased pressures to cut costs, among them passenger operations, and this in turn would create problems for pro-passenger SCL.

In contrast to PC, SCL was intelligently implementing some of the cost-saving measures made possible by merger. The new railroad had only tinkered with schedules in its first year, but more substantial changes began to occur in spring 1968. Effective April 28, 1968, the following major changes took place:

CONSIST OF NOTE 7-A
PRR train 100, *Champion*
On the PRR
Dec. 21, 1967

Car	Type
[PRR 4906]	[GG1 electric locomotive]
ACL 103	Baggage-dorm
ACL *Humming Bird*	7-2 sleeper
ACL *Surf Bird*	7-2 sleeper
B&O *Thrush*	16-4 sleeper
SAL *Jacksonville*	10-6 sleeper
SAL *Glynn County*	10-6 sleeper
ACL *Ponte Vedra Beach*	6-double-bedroom lounge
ACL 224	54-seat coach
SAL 6114	Diner
ACL 256	Tavern-lounge
SAL 6224	52-seat coach
ACL 207	52-seat coach
ACL 238	54-seat coach
SCL 5122	52-seat coach
ACL 239	54-seat coach
RF&P 806	54-seat coach
ACL *Atlanta*	Diner
SAL 6229	50-seat coach
SAL 6200	60-seat coach
RF&P 804	54-seat coach

1. The *Silver Meteor*, trains 57 and 58, began operating to the East Coast of Florida only. What had been the *Meteor*'s West Coast sections, operated between Wildwood and Tampa/St. Petersburg and between Tampa and Venice, were discontinued and the car lines transferred to the *Champion*.

2. The *Silver Star*, trains 21 and 22, formerly an East Coast-only train, began operating to both Florida coasts. The new West Coast section began operating between Jacksonville and St. Petersburg via Orlando and Tampa as train Nos. 23 and 24.

3. The *Champion*, trains 91-92, operated from Jacksonville into Tampa via the old ACL route, and from Tampa to St.Petersburg on the former SAL route via Clearwater. No longer would the *Champ* feature a separate St. Petersburg section operating over the ACL line via Gainesville, Fla.

4. The *Champion*'s handling of *South Wind* and *City of Miami* cars ended. Instead, through cars from these alternating-day Chicago-Florida trains began operating as separate trains to St. Pete via the old ACL Jacksonville-St. Petersburg route which the *Champion* had abandoned.

5. The spring timetable saw the addition of two shortlived Richmond- Miami cars, a coach and a 10-6 sleeper on the *Champion*.

6. The ex-SAL *Sunland* was consolidated with the *City of Miami/ South Wind* between Jacksonville and Miami.

While some trains were being consolidated, a new one was being born. Passenger loadings on the premier trains were high enough for the railroads to run an extra section of the *Champion* between New York and Jacksonville in the summer of 1968, operating northbound on Thursdays, Fridays and Saturdays and southbound on Fridays, Saturdays and Sundays. The *Weekend Champion* carried coaches, a diner, tavern-lounge and 10-6 sleepers between New York and Jacksonville. In addition, the train handled a New York-Augusta 10-6 sleeper and the New York-Montgomery coach.

Although the premier trains were still heavily patronized, secondary runs were coming under increasing scrutiny as express and mail revenues continued to

CONSIST OF NOTE 7-B
SCL train 58, northbound *Silver Meteor*

At Jacksonville, Fla.

Car	Type
[SCL 597]	[Ex-SAL E8A No. 3058]
[SCL 571]	[Ex-SAL E7A No. 3046]
[SCL 668]	[Ex-SAL E7B No. 3106]
SAL 6050	Baggage-dorm
SAL *Miami*	10-6 sleeper
C&O *City of Logan*	10-6 sleeper
SAL *Tallahassee*	11-double-bedroom sleeper
SAL *Clearwater*	5-2-2 sleeper
PRR *Clinton*	10-6 sleeper
SCL *Sun Beam*	5-double-bedroom Sun Lounge
SAL 6111	Diner
SAL *Petersburg*	10-6 sleeper
PRR *Mahoning Rapids*	10-6 sleeper
SAL 6208	56-seat coach
SAL 6115	Diner
SCL 5619	56-seat coach
SCL 5617	56-seat coach
RF&P 856	52-seat coach
RF&P 854	52-seat coach
SAL 6229	50-seat coach
SCL 5841	Tavern-observation

Triple E-units, including two ex-Seaboard units and an ACL locomotive, lead a very healthy-looking *Silver Meteor* consist southbound over the Trout River upon entering Jacksonville at 8:30 a.m. on March 17, 1968. C&O 10-6 sleeper *City of Logan* stands out in the crowd.—DAVID W. SALTER.

plummet. In late May 1968, the *Palmland* was cut back to a New York-Columbia (S.C.) operation. Likewise, trains 7 and 8, the *Sunland*, was eliminated southbound from Hamlet to Jacksonville and northbound from Jacksonville to Washington. By the end of the year, SCL operated 21 fewer passenger trains than it had the previous year.

Still other, more-ominous clouds gathered. By mid 1968, the Pullman Company, an American institution for over 100 years, was in serious trouble. The sleeping-car operator which, at its zenith in the 1920's had provided rolling, nightly lodging for better than 100,000 guests, had been hit hard by the post-World War II proliferation of airlines and the appearance of new hotels and motels along a growing network of public-funded interstate highways. As a result, by 1968 only a handful of carriers still belonged to Pullman.

To be sure, there were still advantages to continued association with the company. Pullman maintenance was second to none, and it kept the cars rolling. Although several railroads were reluctant to take on the substantial headaches of maintaining their sizable sleeping-car fleets themselves, a number were terminating their association with Pullman—and sleeping-car service altogether—mostly to defray costs.

For SCL, basically content with Pullman's service, the problem started with its northernmost partner. In the spring of 1968, Penn Central served notice of its intention of quitting Pullman altogether. Not content with carrying out this action alone, PC tried to influence those interline carriers who still ran Pullman-operated cars into New York over its lines to do the same. By the latter part of 1968, this philosophy was catching on in the industry in general, with predictable results. At midnight on Dec. 31, 1968, the once mighty company ceased all sleeping-car operations on U.S. rails, and by Aug. 1, 1969, all Pullman maintenance of sleeping cars came to an end. SCL had stuck it out to the bitter end, assuming the operation of sleeping cars on its lines on Jan. 1, 1969.

It wasn't all doom and gloom, though. Despite the elimination of secondary runs and the loss of Pullman, SCL took an aggressively positive stance toward marketing its top streamliners. Proof positive could be found in print and on the rails. A series of catchy ads began to make the rounds in the press. Poking fun at recent airliner hijackings to Cuba, the railroad announced: "If you want to go to Miami without a stopover in Havana, call us."

The *Florida Special*, SCL's "fun" train, still offered free champagne, the Candlelight Dinner, movies, TV and telephone service as well as a consist heavily laden

The *Weekend Champion* was yet another New York-Florida train, but it only operated as far as Jacksonville. Inaugurated for the 1968 summer season, the weekend run was quite popular. SCL and RF&P intended to operate it again for the summer of 1969, but Penn Central refused to cooperate, short-circuiting the newcomer's career.—AUTHOR'S COLLECTION.

CONSIST OF NOTE 7-C

PRR train 127, southbound *Silver Star*

North of Washington
Dec. 15, 1967

Car	Type
[PRR 4926]	[GG1 electric locomotive]
SCL 5025	Baggage-dorm
SAL 6229	50-seat coach
SAL 6268	56-seat coach
SCL 5840	Tavern-observation
RF&P 806	54-seat coach
SAL 6253	60-seat coach
ACL *Tarboro*	Diner
RF&P 855	52-seat coach
SAL 6114	Diner
SAL *Birmingham*	10-6 sleeper
B&O *Wren*	16-4 sleeper
SAL *Sebring*	11-double-bedroom sleeper
SCL *Palm Beach*	6-double-bedroom lounge
PRR *Greenwood*	10 6 sleeper
SAL *Jacksonville*	10-6 sleeper

Not shown: RVR-MIA 5-1-4-4 sleeper and WAS-MIA 10-6

CONSIST OF NOTE 7-D

SCL train 2, northbound *Florida Special*

Jacksonville, Fla.
March 18, 1968

Car	Type
[SCL 525]	[E7A locomotive]
[SCL 657]	[E7B locomotive]
[SCL 515]	[E6A locomotive]
ACL 106	Baggage-dorm
SCL 5405	56-seat coach
ACl 228	54-seat coach
ACL 236	54-seat coach
SCL 5906	Diner
SCL 5992	Recreation car
PRR *French Rapids*	10-6 sleeper
ACL *Ponte Vedra Beach*	6-double-bedroom lounge
SCL 5913	Diner
ACL *Magnolia Gardens*	11-double-bedroom sleeper
SOU *Rappahannock River*	10-6 sleeper
UP *Sun Rest*	11-double-bedroom sleeper
PRR *Imperial Ridge*	4-4-2 sleeper
PRR *H. J. Heinz*	4-4-2 sleeper
PRR *Mountain View*	2-m.r., 1-d.br. lounge-obs

CONSISTS OF NOTE/7-E

SCL train 75, *Gulf Coast Special*

Arriving Jacksonville, Fla.
March 18, 1968

Car	Type
[SCL 530]	[E?? locomotive]
[SCL 653]	[E?? locomotive]
[SCL 539]	[E?? locomotive]
REA 6790	Express box car
REA 6168	Express box car
ACL 587	Express baggage
ACL 3	RPO
SAL 329	Mail-storage
SOU 512	Mail-storage
PRR 9294	Baggage
ACL 1085	54-seat coach (rebuilt hvywt.)
ACL 1075	54-seat coach (rebuilt hvywt.)
ACL *Osceola County*	10-6 sleeper

with premium room accommodations. For the winter of 1968-69, the B&O dome sleepers returned between Richmond and Miami, replacing observation cars. The *Silver Meteor* carried a round-end tavern observation, and passengers in any of its seven or eight regularly assigned sleepers could still enjoy the Sun Lounge. High-quality meals continued to be a keynote in the dining car.

But even SCL couldn't escape the inevitable. Its passenger revenues were more than 7 percent lower than those of the previous year, and the railroad made some concessions to the realities of the market. For the 1968-69 winter season, Budget Meal Cars supplemented diners on the *Meteor* and *Star*. Essentially a stripped down, no frills diner, the cars were a similar economy measure to the Budget Room Coach. Mercifully, they proved less popular, disappearing after the winter season.

Then, in May 1969, SCL sought to discontinue its portion of the *Silver Comet* between Richmond and Atlanta after the train was discontinued by PC and RF&P between New York and Richmond. According to SCL, the service cutbacks cheated the train of 69 percent of its ridership. The result from mail, express and passenger shortfalls was predicted to be a yearly

loss of $ 350,000. By June, the *Comet* was gone.

Next on the block was the *Everglades,* which SCL and RF&P filed to discontinue on Nov. 7. What the railroads hoped would be a quiet discontinuance turned into an unusual train-off battle. Ironically, neither the general public nor the newly formed National Association of Railroad Passengers (NARP) seemed to be preoccupied with the case. The real problem for the railroads was the State of Virginia, which owned a large percentage of RF&P and didn't take a cotton to the only conveniently scheduled afternoon train linking Richmond and Washington being discontinued.

Although the railroads had a legitimate beef about the loss of express earnings, they were forced to admit that they, not the post office, had requested the shift in mail traffic to the *Silver Star*, which had worsened

RIGHT: The *Everglades* and the *Gulf Coast Special* were the only two remaining secondary New York-Florida trains that lasted until Amtrak's startup on May 1, 1971, at which time Penn Central, RF&P and SCL were allowed to drop them. A week before Amtrak, the photographer—en route to Petersburg on the *Everglades*—records the train being serviced during its layover at Broad Street Station in Richmond.—MIKE SCHAFER. BELOW: SCL's *Silver Star* (left) waits patiently in the siding at Lake Worth, Fla., while the *Meteor* zips by. This venerable duo survived as this book went to press in 1994, but their one-time rival *Champion* had vanished 15 years earlier.—KARL ZIMMERMANN.

the *Everglade*'s earning power. Passenger complaints about accommodations on the train didn't help either. The ICC ordered the railroads to continue running the train.

PC continued to make trouble for SCL. Spurred by encouraging ridership, SCL and RF&P sought to reinstate the *Weekend Champion* for the summer of 1969. PC flatly refused, citing low ridership! SCL was powerless to force the issue and, without access to lucrative northern markets like Philadelphia and New York, the railroad opted not to run the train.

There were other challenges, too. Suddenly faced with the chore of maintaining perhaps the largest fleet of sleeping cars in the U.S. (79 at the time), SCL took a novel approach. In July 1969, the railroad sold its entire sleeping-car fleet to Hamburg Industries of Augusta, Ga., which performed the maintenance and leased the cars back to SCL. Then SCL did something even more unusual: As one of few roads in the country still faced with a large demand for sleeper space, it arranged for Hamburg to purchase several secondhand sleepers. There wasn't another railroad in the country adding sleeping cars to its roster in 1969!

In September 1969, Hamburg purchased eight B&O 16-4 cars, three ex-B&O dome sleepers it had been leasing from C&O/B&O and three 11-double-bedroom sleepers—*Greenbrier, Monticello* and *Natural Bridge.* In March 1970, two more 11-double-bedroom C&O cars, *Homestead* and *Mount Vernon,* joined the roster. The all-bedroom cars worked the *Florida Special* that winter, and the domes were assigned to the *Special* every season until Amtrak. The domes also operated on the *Silver Star* in the spring, summer and fall of 1969. In the winter of 1969-70, the *Silver Meteor* began carrying the Budget Room Coach formerly found on the *Silver Star.*

For the spring and summer of 1970, passenger operations proceeded with few obvious changes from the previous summer, but, behind the scenes, significant events were taking place which would change the future forever. By now the "passenger problem," from a national standpoint, had taken such a serious turn for the worse that the cash-starved railroad industry beseeched Congress and the Department of Transportation for help. Even on pro-passenger Seaboard Coast Line, which had admirable passenger traffic levels for those troubled times, the numbers were frightening. According to the ICC, SCL had taken in $22.2 million dollars in passenger revenues in 1968, but still had lost a whopping $19.3 million.

On Jan. 18, 1970, the Department of Transportation announced plans for "Railpax," a semi-public corporation set up to run the nation's rail passenger system. The result was the eventual signing of the Rail Passenger Service Act by President Nixon on Oct. 30, 1970. The Act created the National Railroad Passenger Corporation, which officially was dubbed Amtrak on April 19, 1971. SCL made its intentions of joining Railpax known in its 1970 annual report.

Despite the fact that the railroad intended to rid itself of the service which had been part of its history for close to a century, SCL showed a lot of class. As long as its top trains still ran, there'd be no serious downgrading of service. In fact, the railroad had actually been fighting to continue the operation of one of its best trains. In July 1970, Penn Central notified SCL that it did not intend to operate the seasonal *Florida Special* that coming winter because it felt passenger loadings wouldn't be sufficient. SCL Vice President of Passenger Traffic J. R. Getty took exception, saying ". . . we do not believe it would be in the best economic or overall interest of all of us to not operate this famous train in the best manner possible again this coming winter season." SCL prevailed, and the *Florida Special* returned for another glorious season.

In spring 1971, SCL formally announced that the new National Railroad Passenger Corporation, which it would joint along with 19 other railroads, would include in its route structure New York-Miami, New York-Tampa-St. Petersburg and Chicago-Florida endpoints. On April 16, 1971, with the legal details finalized, SCL officially signed a contract to join NRPC.

By its very nature, as first aid for an ailing patient, Amtrak would become the "great leveler," spreading the wealth (what little was left in the nation's ailing passenger network) and patching up the national system, primarily with the equipment of those roads who had maintained their fleets instead of neglecting them. Thus, Santa Fe, Union Pacific, Burlington Northern and Seaboard Coast Line cars would provide the backbone of the new Amtrak system.

It was particularly appropriate that the train that had started it all—the *Silver Meteor*—exited the private railroad scene on April 30, 1971, much as it had entered it a little over 32 years earlier. A legendary GG1 electric still handed the train over to trusty EMD E-units; a stainless-steel, fluted-side Budd observation punctuated its end; while aboard, passengers anticipated a vacation land of palm trees and surf.

It was as much a symbol of what was wrong with the passenger train as what we would miss about it. Change hadn't come quick enough or often enough to the railroad passenger business. When it did come, it did so on the coattails of necessity. Now again, born of necessity, a change would come. This time it symbolized a loss as well as a new beginning.

Impervious to regret, the Mars light of its locomotive scouring the darkness, the last SCL *Silver Meteor* charged southward through the Virginia night. Inside its 1000-foot cocoon of stainless steel, a moving city went about its business. In the diner's kitchen, cooks prepared for the following morning's breakfast as a handful of latecomers finished a night cap in the Sun Lounge. A white-jacketed porter moved with practiced gait down the hushed corridor of a sleeper as inside one of its rooms a passenger turned out his night light and snuggled down under crisp linens. Outside, trackside, the *Meteor* screamed past the signal, the roar of its passing replaced only by an eerie silence and the piercing, red eye of the lonely sentinel.

Southbound SCL *Silver Meteor* at La Crosse, Va.—Mel Patrick photo

ATLANTIC COAST LINE ROUTE/prewar cars, shown as delivered

Railroad	Name/number	Type	Builder	Date
ACL	100, 101	22-seat coach-bag-dorm	Budd	11/39
FEC	*Stuart**	22-seat coach-bag-dorm	Budd	11/39
FEC	*New Smyrna***	22-seat coach-bag-dorm	Budd	11/39
FEC	*Hollywood*	60-seat coach	Budd	11/39
FEC	*Cocoa Rockledge*	60-seat coach	Budd	11/39
FEC	*Hobe Sound@*	60-seat coach	Budd	11/39
FEC	*Melbourne*	60-seat coach	Budd	11/39
FEC	*Pompano*	60-seat coach	Budd	11/39
FEC	*Boca Raton*	60-seat coach	Budd	11/39
ACL	200-205	60-seat coach	Budd	11/39
FEC	*Vero Beach*	52-seat coach/host. rm.	Budd	11/39
FEC	*Delray Beach*	52-seat coach/host. rm.	Budd	11/39
ACL	206, 207	52-seat coach/host. rm.	Budd	11/39
FEC	*Fort Pierce*	48-seat diner	Budd	11/39
FEC	*Fort Lauderdale*	48-seat diner	Budd	11/39
ACL	*New York*	48-seat diner	Budd	11/39
ACL	*Philadelphia*	48-seat diner	Budd	11/39
FEC	*Bay Biscayne*	Lounge-observation#	Budd	11/39
FEC	*Lake Worth*	Lounge-observation#	Budd	11/39
ACL	250, 251	Lounge-observation#	Budd	11/39
ACL	102-104	14-seat coach-bag-dorm	Budd	12/40
ACL	*Boston*	48-seat diner	Budd	12/40
ACL	*Newark*	48-seat diner	Budd	12/40
ACL	*Baltimore*	48-seat diner	Budd	12/40
ACL	208-215	56-seat coach	Budd	12/40
ACL	252-254	Lounge-observation†	Budd	12/40
PRR	4026-4029	60-seat coach	Budd	12/40

ATLANTIC COAST LINE ROUTE/postwar cars delivered

Railroad	Name/number	Type	Builder	Date
ACL	105-107	14-seat coach-bag-dorm	Budd	4/47
FEC	*Banana River*	14-seat coach-bag-dorm	Budd	4/47
FEC	*St. John's River*	28-seat coach-bag-dorm	Budd	4/47
FEC	*Jacksonville*	56-seat coach	Budd	6/46
FEC	*Stuart*	56-seat coach	Budd	6/46
FEC	*Eau Gallie*	56-seat coach	Budd	6/46
FEC	*Dania*	56-seat coach	Budd	6/46
FEC	*Ormond*	56-seat coach	Budd	6/46
FEC	*Wabasso*	56-seat coach	Budd	6/46
FEC	*Boynton*	56-seat coach	Budd	6/46
FEC	*Bunnell*	56-seat coach	Budd	6/46
FEC	*Titusville*	56-seat coach	Budd	6/46
FEC	*Homestead*	56-seat coach	Budd	6/46
FEC	*Belleglade*	56-seat coach	Budd	6/46
ACL	216-227	54-seat coach	Budd	5-6/46
RF&P	801-806	54-seat coach	Budd	5-6/46
PRR	4046-4054	54-seat coach	Budd	5-6/46
ACL	221-223	46-seat coach/host. rm.	Budd	5/46
ACL	*Washington*	48-seat diner	Budd	4-5/47
ACL	*Tampa*	48-seat diner	Budd	4-5/47
FEC	*Fort San Marco*	48-seat diner	Budd	4-5/47
FEC	*Fort Dallas*	48-seat diner	Budd	4-5/47
FEC	*Fort Matanzas*	48-seat diner	Budd	4-5/47
ACL	*St. Petersburg★*	18-seat diner/14-seat lge.	Budd	5/47
FEC	*Lake Okeechobee*	Bar-lounge observation†	Budd	5/47
ACL	255-257	Bar-lounge observation†	Budd	5/47
FEC	*Hobe Sound*	Bar-lounge observation#	Budd	5/47
FEC	*St. Lucie Sound*	Bar-lounge observation#	Budd	5/47
FEC	*Port Everglades*	Chair-lounge	Budd	3/48
ACL	*Cordele*	36-seat diner	P-S	2-5/50
ACL	*Atlanta*	36-seat diner	P-S	2-5/50
ACL	*Birmingham*	36-seat diner	P-S	2-5/50
ACL	*Fitzgerald*	36-seat diner	P-S	2-5/50
ACL	*Greenville*	36-seat diner	P-S	2-5/50
ACL	*LaGrange*	36-seat diner	P-S	2-5/50
ACL	*Moultrie*	36-seat diner	P-S	2-5/50
ACL	*Plant City*	36-seat diner	P-S	2-5/50
ACL	*Talladega*	36-seat diner	P-S	2-5/50
ACL	*Tarboro*	36-seat diner	P-S	2-5/50
FEC	*Fort Drum*	36-seat diner	P-S	2-5/50
FEC	*Fort Ribault*	36-seat diner	P-S	2-5/50
RF&P	*Henrico*	36-seat diner	P-S	2-5/50
ACL	228-247	54-seat coach	P-S	11/49-1/50
RF&P	810-812	54-seat coach	P-S	11/49-1/50
FEC	*Canal Point*	56-seat coach	P-S	11/49-1/50
FEC	*Hypoluxo*	56-seat coach	P-S	11/49-1/50
FEC	*Salerno*	56-seat coach	P-S	11/49-1/50
FEC	*Sebastian*	56-seat coach	P-S	11/49-1/50
FEC	*Lantana*	56-seat coach	P-S	11/49-1/50
ACL	*Alachua County*	10-6 sleeper	P-S	9-10/49
ACL	*Beaufort County*	10-6 sleeper	P-S	9-10/49
ACL	*Berkeley County*	10-6 sleeper	P-S	9-10/49

Railroad	Name/number	Type	Builder	Date
ACL	*Chatham County*	10-6 sleeper	P-S	9-10/49
ACL	*Clarendon County*	10-6 sleeper	P-S	9-10/49
ACL	*Colleton County*	10-6 sleeper	P-S	9-10/49
ACL	*Cumberland County*	10-6 sleeper	P-S	9-10/49
ACL	*Darlington County*	10-6 sleeper	P-S	9-10/49
ACL	*Duval County*	10-6 sleeper	P-S	9-10/49
ACL	*Edgecombe County*	10-6 sleeper	P-S	9-10/49
ACL	*Glynn County*	10-6 sleeper	P-S	9-10/49
ACL	*Harnett County*	10-6 sleeper	P-S	9-10/49
ACL	*Hillsboro County*	10-6 sleeper	P-S	9-10/49
ACL	*Marion County*	10-6 sleeper	P-S	9-10/49
ACL	*Nash County*	10-6 sleeper	P-S	9-10/49
ACL	*Nassau County*	10-6 sleeper	P-S	9-10/49
ACL	*Northampton County*	10-6 sleeper	P-S	9-10/49
ACL	*Osceola County*	10-6 sleeper	P-S	9-10/49
ACL	*Pinellas County*	10-6 sleeper	P-S	9-10/49
ACL	*Polk County*	10-6 sleeper	P-S	9-10/49
ACL	*Prince George County*	10-6 sleeper	P-S	9-10/49
ACL	*Putnam County*	10-6 sleeper	P-S	9-10/49
ACL	*Seminole County*	10-6 sleeper	P-S	9-10/49
ACL	*Sumter County*	10-6 sleeper	P-S	9-10/49
ACL	*Ware County*	10-6 sleeper	P-S	9-10/49
RF&P	*Caroline County*	10-6 sleeper	P-S	9-10/49
RF&P	*Hanover County*	10-6 sleeper	P-S	9-10/49
RF&P	*Spotsylvania County*	10-6 sleeper	P-S	9-10/49
RF&P	*Stratford County*	10-6 sleeper	P-S	9-10/49
FEC	*Bahamian*	10-6 sleeper	P-S	9-10/49
FEC	*Caparra*	10-6 sleeper	P-S	9-10/49
FEC	*Columbia*	10-6 sleeper	P-S	9-10/49
FEC	*Cuba*	10-6 sleeper	P-S	9-10/49
FEC	*Havana*	10-6 sleeper	P-S	9-10/49
FEC	*Honduras*	10-6 sleeper	P-S	9-10/49
FEC	*Oriente*	10-6 sleeper	P-S	9-10/49
PRR	*Chester County*	10-6 sleeper	P-S	9-10/49
PRR	*Baltimore County*	10-6 sleeper	P-S	9-10/49
PRR	*Bucks County*	10-6 sleeper	P-S	9-10/49
PRR	*Delaware County*	10-6 sleeper	P-S	9-10/49
PRR	*Hudson County*	10-6 sleeper	P-S	9-10/49
PRR	*Union County*	10-6 sleeper	P-S	9-10/49
PRR	*Governors Island*	21-roomette sleeper	P-S	9-10/49
PRR	*Staten Island*	21-roomette sleeper	P-S	9-10/49
RF&P	*Byrd Island*	21-roomette sleeper	P-S	9-10/49
ACL	*Edisto Island*	21-roomette sleeper	P-S	9-10/49
ACL	*Parris Island*	21-roomette sleeper	P-S	9-10/49
ACL	*Roanoke Island*	21-roomette sleeper	P-S	9-10/49
ACL	*St. Simons Island*	21-roomette sleeper	P-S	9-10/49
ACL	*Sullivans Island*	21-roomette sleeper	P-S	9-10/49
FEC	*Salvador*	21-roomette sleeper	P-S	9-10/49
FEC	*Uruguay*	21-roomette sleeper	P-S	9-10/49
ACL	*Myrtle Beach*	6-dble. bedroom lounge	ACF	11-12/49
ACL	*Pass-a-Grille Beach*	6-dble. bedroom lounge	ACF	11-12/49
ACL	*Ponte Vedra Beach*	6-dble. bedroom lounge	ACF	11-12/49
ACL	*Sea Island Beach*	6-dble. bedroom lounge	ACF	11-12/49
ACL	*Virginia Beach*	6-dble. bedroom lounge	ACF	11-12/49
ACL	*Wrightsville Beach*	6-dble. bedroom lounge	ACF	11-12/49
FEC	*Magnolia*	6-dble. bedroom lounge	ACL	11/12-49
FEC	*Oleander*	6-dble. bedroom lounge	ACL	11/12-49
RF&P	*Colonial Beach*	6-dble. bedroom lounge	ACF	11-12/49
RF&P	*Fairfax River*	14-2 sleeper	ACF	2-3/50
FEC	*Panama*	14-2 sleeper	ACF	2-3/50
ACL	*Ashley River*	14-2 sleeper	ACF	2-3/50
ACL	*Cape Fear River*	14-2 sleeper	ACF	2-3/50
ACL	*Cooper River*	14-2 sleeper	ACF	2-3/50
ACL	*Manatee River*	14-2 sleeper	ACF	2-3/50
ACL	*Ogeechee River*	14-2 sleeper	ACF	2-3/50
ACL	*Suwanee River*	14-2 sleeper	ACF	2-3/50
PRR	*Anacostia River*	14-2 sleeper	ACF	2-3/50
PRR	*Hackensack River*	14-2 sleeper	ACF	2-3/50
ACL	150-151	Baggage	ACF	2-3/50
FEC	501	Baggage	ACF	2-3/50

ATLANTIC COAST LINE ROUTE/cars acquired from other roads (date shown is date acquired)

Ex-Chesapeake & Ohio

Railroad	Name/number	Type	Builder	Date
ACL	*Bryan County*	10-6 sleeper	P-S	10/50
ACL	*Dillon County*	10-6 sleeper	P-S	10/50
ACL	*Halifax County*	10-6 sleeper	P-S	10/50
ACL	*Volusia County*	10-6 sleeper	P-S	10/50
ACL	270-275	36-seat coach-lounge	Budd	10/50
ACL	125/*Port Tampa*	Kitchen-dorm/diner	P-S	12/50
ACL	126/*Winter Park*	Kitchen-dorm/diner	P-S	12/50
ACL	127/*St. Petersburg*	Kitchen-dorm/diner	Budd	12/50
ACL	128/*Winter Haven*	Kitchen-dorm/diner	Budd	12/50
ACL	129/*Fort Meyers*	Kitchen-dorm/diner	Budd	12/50

Railroad	Name/number	Type	Builder	Date
Ex-New York Central❖				
ACL	Cape Fear River	4-4 sleeper	P-S	10/62
ACL	Kissimmee River	4-4 sleeper	P-S	10/62
ACL	Manatee River	4-4 sleeper	P-S	10/62
ACL	Ortega River	4-4 sleeper	P-S	10/62
ACL	Savannah River	4-4 sleeper	P-S	10/62
ACL	Suwanee River	4-4 sleeper	P-S	10/62
Ex-Nickel Plate				
ACL	260-263	52-seat coach	P-S	8/64

ATLANTIC COAST LINE ROUTE/rebuilt cars

Railroad	Name/No.	New configuration	Former Name/No.	Date rblt.
ACL	100	Baggage-dorm	Same	7/47
ACL	101	Baggage-dorm	Same	9/47
ACL	102-107	Baggage-dorm	Same	3/62
ACL	Rice Bird	7-2 sleeper	Manatee River (14-2)	4/61
ACL	Blue Bird	7-2 sleeper	Cape Fear River (14-2)	7/61
ACL	Humming Bird	7-2 sleeper	Ogeechee River (14-2)	7/61
ACL	Surf Bird	7-2 sleeper	Suwanee River (14-2)	7/61
ACL	Honey Bird	7-2 sleeper	Ashley River (14-2)	9/61
ACL	Jay Bird	7-2 sleeper	Cooper River (14-2)	10/61
ACL	Magnolia Gardens	11-dble. bdrm. sleeper	Parris Island (21-rmt)	7/62

ATLANTIC COAST LINE ROUTE/homebuilt cars; car shells built by Pullman-Standard

Railroad	Name/number	Type	Builder	Date
ACL	Naples	36-seat diner	ACL	1959
ACL	152	Baggage	ACL	1959

SEABOARD AIR LINE ROUTE/prewar cars delivered as shown

SAL	6000	22-seat coach-bag-dorm	Budd	1/39
SAL	6100	48-seat diner	Budd	1/39
SAL	6200-6202	60-seat coach	Budd	1/39
SAL	6300	30-seat coach-tavern	Budd	1/39
SAL	6400	48-seat coach-tavern-obs#	Budd	1/39
PRR	4014☆	66-seat coach	Budd	11/39
SAL	6001-6002	22-seat coach-bag-dorm	Budd	11/39
SAL	6101-6102	48-seat diner	Budd	11/39
SAL	6203-6207	60-seat coach	Budd	11/39
SAL	6301-6302	30-seat coach-tavern	Budd	11/39
SAL	6103	32-seat diner-lounge	Budd	11/39
PRR	4015-4017	60-seat coach	Budd	11/39
SAL	6003-6005	18-seat coach-bag-dorm	Budd	11/40
SAL	6104, 6105	48-seat diner	Budd	11/40
SAL	6208-6214	56-seat coach	Budd	11/40
SAL	6500-6502	30-seat coach-buffet-obs†	Budd	11/40
PRR	4018☆	60-seat coach	Budd	11/40
PRR	4024, 4025	60-seat coach	Budd	12/40

SEABOARD AIR LINE ROUTE/postwar

SAL	6215-6226	52-seat coach	Budd	1-4/47
PRR	4058-4067	52-seat coach	Budd	1-4/47
RF&P	850-857	52-seat coach	Budd	1-4/47
SAL	6050-6053	Baggage-dormitory	Budd	6/47
SAL	6106-6114	48-seat diner	Budd	6/47
SAL	6600-6605	Tavern-observation#	Budd	7/47
SAL	Charlotte	10-6 sleeper	P-S	5-6/49
SAL	Columbia	10-6 sleeper	P-S	5-6/49
SAL	Jacksonville	10-6 sleeper	P-S	5-6/49
SAL	Norfolk	10-6 sleeper	P-S	5-6/49
SAL	Orlando	10-6 sleeper	P-S	5-6/49
SAL	Petersburg	10-6 sleeper	P-S	5-6/49
SAL	Portsmouth	10-6 sleeper	P-S	5-6/49
SAL	Raleigh	10-6 sleeper	P-S	5-6/49
SAL	Richmond	10-6 sleeper	P-S	5-6/49
SAL	Savannah	10-6 sleeper	P-S	5-6/49
SAL	Tampa	10-6 sleeper	P-S	5-6/49
RF&P	Chester	10-6 sleeper	P-S	5-6/49
RF&P	Essex	10-6 sleeper	P-S	5-6/49
RF&P	Lancaster	10-6 sleeper	P-S	5-6/49
SAL	Lake Wales	10-6 sleeper	Budd	6-8/49
SAL	Miami	10-6 sleeper	Budd	6-8/49
SAL	Sarasota	10-6 sleeper	Budd	6-8/49
SAL	Petersburg	10-6 sleeper	Budd	6-8/49
SAL	West Palm Beach	10-6 sleeper	Budd	6-8/49
SAL	Winter Haven	10-6 sleeper	Budd	6-8/49
PRR	Athens	10-6 sleeper	Budd	6-8/49
PRR	Bradenton	10-6 sleeper	Budd	6-8/49
PRR	Chester	10-6 sleeper	Budd	6-8/49
PRR	Clinton	10-6 sleeper	Budd	6-8/49
PRR	Elberton	10-6 sleeper	Budd	6-8/49

Railroad	Name/number	Type	Builder	Date
PRR	Greenwood	10-6 sleeper	Budd	6-8/49
SAL	Kennesaw Mountain	6-dbl.-bedroom lounge	ACF	8/49
SAL	Red Mountain	6-dbl.-bedroom lounge	ACF	8/49
SAL	Stone Mountain	6-dbl.-bedroom lounge	ACF	8/49
SAL	Bay Pines	5-1-4-4 sleeper	Budd	11/55
SAL	Camden	5-1-4-4 sleeper	Budd	11/55
SAL	Cedartown	5-1-4-4 sleeper	Budd	11/55
SAL	Henderson	5-1-4-4 sleeper	Budd	11/55
SAL	Pinehurst	5-1-4-4 sleeper	Budd	11/55
SAL	Southern Pines	5-1-4-4 sleeper	Budd	11/55
SAL	6235-6241	52-seat coach/10-seat lge.	P-S	12/55
RF&P	861-862	52-seat coach/10-seat lge.	P-S	12/55
SAL	Avon Park	11-dbl.-bedroom sleeper	P-S	12/55-1/56
SAL	Hialeah	11-dbl.-bedroom sleeper	P-S	12/55-1/56
SAL	Ocala	11-dbl.-bedroom sleeper	P-S	12/55-1/56
SAL	Sebring	11-dbl.-bedroom sleeper	P-S	12/55-1/56
SAL	Tallahassee	11-dbl.-bedroom sleeper	P-S	12/55-1/56
SAL	Venice	11-dbl.-bedroom sleeper	P-S	12/55-1/56
SAL	Hollywood Beach	5-dbl. br. Sun Lounge	P-S	1/56
SAL	Miami Beach	5-dbl. br. Sun Lounge	P-S	1/56
SAL	Palm Beach	5-dbl. br. Sun Lounge	P-S	1/56
SAL	Boca Grande	5-2-2 sleeper	P-S	1/56
SAL	Clearwater	5-2-2 sleeper	P-S	1/56
SAL	Fort Lauderdale	5-2-2 sleeper	P-S	1/56

SEABOARD AIR LINE ROUTE/cars acquired from other roads (date is date acquired)

Ex-Chesapeake & Ohio

SAL	6227-6231	50-seat coach	Budd	8/50
SAL	6232-6234	36-seat coach/8-seat lge.	Budd	8/50
SAL	6242-6251	52-seat coach	P-S	6/58

Ex-Florida East Coast (see ACL roster for builder)

Railroad	Number	Type	Former name/No.	Date acqrd.
SAL	6070	Baggage	501	11/65
SAL	6057	Baggage-dorm	Halifax River	11/65
SAL	6058	Baggage-dorm	St. Johns River	11/65
SAL	6006	Baggage-dorm-coach	Indian River	11/65
SAL	6252	52-seat coach/host. rm.	Delray Beach	11/65
SAL	6253	56-seat coach	New Smyrna Beach	11/65
SAL	6254	60-seat coach	Melbourne	11/65
SAL	6255	52-seat coach/host. rm.	Vero Beach	11/65
SAL	6256	60-seat coach	Pompano	11/65
SAL	6257	60-seat coach	Boca Raton	11/65
SAL	6258	56-seat coach	Dania	11/65
SAL	6259	56-seat coach	Eau Gallie	11/65
SAL	6260	56-seat coach	Ormond	11/65
SAL	6261	56-seat coach	Wabasso	11/65
SAL	6262	54-seat coach	Belleglade	11/65
SAL	6263	56-seat coach	Jacksonville	11/65
SAL	6264	56-seat coach	Stuart	11/65
SAL	6265	52-seat coach	Pahokee	11/65
SAL	6266	56-seat coach	Sebastian	11/65
SAL	6267	56-seat coach	Canal Point	11/65
SAL	6268	56-seat coach	Salerno	11/65
SAL	6269	56-seat coach	Lantana	11/65
SAL	6270	56-seat coach	Hypoluxo	11/65
SAL	6271	56-seat coach	St. Augustine	11/65
SAL	6272	56-seat coach	Miami	11/65
SAL	6273	56-seat coach	Hollywood	11/65
SAL	6274	56-seat coach	Cocoa-Rockledge	11/65
SAL	6115	Diner	Fort Lauderdale	11/65
SAL	6116	Diner	Fort Dallas	11/65
SAL	6117	Diner	Fort Matanzas	11/65
SAL	6118	Diner	Fort San Marco	11/65
SAL	6119	Diner	Fort Ribault	11/65
SAL	6120	Diner	Fort Drum	11/65
SAL	6620	Diner-lounge	South Bay	11/65
SAL	6621	Tavern-lounge-obs	Lake Worth#	11/65
SAL	6622	Tavern-lounge-obs	Bay Biscayne#	11/65

NOTES

*Renamed Indian River in 1946
**Renamed Halifax River in 1947
@Renamed New Smyrna Beach in 1947
#Round-end
†Blunt-end
★Renamed Orlando in 1950; rebuilt to 48-seat diner
❖Rebuilt before delivery to ACL from 4-4-2 to 4-4
☆World's Fair demonstrator cars

This roster shows only equipment built, rebuilt and/or purchased expressly for Northeast-Florida service and the New York-Atlanta-Birmingham Silver Comet.

The solitude of a Virginia night is briefly ruffled at the burgh of Newington, long since a stop for any passenger train, as the southbound *Florida Special* blares by on the RF&P main line. One can imagine that mention of the impending "Amtrak" was perhaps among news items in the Sunday morning papers bundled on the bench in front of Pearson's Store and Newington post office. Bottle caps paving the "front yard" attest to a time when soda pop in returnable glass bottles was still a way of life—just like the passenger train.—MEL PATRICK.

ACKNOWLEDGEMENTS

NOTHING IS MORE VALUABLE than friendship. Through this enterprise I have formed several lasting friendships whose value far outweighs the material or information shared. Without the help of these new and old acquaintances, this book could simply not have been produced. All errors, however, should be addressed to the author. I am especially indebted to Ken Ardinger, Frank Ardrey Jr., Chris Baer, Anne Bennof, Ted Benson, Sam Boldrick, O. Harry Borsum, Seth Bramson, Wiley Bryan, Bill Burkhardt, Warren Calloway, Bill Caloroso, Mark Cedek, Hugh Comer, Mac Connery, William Connolly, Dennis Conniff, Thomas W. Dixon Jr., George Drury, George Eichelberger, Steve Fitzgerald, William Girard, Larry Goolsby, Howard Griffin, William E. Griffin Jr., Foster Gunnison, Victor Hand, Herb Harwood Jr., Ed Hawkins, Bill Heisler, Joseph A. Hueber, Kenneth L. Howes, William F. Howes Jr., John Humes, William J. Husa Jr., Sam Jennings, Paul Joslin, John Kuehl, Tom King, Stan Kistler, William Klepinger, Max Knoecklein, Dennis Kogan, John Krug, J. Parker Lamb, Mike Leinenbach, Lloyd D. Lewis, Robert G. Lewis, Bruce MacGregor, Peter Maiken, Bob Malinoski, Dr. Louis Marre, Ken Marsh, Gordon Mott, Tom Martorano, Peter McLachlan, Bill Middleton, Rudy Morgenfruh, Frank Moore, Jonathan Nelson, Mel Patrick, Bob Penisi, Vic Rafanelli, Dave Randall, Art Riordan, Howard Robins, David Salter, Mike Schafer, Jim Scribbins, El Simon, J. C. Smith Jr., Jack Swanberg, Carl Swanson, Peter V. Tilp, Susan Tolbert, Harold K. Vollrath, George Votava, Chuck Yungkurth, Richard R. Wallin, Robert Wayner, W. C. Whittaker, Jay Williams, Douglas Wornom and Karl Zimmermann.

In addition, the following organizations contributed to this effort: Association of American Railroads; American Car & Foundry; ACL/SAL Historical Society; Bombardier Corporation; Brotherhood of Locomotive Engineers; Budd Company; California State Railroad Museum; CSX Corporation; De Goyler Library, Southern Methodist University; Flagler Museum; Florida East Coast Industries; Florida State Archives; Gold Coast Railroad Museum; Hagley Museum Library; Jacksonville Chapter-National Railway Historical Society; Miami-Dade Public Library; Miami Herald; Pullman Technology Inc.; Richmond, Fredcricksburg & Potomac Railroad; Smithsonian Institution; St. Louis Mercantile Library Barriger Collection; Timken Roller Bearing; Lawrence Williams Photography.

And, last but not least, I wish to thank my wife Janis and daughters Katie and Kellie for their love and support.
—Joseph M. Welsh